From Tapas to Meze

From Tapas

to Meze

FIRST COURSES FROM
THE MEDITERRANEAN SHORES OF
SPAIN, FRANCE, ITALY, GREECE, TURKEY,
THE MIDDLE EAST, AND NORTH AFRICA

Joanne Weir

CROWN PUBLISHERS, INC. NEW YORK

This book is dedicated to Paul,
for driving me to New Hampshire
that snowy January day in 1985.

Published by Crown Publishers, Inc., 201 East 50th Street,
New York, New York 10022. Member of the Crown Publishing Group.

Random House, Inc. New York, Toronto, London, Sydney, Auckland

CROWN is a trademark of Crown Publishers, Inc.

Manufactured in the U.S.A.

Library of Congress Cataloging-in-Publication Data
Weir, Joanne.
From Tapas to Meze: first courses from the Mediterranean shores
of Spain, France, Italy, Greece, Turkey, the Middle East,
and North Africa / Joanne Weir. — 1st ed.
p. cm.
Includes index.
1. Cookery, Mediterranean. 2. Entrées (Cookery) I. Title.
TX725.M35W45 1994
641.591822—dc20   93-30139
CIP

ISBN 0-517-589621
10 9 8 7 6 5 4 3 2 1
First Edition

Acknowledgments

Without my friends and family this book would not have been possible. For lifelong culinary lessons and fond memories around the table, my thanks go to my mother, Jean Tenaces. I would like to thank those who have stood beside me, traveled along with me, and only a few times asked if they could have a main course: Kathy Weir, Charlotte Robinson, Rand Hoffman, and Gianni D'Alo. My thanks go to recipe testers Annie Bone, Mark Lindsey, Diana Colby, and the incomparable Anita Anderson, who showed up each day with a basket of vegetables and lots of energy. My sincere thanks go to Daphne Zepos, who tested recipes, escorted me in Greece, translated for me, and allowed me to lean on her. Thanks to Angel and Georgi Stoyanof and Stoyanof's, San Francisco, and Sotiris and Lidia Kitrilakis of Peloponnese for sharing so much of Greece and Turkey with me. My thanks to Mary Risley, Peggy Lynch, and Tante Marie's Cooking School for years of support. I thank Jan Langone at the Wine and Food Library, the National Olive Oil Council, and Schlesinger Library at Radcliffe for providing valuable resources. And a special thanks to Barbara Ignatius for her superb editing abilities and sense of humor.

I thank my friends and associates around the Mediterranean who provided unmeasurable information, recipes, and help: Amalia Zepos, Dimitri and Maria Likouressis "Sofouli," Sophie and Stavroula Spyrou, Harisis Voyiatsis, Diane Kochilas, Boutari Wines, Electra Palace Thessaloniki, Grande Bretagne Athens, Mitko Stoyanof, Marimar Torres and Torres Wines Spain, Jaume Subiros, Marisol, Mamen and Lelis Guirao Sanchez, Beatriz and Jose Luis Tamarit Lopez, Mohammed Bourski, Said Ziani, Mourad Lahlou, Magaly and Raymond Fabre, Lulu and Lucien Peyraud, Nino Del Papa, Antonella Panarello, and Astoria Palace.

Many thanks to my patient and hard-working tour agent Lila Spencer and her assistant, Kathy Piskulic, for believing in me and handling my complicated schedules. My heartfelt thanks to my teacher and friend Madeleine Kamman, who taught me the fine art of teaching cooking and that food is so much more than what we put in our mouths. I thank Alice Waters and Chez Panisse. Working there inspired this book in the first place. I thank my literary agent, Julie Fallowfield, and her assistant, Louise Quayle, for initially taking my call and holding my hand all along the way. At Crown, my thanks go to Renana Meyers for keeping me on schedule and to Ken Sansone for his beautiful book design. Special gratitude to my editor, Erica Marcus, for her support, patience, insight, and encouragement with this project. She allowed the book to be mine and for that I am grateful.

And, of course, this book would not be here if it weren't for the loyal support of my husband, Paul, who has understood my difficult schedule, enthusiastically tasted a million first courses, and put up with my preoccupation with this project for years. From my heart, thank you.

Contents

Introduction

One autumn evening I sat with friends around my dining room table enjoying a hearty Tuscan white bean soup followed by a pizza with wild mushrooms and pancetta. I had been thinking of writing a book about the food of the Mediterranean for some time, but I had not yet decided what my focus should be. Inspiration came to me that night: *first courses* from the Mediterranean!

When I began working on the book, I knew I wanted to include all of my favorite foods—pizzas, salads, pastas, risottos, flatbreads, polenta, and soups. But where should I stop? Should I include Turkey? The Middle East? Morocco? As I looked at maps of the Mediterranean and studied the foods common to the countries that border it, I realized my book wouldn't be complete without the foods of Turkey and the Middle East, areas that had fascinated me since I was eighteen years old. Nor could I ignore the exotic countries of North Africa that I'd longed to visit ever since reading Paula Wolfert and Robert Carrier.

I traveled to the Mediterranean to learn about the food, but on my first trip there I discovered that there was much more to first courses than met the mouth. I was in Spain, standing against the tapas bar at Las Truchas in Madrid eating *boquerones*—tiny deep-fried fish—and wiping my fingertips on flimsy napkins a bit larger than a playing card. Why was it that the bar was packed five-feet deep with people? The fish was delicious, but there was more going on here than mere consuming.

In Greece, friends and I sat for hours at rustic outdoor tavernas and ordered plate after plate of sumptuous *meze*: mussels with feta cheese, *taramasalata*–a heavenly puree of cod fish roe, *saganaki*–fried cheese that comes to the table aflame, and pickled squid. In Sicily and again in Apulia, as the sun met the horizon, we shared bowls of pasta, grilled artichokes and sardines, or a pizza. All of these evenings had more to do with feeding our hearts and souls than our stomachs. Indeed, life at the table appeared very different around the Mediterranean than in central Europe or in America. I soon realized that my simple subject matter was really much more than a collection of recipes.

Mealtime around the Mediterranean is a major part of daily life. Drinking is not excessive here, and one wouldn't think of drinking without eating. In every country that touches the Mediterranean, small plates of flavorful foods provide a perfect accompaniment to the local drink, be it sherry, pastis, wine, ouzo, or raki. In Spain we find *tapas*; in France, hors d'oeuvres and entrées; in Italy, antipasti and *primi piatti*; in Greece, Turkey, and the Middle East, *meze*; and in North Africa, *mukabalatt*. Small plates of first courses are meant to stimulate the appetite, not satiate it. The host often prepares them ahead of time to avoid being trapped in the kitchen when the guests arrive and missing all the fun. First courses are most often served at room temperature, so flavors are not dulled by extremes of hot and cold, and so they can be consumed at leisure. The first course of a meal is a savored one, and the memories of these small plates linger long after the table has been cleared.

The countries that surround the Mediterranean Sea share the azure waters and are linked by a sun-baked landscape with a temperate climate. Generally, Mediterranean summers are hot and dry, and the winters are mild and wet, punctuated by the dusty African sirocco and the chilling winds of the French mistral. Blessed by the strong southern sun and the gentle waters that lap the shores, the arid land can be made—with considerable effort—to yield unsurpassed results. This bounty is seen in the tiniest home garden plots or in sprawling outdoor markets, and in the exquisite produce, cheeses, meats, and seafood that grace the table.

Spain, France, Italy, Greece, Turkey, the Middle East, and North Africa produce dishes that are loyal to the seasons. In summer, eggplants, peppers, tomatoes, onions, garlic, and squash abound. In the fall, artichokes, squash, and fennel are grown, and wild mushrooms are hunted by the intrepid. In the winter perfumed groves of lemons and oranges produce a wealth of citrus, and in the spring radishes, lettuces, and asparagus flourish. The makeshift stalls at the outdoor markets of Barcelona, Nice, Palermo, Istanbul, Cairo, and Fez are flooded with seasonal produce that implicitly instruct the cook what she should serve today. To round out the menu and extend the seasons, legumes are dried, wines and spirits are distilled, fish is salted and cured, fruits and vegetables are preserved, fresh milk is made into cheese, bundled herbs are hung in kitchens to dry, and olives are both cured for the table and pressed for their oil.

The symbol of Mediterranean agriculture and the most fundamental element of the larder is the olive and the green-gold oil it produces. A small amount of other fats—lard and butter—are used in the region, but olive oil is used almost exclusively in cooking. Olive oil brings out the flavor of other ingredients and imparts its own fruity qualities, and is a natural complement to the robust regional ingredients–tomatoes, onions, peppers, eggplant, and garlic.

The precise origin of the olive tree has been lost over time. There is speculation that the original home of the olive tree is Syria, but some hypothesize that it is indigenous to the entire Mediterranean basin. Then again, others say it was brought to Egypt by the Hyksos, a nomadic Asian tribe. The Greeks say that the goddess Athena produced the olive tree as her most sacred gift to man. In the Book of Genesis, Noah sent a dove from the Ark and it returned with an olive branch, which has since become an international symbol of peace. Wherever its origins lie, the olive tree holds a unique symbolic position in each Mediterranean country's culture.

The Syrians were the first to cultivate the trees and produce olive oil, but the Greeks and Romans were unrivaled in spreading the cultivation of the olive around the Mediterranean and producing vast quantities of olive oil. Early on, olive oil was used in religious rites, as medicine, ointment, and fuel for oil lamps. Its leaves were winter fodder for the goats and sheep, its branches and roots a source of heat. It wasn't until later that olive oil became a significant part of the Mediterranean diet.

The extraction of oil from the olive requires a specific series of operations to obtain a high-quality product. Around the Mediterranean, olives are harvested from the fall to winter, depending upon the country and whether they are picked green, brown, deep-violet or black. Optimally, the olives are sorted and washed within hours of picking. Next they are crushed to produce a paste that is traditionally spread between hemp mats. The mats are layered one on top of another and pressed, resulting in a water and olive oil mixture. The oil, being lighter than the water, rises to the surface and is decanted. (Today, due to higher demand and mechanization, the paste is either pressed hydraulically or put through a centrifuge to extract the oil. New automated oil mills are bright with stainless steel and operated by computers—a bit less romantic, but the results bring a higher consistency to the finished product.)

Extra virgin olive oil is made from the first pressing of the olives. This pressing produces a darker, purer, fruitier olive oil, one which is cleaner on the palate. More expensive than lesser grades, extra virgin oil is usually saved for special dishes, mainly uncooked ones, where the flavor of the oil is on display. The oil that is extracted from the second, third, and fourth pressings of the olive paste deteriorates progressively. These oils must be treated chemically to neutralize high acid levels, and extra virgin olive oil is added to them to boost their flavor.

Olive oil has an honored place in the Mediterranean diet but so do table or eating olives. To remove their bitterness and render them palatable, raw olives must be either brined (soaked in an alkaline solution) or salt cured (layered in a basket with salt). Olives are then marinated, stuffed, cooked, or simply served on a small plate with drinks. The most common eating olives grown around the Mediterranean are Niçoise and Picholine (France), Frantoio (Italy), Manzanilla and Arbequina (Spain), and Kalamata (Greece).

The trinity that forms the backbone of Mediterranean cuisine is comprised of olive oil, garlic, and tomatoes, and there is hardly a regional dish that doesn't include at least one of these ingredients. Garlic has been used here for eons and appears with olive oil as an inseparable and incomparable partner: *allioli* and *romesco* from Spain; *anchoiade, aioli, aillade,* and *tapenade* from the south of France; *agliata* and *aglio e oglio* from Italy; *skorthalia* from Greece; *tarator* from Turkey; *tahini* in the Levant; and *harissa* and *chermoula* from North Africa. Tomatoes are relative newcomers to the Mediterranean, arriving from the Americas in the early sixteenth century. They took the area by storm, not only for their versatility and flavor, but as a natural complement to olive oil.

Other vegetables that give form and flavor to Mediterranean cuisine are onions, leeks, greens, beans, peppers, artichokes, eggplant, squash, mushrooms, and fennel. Herbs figure prominently in Mediterranean cuisine— parsley, basil, oregano, dill, bay leaves, mint,

marjoram, rosemary, thyme, and sage on the northen shores, and in the southern Mediterranean, the aforementioned plus coriander. A liberal hand with spices makes use of saffron, black pepper, and crushed red pepper, and especially around the southern and eastern Mediterranean, paprika, ginger, cumin, cinnamon, allspice, and turmeric. Other essentially Mediterranean ingredients include capers, almonds, pine nuts, aromatic honeys, orange and rose waters, figs, citrus, lamb, anchovies, fish, shellfish, salted fish, grapes, and a tremendous assortment of rice, legumes, and grains.

The Mediterranean shores have produced a relatively narrow variety of cheeses, but nowhere is quality higher. These cheeses— made from the milk of cows, goats, and sheep—are gutsy and staightforward and tend to be, as much as cheeses can, on the lean side. Italy boasts Ricotta, Mascarpone, Gorgonzola, Fontina, Bel Paese, Provolone, Asiago, the famed buffalo milk Mozzarella, and the incomparable eating and grating cheeses, Parmesan and Pecorino. Southern France produces a wide variety of goat cheeses and Roquefort, and Coriscans make a ricotta-like cheese, Broccio. Greece is famed for its briny Feta, Kasseri and Kefalotyri and Spain for its Manchego, a hard, sheep's milk cheese. Turkey is noted for Kajmak, a soft, fresh incredibly rich cheese, and Tulim, a sheep's milk cheese. Egypt makes Domiati, a cow's milk cheese. The Eastern shores of the Mediterranean produce some delicious thick yogurt, which when drained produces a creamy spreadable yogurt cheese called Labneh.

Mediterranean ingredients are not particularly unusual ones; most are available in the United States. But what makes the food interesting is the way that each country puts the ingredients together to form its own unique cuisine with its own nuances and flavors. Ingredients are treated with integrity; each dish strives to maintain the full and pure flavor of the separate components.

With an abundance of fish, vegetables, pulses, rice, and legumes, liberal use of olive oil and limited red meat and dairy products, Mediterranean cuisine is a healthy one. Olive oil, monounsaturate-rich and containing no cholesterol, is the most nutritionally beneficial fat in the pantry. Onions and garlic cleanse the bloodstream and are known to have curative and protective qualities. The moderate consumption of wine aids digestion, stimulates the appetite, and reduces stress. The gentle pace of daily life around the Mediterranean leaves time for social and sensual pleasures. With this healthy cuisine and a relaxed atti-

tude, it is no wonder that the countries of the Mediterranean have the lowest incidence of heart disease and cancer in Europe

The Mediterranean embraces fifteen countries and touches three continents, Europe, Africa, and Asia. It is a vast sea stretching from the Strait of Gibraltar to the Bosphorus, from Marseilles to Tunis. Of the Christians, Jews, and Muslims who live there, some look to the vast desert, some look to the mountains, and some look to the sea. Some see fishing villages clinging to the rocks, some see ancient ruins, some see the perimeters of their own island. But everywhere one looks, one appreciates the robust Mediterranean spirit, its unparalleled history, and the hospitality with which it offers its remarkable cuisines. As you sample these dishes, imagine that you are sitting under an arbor sipping wine, or passing time in a small café, caught in conversation, or standing with friends and enjoying morsels of food at the bar. Food isn't separate from life around the Mediterranean, and so it can be in your own home: a simple table set with many small plates and perhaps a jug of wine, at which friends may gather at the end of the day.

About the Recipes

First courses from the countries that border the Mediterranean are so numerous that a comprehensive collection of them would produce a book many times longer than the one you're reading. So, for *From Tapas to Meze*, I chose the dishes that I most like to cook and eat. I tried to include recipes that for the most part are simple and uncomplicated. This is not food to be fussed over—you will find no turned vegetable garnishes or piped purees. Rather, these are dishes to delight all of the senses, not to intimidate the eyes or tax the stomach.

My goal in writing this book was to present the real flavors of the Mediterranean. Are all the recipes here completely authentic? Some indeed are written exactly as I ate them in their kitchens of origin, while others involving arcane ingredients and/or methods have been adapted for the American cook. However, none of the recipes here is etched in stone. You should use each of them as a guide to incorporating your own tastes and the freshest available ingredients—just as a Mediterranean cook would. To help you in this culinary improvisation, I have made suggestions for substitutions wherever possible.

Meze, tapas, antipasti, *primi piatti,* entrées, and hors d'oeuvres are infinitely adaptable. When grouped together in abundance, they provide a terrific alternative to a traditional meal of first course, main dish, and side dishes. You can set them all out for a buffet, or serve them in succession, for an elegant dinner party. If you increase the serving size, many of these recipes make wonderful main courses. And since most of these dishes are served at room temperature, they're perfect for a meal-away-from-home.

Of course, you can always serve first courses traditionally—as the exotic and evocative overture to a dramatic meal.

The Mediterranean Kitchen

I've included this section on useful cooking utensils not because it is extensive but rather because it is not. Around the Mediterranean, it amazes me how few utensils are actually needed to turn out such interesting and flavorful foods. The Mediterranean home kitchen is a simple one, lending itself to straightforward techniques. The weather invites cooking out-of-doors. Dishes are mainly grilled or spit roasted over a wood fire outside or in an indoor hearth, or slowly simmered or deep-fried.

Cast-Iron Pan. This pan is very useful for roasting vegetables on top of the stove. For example, it can be used for tomatoes, peppers, and even eggplant. In the Levant section, one of my favorites is a recipe for Red Hot Smoked Tomato Relish (page 223). In this recipe, I smoke the tomatoes and peppers in a very hot cast-iron pan. Other pans such as anodized aluminum or stainless steel, which are not as heavy as cast iron, cannot withstand the heat and are unsuitable for this technique. Cast-iron pans are very inexpensive and can be purchased at a cookware shop, a hardware store, or even a well-stocked grocery store.

Food Processor or Blender. I often use a blender as opposed to a food processor for various recipes, especially pureed soups. The blender aerates the mixture, yielding a silky smooth texture. I also recommend a food processor for many things like chopping nuts and making bread crumbs. You will find it especially invaluable for the Caramelized Onion Omelette from Andalusia (page 33) where three pounds of chopped onions are needed.

Mortar and Pestle. Despite the convenience of a food processor or blender, I find the mortar and pestle to be an absolute necessity in the Mediterranean kitchen. It is extremely efficient to grind spices and nuts to a fine dust and pulverize ingredients to a smooth paste like garlic for a garlic mayonnaise, pistou, pesto, anchoiade, brandade, garom, kibbeh or olives for tapenade. I have various sizes and materials—brass, ceramic, and marble. My favorite ones are made of marble. To start, a 2-cup capacity will suffice. These can be purchased at any good cookware shop.

Cheese Grater. I recommend a fine and

coarse grater for grating hard and semisoft cheeses.

Pasta Machine. My favorite pasta machine is the traditional hand crank pasta machine available in Italian cookware stores, specialty cookware shops, and by mail order. It is inexpensive and simple to use. It is usually sold with at least two cutting blades—for fettuccine and linguine. My favorite brand is Imperia—it has excellent roller calibration, which makes the entire process a breeze. I do not recommend electric pasta machines for two reasons: They are expensive, and the finished product is extruded (forced out of the holes) rather than rolled, which yields a tougher pasta. The traditional hand crank pasta machines cost between $40 and $60, depending upon the brand and model.

Pizza Stone, Bricks, or Tiles. I always cook my pizzas on a pizza stone and not in a pan to achieve a desired crispy finished product. A pizza stone or pizza bricks can be purchased in a specialty kitchen shop. A pizza stone is one piece and is placed on the bottom shelf of the oven. Pizza bricks are set in a large metal tray and placed on the bottom shelf of the oven. The least expensive alternative is to purchase unglazed quarry tiles at a tile manufacturer and place them close together on the bottom shelf of the oven.

Pizza Peel or Paddle. A pizza peel or paddle is made of metal or wood, wood being less expensive. This is used to transfer pizzas, flatbreads, and calzones to the tiles in the oven. If a peel or paddle is unavailable, the bottom side of a baking sheet can be substituted.

Food Mills. I use a food mill often when I want to pulverize a mixture and extract something like tomato seeds, garlic skins, or fish bones at the same time. A food mill breaks down the pulp so some texture remains. It is usually sold with three disks of various perforation size, allowing the cook to vary the resultant consistency.

Gas, Electric, and Charcoal Grills. In the Mediterranean, all food is grilled over hardwoods as opposed to gas or electric grills. I prefer grilling with hardwoods or mesquite because they impart a smoky flavor characteristic of the Mediterranean. A gas or electric grill will not impart a smoky flavor to the finished product. There is also a Tuscan Grill available that can be set inside an indoor fireplace. It has adjustable shelves and costs about $100. If you do not have any type of grill available to you, you can also use the broiler to your stove as directed in various recipes throughout the book.

From Tapas to Meze

Cold Iced Tomato Soup
from Andalusia

Chilled White Gazpacho with
Almonds and Grapes

Smoked Ham Soup with
White Beans and Mint

Veal and Green Pepper
Turnovers of Murcia

Quick Puff Pastry

Summer Vegetable Flat Bread

Grilled Bread with Ripe Tomatoes
and Olive Oil

Chorizo and Cheese Puffs

Fried Vegetable Pancake
Ca La Maria

Baked Semolina Pasta
with Garlic Mayonnaise

Caramelized Onion Omelette
from Andalusia

Wild Mushroom and
Roasted Garlic Flan

Spanish Omelette, Gypsy-Style

Tiny Spiced Meatballs
with Tomatoes

Pork Dumplings Wrapped
in Cabbage Leaves

Spicy Pork Kebabs with
Moorish Flavors

Pork Tenderloin Stuffed with
Onion Marmalade

Stewed Chick-Peas with Chorizo

Roasted Potatoes with
Spicy Tomato Sauce

Braised Spring Vegetables Stew
from Alicante

Stuffed Eggplant with
Oregano and Mint

Wilted Greens with Raisins,
Pine Nuts, and Fried Bread

Spain

Grilled Leeks and Scallions
with Romesco

Warm Charcoal-Grilled
Vegetable Salad

Fava Bean Salad
with Fresh Mint

Shredded Cod Salad with
Tomatoes, Peppers, and Onions

Salt Cod Salad with
Oranges and Olives

Salad of Marinated Chicken,
Pickled Vegetables, and Herbs

Clams Stewed with Tomatoes
and Garlic

Stuffed Mussels with Roasted
Garlic Mayonnaise

Shrimp and Green Onion
Pancakes

Menorcan Lobster Stew

Catalan Black Rice with Squid

Grilled Tuna with
Green Olive Relish

hy is it that on a side street in Seville or Malaga or even Murcia, it is nearly impossible to walk past a certain *tasca,* or tavern, due to the multitude of people spilling out into the streets? Wading through the people and arriving at the bar is a feat for an acrobat. People are jammed against the bar in a sea of glasses, conversation, and small plates of food. All around, there is commotion. What is the attraction that has people crowded next to one another screeching with excitement?

In Spain first courses are called *tapas,* and indulging in them is Spain's favorite sport. The pleasurable and congenial Spanish tradition of offering many small dishes began in the mid-1800s when tavern owners would put a slice of ham or a simple plate of almonds over the top of a sherry glass to keep the flies out. *Tapa* means "to cover," and those early *tapas* were free of charge. *Tapas* were meant to promote thirst and increase drink sales. Over the next hundred years, *tapas* evolved to the point where they have become part of everyday life, not only as a covering for the glass of sherry, but as the main event of a visit to the tavern.

But *tapas* are really more than an appetizer. They are a way of life. Conviviality and *tapas* go hand in hand. This congenial custom draws people together to discuss the day's events passionately; to talk philosophy, theater, and the arts; to exchange views on film, poetry, maybe even food, all the while drinking and savoring the variety of flavors of the various *tapas* amid a lively, animated crowd. Each *tasca* has its own specialty reflecting the season's offerings and local cooking styles so it is common to partake in "*tasca*-hopping." A typical conversation in Spain goes as follows: "I found a wonderful little *tapas* bar where they serve the very best *pastel.*"

"Great! After that, let's go to that tiny little place on the corner where they serve *patates bravas* just like my mother used to make."

Thus dinner gets put on the back burner.

Today, *tapas* are served all day in Spain but are most popular before meals. Both lunch and dinner are eaten quite late, so *tapas* are meant to stave off hunger, whet the appetite, and bring immediate gratification. *Tapas* are not something to be lingered over but instead consumed in haste so as to move on to the next flavorful morsel. They are washed down with a cool glass of sherry, beer, or wine. The *tapas* bar usually has a few glass cases filled with various *tapas* and a blackboard of daily specials ranging from simple to complex—from a plate of perfectly salted and roasted almonds, bright red radishes, or glistening meaty green olives to golden deep-fried anchovies, a salad of salt cod, olives, and oranges, or even a chick-pea and roasted garlic soup. Choices are made and within seconds the plates appear. The bartender runs back and forth, taking care of everyone at the same time. He also has the difficult task of keeping a running tally in his head of what everyone has eaten and in the end presenting the patron with a grand total. It makes for an enjoyable evening in a country where the people know how to live.

But life in Spain hasn't always been so carefree and easy. Spain is a country that has seen many invasions, the Romans and the Arab Moors of North Africa leaving the most profound effect. In the first half of the first millennium, the occupying Romans instituted the first large-scale propagation of olive trees and grapevines and taught the Spanish the fine art of curing Serrano hams, similar to Italian prosciutto. The Moors ruled for eight hundred years, from 711 to 1492, and left the most pervasive cultural imprint on Spain. The Arab Moors introduced eggplant, almonds, hazelnuts, citrus, sugarcane, and spices like cumin, cinnamon, black pepper, saffron, and nutmeg. They perfected the Roman irrigation system, making the land around Valencia perfect for growing rice. The Moors were expelled in 1492, the same year that Columbus set sail for the New World in search of gold and silver. Columbus returned to Spain, and in subsequent years the direction of the cooking in Spain and the rest of the Mediterranean was changed by the introduction of foods from the New World: tomatoes, peppers, potatoes,

corn, varieties of squash, various dried beans, avocado, chocolate, and turkey.

The Spanish states that border the Mediterranean—Catalonia, Valencia, Murcia, Andalusia, and the Balearic islands—vary immensely. Catalonia, which inhabits the northeast corner of Spain, is a cultural kingdom whose loyalties cross political borders to include parts of Roussillon in the southwest corner of France, a portion of Valencia, Andorra, and even a single city on the Italian island of Sardinia. More closely related to Languedoc and Provence than Spain, Catalonia has its own distinct style of food, which is highly aromatic and flavorful, employing unexpected combinations of taste. Some believe that it is the most sophisticated and original food of Spain. Eating is taken seriously in Catalonia and due to the influence of bordering France, Catalans do not feel that they have consumed a "proper" meal if they have to take it standing up. Thus first courses are taken at the table and *tapas* are not so much a part of daily life.

The Balearic islands—Majorca, Minorca, Ibiza, and Formentera—are a haven for romantics. With serrated coasts, coves, and cliffs descending to the sea, it is not surprising that the main culinary focus is the Mediterranean. Fish and shellfish, especially a spiny type of lobster called *llogosta*, and capers that grow wild on the island make their way into much of the cuisine. With strong ties to Catalonia, many of the dishes are similar in nature, both down-to-earth and flavorful. It is thought that mayonnaise or *salsa* mahonesa—a sauce served with many *tapas*—originated here in Port Mahon on Minorca.

Heading further south along the east coast of Spain, Valencia is a fertile, semitropical plane of sugarcane, date palms, citrus groves, and most importantly rice fields. Rice has been grown here since Moorish times, and many recipes are based around it. Paella, the national dish of Spain, is made with short-grain rice and saffron grown in nearby Murcia. This quasirisotto of Spain is occasionally eaten as *tapas* or a first course but mostly it is eaten as a dramatic main course. As we head further south to Murcia, rice paddies give way to vegetable fields, fruit orchards, and groves of date palms. Murcia relies heavily on the *huerta*, or garden. The strong Arabic influence is seen in the generous use of sweet spices and chick-peas, and the tremendous array of seafood helps to mold a unique and varied cuisine.

Andalusia is the home of horses, dancing, flamenco guitar, and merrymaking. The Andalusian has a real zest for life. Food is not generally the cerebral art that it is in other parts of Spain like Catalonia, but Andalusians take their *tapas* seriously, especially in Seville. The most popular *tapa* over all of Spain is a simple plate of paper-thin slices of Serrano ham from Andalusia, Jabugo being the finest. The pigs are fattened for a year on acorns and then slaughtered. The haunches and shoulders of the pig are cured by salting, washing, and drying and then matured in underground cellars for one to three years where they acquire a distinctive aroma and flavor. But the Andalusian *tapas* don't end with ham. Andalusia is renowned for its perfectly deep-fried fish, and egg dishes abound, especially the tortilla. Gazpacho, the cold liquid salad introduced by the Moors, was born here, and the Moorish influence can also be tasted in highly spiced Andalusian kebabs.

The rich historical legacy of many classical Mediterranean countries is seen both in Spain's culture and in its food. It is not a peppery or hot cuisine; instead, it is colored with the subtlety of saffron and paprika and the perfume of olive oil, the mild sweetness of pimiento, almonds, tomatoes, and caramelized onions, the earthiness of wild asparagus, mushrooms, and herbs, and the zest of lots of sherry vinegar and garlic. Pork products like Serrano ham and chorizo sausages, game, fish, shellfish, and salt cod are mainstays, while citrus and other fruits make their way into both sweet and savory dishes. Spain's is an uncomplicated cuisine, composed of the best ingredients and the simplest techniques, virtues that are heroically evident in *tapas*.

Cold Iced Tomato Soup from Andalusia

In Spain, there are over thirty varieties of gazpacho, all containing soaked bread. The dish originally came to Andalusia via the Romans, who made it with garlic, bread, olive oil, water, and salt. When Columbus returned to Spain from the New World, he brought with him the tomato and pepper. With these new ingredients, the face of gazpacho changed and became more rosy.

2½ pounds fresh ripe tomatoes, peeled, seeded, and chopped (page 278), or 3 cups (1 28-ounce can) Italian plum tomatoes, chopped, juice reserved
1 green pepper, seeded and coarsely chopped
1 medium red onion, coarsely chopped
1 large cucumber, peeled, halved, seeded, and coarsely chopped
5 to 6 tablespoons red wine vinegar
3 large garlic cloves, minced
1¼ cups tomato juice
¼ cup extra virgin olive oil
1 slice bread, crusts removed, soaked in water and squeezed dry
Salt and freshly ground pepper

Garnish
1 tablespoon olive oil
1 tablespoon butter
3 garlic cloves, peeled and crushed

6 slices white bread, crusts removed, cut into small cubes
¼ cup peeled, seeded, and chopped cucumber
¼ cup diced green pepper
½ tomato, diced
¼ cup diced red onion

1 In a bowl, mix the tomatoes, green pepper, onions, cucumber, vinegar, garlic, tomato juice, olive oil, and bread. Put the mixture in batches in a blender and blend on high speed for 3 to 4 minutes, until very smooth. Strain through a coarse strainer. Season with salt, pepper, and vinegar as needed. Chill.

2 Heat the olive oil and butter in a skillet. Add the crushed garlic and cook until the garlic is golden brown, about 4 to 5 minutes. Remove the garlic and discard. Add the bread cubes and stir to coat. Sauté slowly, stirring occasionally, for 20 to 30 minutes, until the bread cubes are golden. Cool.

3 Serve the soup garnished with cucumbers, green peppers, tomato, red onion, and the homemade croutons.

Serves 6

Chilled White Gazpacho with Almonds and Grapes

Also known as white garlic soup, ajo blanco *is a highly original soup that has not received its due credit. Originally a noon meal for peasants, it was prepared in wooden bowls in the fields and eaten directly from the bowl with wooden spoons. This seductive blend of garlic, almonds, sherry vinegar, and ice water goes back 1,000 years to the Moorish occupation. A must is the splash of sherry vinegar, which comes from Jerez, a very quick jaunt west of the Strait of Gibraltar. I've chosen a version of* ajo blanco *that comes from Málaga, where it is garnished with sweet muscat grapes.*

¾ cup almonds, blanched

3 garlic cloves, peeled

Salt

4 slices (4 ounces) stale hearty white bread,
 crusts removed

4 cups ice water

7 tablespoons olive oil

2 to 3 tablespoons white wine vinegar

2 tablespoons sherry vinegar

1 tablespoon butter

6 thick slices (6 ounces) white bread, crusts
 removed, cut in cubes

1½ cups seedless green grapes

1 Grind the almonds, 2 garlic cloves, and ½ teaspoon salt to a fine consistency in a food processor or blender. Soak the stale bread in 1 cup ice water and squeeze to extract the moisture. Add the bread to the processor. With the processor running, add 6 tablespoons oil and 1 cup ice water slowly in a steady stream. Add the vinegars and mix on high speed 2 minutes. Add 1 cup ice water and mix 2 more minutes. Place in a bowl, add the remaining ice water, and mix well. Adjust the seasonings with the salt and vinegar. Chill.

The soup can be made to this point and chilled for up to 6 hours before serving.

2 Melt the butter and the remaining 1 tablespoon olive oil in a skillet. Crush the remaining garlic clove and add to the pan with the bread cubes, tossing to coat with the butter and oil. Cook over very low heat, stirring occasionally, 20 to 30 minutes, or until the cubes are golden.

3 Serve the soup ice cold garnished with the croutons and grapes.

Serves 6

Smoked Ham Soup with White Beans and Mint

It was really chilly that evening in November. When we arrived for dinner at Beatriz and Jose Luis's in Ecija in southern Spain, the table was already set. Jose Luis greeted us at the door while Beatriz was in the kitchen checking the progress of the soup. When Beatriz came back to the room, we took our seats at the table. Curiously, they both covered their laps with the overhanging edges of the tablecloth, so I followed suit. Much to my delight, it was heated, like an electric blanket. I laughed to myself and wondered why we didn't have such a creation in the United States to keep the winter chill away from the table. This soup was perfect that evening, and I never felt another chill.

¾ cup (5 ounces) dry white beans
6 parsley stems
Pinch of dried thyme
2 bay leaves
1 tablespoon olive oil
¼ pound thickly sliced smoked bacon, cut into ¼-inch dice
1 medium onion, chopped
3 garlic cloves, minced
2 smoked ham hocks (1 pound total)
4 tomatoes, peeled, seeded, and chopped (page 278), or 1½ cups canned Italian plum tomatoes, drained and chopped

6 cups chicken stock (page 272)
3 fresh mint stems, bruised with the back of a knife
Salt and freshly ground pepper
5 tablespoons chopped fresh mint

1 Pick over the white beans and discard any stones. Cover with water and soak overnight. The next day, drain, place in a saucepan with the parsley stems, thyme, bay leaves, and enough water to cover by 2 inches. Simmer until the skins just begin to crack and the beans are tender, about 35 to 45 minutes.

2 Heat a soup pot and add the olive oil, bacon, and onions. Sauté until the onions are soft and the bacon is rendered, about 10 minutes. Add the garlic and continue to cook for 3 minutes, until the bacon just begins to turn golden. Add the ham hocks, tomatoes, chicken stock, and mint stems. Simmer 1 hour.

3 Add the beans and continue to simmer 1 hour. Remove and discard the parsley stems, mint stems, and bay leaves. Remove the ham hocks. Discard the skin and bones, cut the ham into bite-size pieces, and add the ham to the soup. Season with salt and pepper. Ladle the soup into bowls and garnish with chopped mint.

Serves 6

Veal and Green Pepper Turnovers of Murcia

The pastel *is a meat pie filled with chopped veal, chorizo, onions, hard-boiled eggs, and spices and covered with a fine layer of puff pastry. Of Moorish influence, the* pastel *dates back to the 1400s when the Moors occupied Spain. The Moors' influence can be seen today in food, architecture, art, music, and even the faces of the people especially in the southern provinces of Andalusia and Murcia. The* pastel *resembles the Moroccan* bastilla, *hence the similarity in spelling.*

2 tablespoons olive oil

1 medium onion, chopped

2 garlic cloves, minced

2 green bell peppers, seeded and finely chopped

4 ounces chorizo sausage, skin removed

4 ounces finely diced Spanish ham, prosciutto, or Black Forest ham

½ pound ground veal

Pinch of saffron

2 large tomatoes, peeled, seeded and chopped (page 278), or ¾ cup canned Italian plum tomatoes, drained and chopped

¼ cup pitted and finely chopped green olives (page 279)

½ teaspoon cumin

2 hard-boiled eggs, finely chopped

Salt and freshly ground pepper

1 recipe Quick Puff Pastry (recipe follows) or 1 10-ounce package frozen puff pastry sheets, defrosted

2 eggs, whisked

1 Heat the oil in a skillet. Add the onions, garlic, and green pepper and sauté over low heat until soft, 7 minutes. Increase the heat to medium and add the chorizo, ham, and veal. Sauté 5 minutes. Heat the saffron in a small skillet over medium heat, shaking the pan frequently, for 1 minute. Add the saffron, tomatoes, olives, and cumin and simmer, covered, 10 minutes. Uncover and continue to cook until the moisture is gone, 3 to 4 minutes. Add the hard-cooked eggs and mix well. Season with salt and pepper.

2 Preheat the oven to 350°F.

3 On a floured surface with a floured rolling pin, roll the puff pastry to ⅛ inch thick. Using a 3½-inch round cookie cutter or a clean empty can, cut circles. Place a tablespoon of filling to the side of the center of each circle. Combine the whisked eggs with 1 tablespoon water. Brush the edges of half the circle with the egg wash. Fold the circle over, enclosing the filling, and seal the edges. Place the turnovers on an ungreased baking sheet and bake until golden brown, 15 minutes.

Makes 24 turnovers

NOTE: These can be made several hours ahead of time, refrigerated, and baked at the last minute. Alternately, they can be made up to a week ahead of time and stored in the freezer. Remove from the freezer and bake frozen. If they are baked frozen, they will cook 5 to 7 minutes longer. If they get cold when serving, reheat in a 350°F. oven.

PASTA DE HOJALDRE

Quick Puff Pastry

This quick and easy recipe dispels any concern you might have about the difficulty in making puff pastry. It is adapted from a recipe by my dear friend, Lisa Saltzman. One note of caution: You must work quickly so that the butter does not get soft. If the dough gets sticky, dust well with flour and place in the refrigerator for 10 minutes.

1 cup all-purpose flour
⅓ cup cake flour
¼ teaspoon salt
12 tablespoons butter
2 teaspoons lemon juice
¼–⅓ cup ice water

1 Mix the flours and salt and place in the freezer 1 hour before using. Keep the butter refrigerated until ready to use.

2 Place the cold flour in a mixing bowl with the cold butter and cut into ½-inch pieces with 2 forks, or place in a food processor bowl and pulse until the butter is cut up into ¼- to ½-inch pieces. Combine the lemon juice and ice water and add it a little at a time, mixing only until the dough is moistened and just begins to hold together.

3 Turn out onto a lightly floured board and press together as best you can to form a rough rectangle shape. There will be large chunks of butter showing. Do not knead. Roll out the dough into a ½-inch-thick rectangle. Fold the narrow ends toward the center to meet in the center. Fold in half again so that there are 4 layers. This is your first turn.

4 Turn the dough a quarter of a turn and roll again to form a rectangle ½ inch thick. Repeat the folding process. This is your second turn. Turn the dough a quarter of a turn and roll again to form a rectangle ½ inch thick. This time, fold into thirds as you would a letter.

5 Cover the dough with plastic wrap and chill 45 to 60 minutes.

Makes ¾ pound

NOTE: The dough can be stored in the refrigerator for up to 3 days or frozen for a month.

Summer Vegetable Flat Bread

*T*raditional fare on the Balearic islands, this "Catalan pizza" is made in a round or long, narrow oval shape and baked in a wood-fired oven. Cheese and herbs are not used as they are in Italy but instead, a coca is topped with a simple combination of either the harvest's bounty or the cook's leftovers.

Dough

1 tablespoon active dry yeast
2 tablespoons plus 1 cup warm water
3 cups all-purpose flour
1 teaspoon salt
¼ cup olive oil

Topping

2 cups tightly packed Swiss chard, washed and dried
3 tablespoons extra virgin olive oil
5 garlic cloves, minced
1 small zucchini, unpeeled, sliced paper-thin
1 large green bell pepper, seeded and thinly sliced
1 large onion, thinly sliced
Salt and freshly ground pepper
2 ripe tomatoes, thinly sliced
2 teaspoons white wine vinegar
¼ cup pine nuts, toasted (page 277)

1 In a bowl, dissolve the yeast in 2 tablespoons warm water. Let stand 10 minutes until frothy. Add the flour, salt, 1 cup warm water, and ¼ cup olive oil. Knead on a floured surface until smooth, elastic, and slightly tacky to the touch, about 7 to 10 minutes. Place the dough in an oiled bowl and turn it over so it is completely coated with oil. Cover with plastic wrap and place in a warm place (75°F.). Allow to rise until doubled in volume, 1 hour.

2 Preheat the oven to 400°F.

3 Pile Swiss chard leaves on top of one another, roll them up, and slice into ½-inch strips. In a skillet, heat 1 tablespoon oil. Add the garlic and the Swiss chard. Cover and sauté 2 minutes. Uncover and continue to cook until the Swiss chard is soft, 2 to 3 minutes. Remove from the pan and reserve. Add 1 tablespoon oil to the skillet, add the zucchini, and sauté, uncovered, 4 minutes, until cooked. Remove and reserve with the chard. Continue with the peppers and onions. Combine all the vegetables together in a bowl and season with salt and pepper. Reserve.

4 Punch down the dough and cut into 2 pieces. Flour a surface and roll each portion into a long, flat oval shape, ⅜-inch thick, 8 × 10 inches. Build up the edges slightly. Place both pieces of dough side by side on a large oiled baking sheet. (See Note if you are using a pizza stone or oven tiles.) Divide the green vegetables between them and distribute evenly, leaving a ½-inch border around the edges. Distribute the tomatoes over the greens. Drizzle with vinegar. Sprinkle pine nuts on top and drizzle each *coca* with ½ tablespoon oil. Season with salt and pepper. Bake 20 to 25 minutes, until golden. (See Note.)

♪ Remove the *coca* from the pan and cut into wedges. Serve immediately or at room temperature.

Makes 2 coca to serve 8

NOTE: Preheat pizza stone or oven tiles to 400°F. Place one dough on a heavily floured pizza peel or paddle. Proceed with the vegetables. Transfer the *coca* from the paddle and place it directly on the stone or oven tiles. Repeat with the other dough. Bake 15 to 20 minutes, until golden.

PAN CON TOMATE

Grilled Bread with Ripe Tomatoes

The cousin to Rome's bruschetta *or Florence's* fettunta, *Catalonia's* pan con tomate *is equivalent to an American snack food like potato chips or pretzels. A slice of country bread is toasted over a wood fire, smeared with fruity olive oil and crushed ripe tomatoes, and sprinkled with salt. The olive oil and tomato act as a moistener that also provides a burst of flavor. It is essential that the tomatoes be ripe, although the garlic is optional. This dish is also delicious as a lunch accompaniment to a salad, especially when topped with paper-thin slices of Manchego cheese or Serrano ham.*

    2 garlic cloves, peeled
    Coarse salt
    ¼ cup extra virgin olive oil
    12 slices rustic country-style bread,
        cut ¾ inch thick
    6 very ripe tomatoes
    Freshly ground pepper

Garnish
    ½ cup green Spanish olives

    12 anchovy fillets, soaked in cold water 10
        minutes and patted dry
    6 paper-thin slices Spanish ham, prosciutto,
        or Black Forest ham
    12 paper-thin slices Manchego or Parmesan
        cheese (see Note)

1 Mash the garlic and a pinch of salt in a mortar and pestle. Mix with the oil. Set aside.

2 Grill the bread until golden brown on a barbecue over a woodburning fire or toast under a broiler, about 45 to 60 seconds, until golden on each side.

3 Cut the tomatoes in half and cupping a half in your palm, rub both sides of the toast with the tomato, squeezing slightly as you go along to leave pulp, seeds, and juice. Drizzle with garlic-olive oil mixture and sprinkle with salt and pepper. Serve immediately garnished with olives, anchovy fillets, ham, and/or cheese.

Serves 6

NOTE: Manchego cheese is a sheep's milk cheese available in specialty cheese shops.

Chorizo and Cheese Puffs

Spain has an affinity for sausages of all kinds, red, black, or white. Botifarra is a simple white pork sausage while botifarra negra is a coarser, fattier sausage made with bread soaked in pig's blood. Morcilla is another blood sausage made with manteca, or red lard (lard heavily seasoned with paprika). Sobrassada, a Majorcan specialty, is a soft, almost pastelike sausage flavored with garlic and paprika that shows up as a favorite tapas spread on bread. But the most popular Spanish sausage is undoubtedly chorizo, a pork sausage heavily spiced with red pepper, cumin, and garlic and made red with paprika. Chorizo and Manchego cheese pair up in this recipe to make a tasty tapa.

1 cup all-purpose flour

¼ teaspoon crushed red pepper

3 eggs, separated

2 tablespoons olive oil

¾ cup warm beer

Salt and freshly ground pepper

1 quart peanut or corn oil

10 ounces chorizo, skinned and finely chopped

3 tablespoons chopped fresh parsley

1 cup grated Manchego or Parmesan cheese (see Note, page 29)

Fresh parsley leaves, preferably Italian

1 Sift the flour into a bowl. Add the red pepper and mix well. Make a well in the center and add the beaten egg yolks, olive oil, beer, ½ teaspoon salt, and pepper. With a spoon, mix well but do not allow the batter to get stringy. Let rest for 1 hour at room temperature.

2 Heat the peanut or corn oil to 375°F. until it sizzles on contact with a drop of batter.

3 Heat a skillet over medium heat and cook the chorizo 3 minutes, uncovered, stirring occasionally.

4 Beat the egg whites until they form stiff peaks. Fold the whites, chorizo, parsley, and cheese into the batter.

5 Drop the batter by heaping tablespoonfuls into the hot oil, turning occasionally until golden, 2 to 3 minutes. Drain on paper towels.

6 Place on a platter and garnish with parsley leaves. Serve immediately.

Makes 25 to 30 puffs to serve 6 to 8

Fried Vegetable Pancake Ca La Maria

This irresistible potato, cauliflower, and cabbage pancake comes from a restaurant called Ca La Maria. Tucked away in the tiny village of Mollet de Peralada in the northeastern corner of Spain, Maria presides over the kitchen and cooks rustic regional specialties from the Ampurdan area. Verdura frita is typically served with golden-fried slab bacon and allioli. Allioli, *or* allyoli, *is just what it says, garlic and oil. Allioli Negat or garlic mayonnaise, as used in this recipe, incorporates an egg yolk and is basically the same as aioli of Provence or* aillade *of Languedoc. Supposedly, mayonnaise or salsa* mahonesa *was first made at Port Mahon on the Spanish island of Minorca. Perhaps it was brought to Minorca by the French who simply left the garlic out of the aioli. Either way, in this recipe, it is a gift.*

1 pound russet baking potatoes, peeled and
    cut in half
½ pound green cabbage, cored and coarsely
    chopped
½ pound cauliflower, cored and cut into
    large pieces
Salt and freshly ground pepper
6 ounces thickly sliced bacon
¼ cup all-purpose flour
2 tablespoons olive oil
½ recipe Spanish Garlic Mayonnaise
    (page 275)

1 Cook the potatoes, cabbage, and cauliflower in boiling salted water until soft. Drain very well and cool completely. Pass through a food mill or puree in a food processor. Season with salt and pepper. Place the mixture in a skillet and sauté, stirring constantly, until the mixture evaporates most of its moisture and is able to hold its shape, 5 to 8 minutes.

2 Cook the bacon in a skillet over medium heat until golden, 6 to 8 minutes. Keep warm and reserve for a garnish.

3 Place the flour on a plate. Make a 3-inch cake with the vegetable mixture and place the pancake on the flour to dust both sides well. Repeat with the remaining vegetable mixture.

4 Heat the olive oil in a large skillet over high heat. Reduce the heat to medium. Sauté the pancakes until golden brown on one side, 5 to 7 minutes. Turn the pancakes and continue to cook until golden on the other side, 5 to 7 minutes.

5 Place the hot pancakes on a plate and garnish with the bacon and Spanish Garlic Mayonnaise. Serve immediately.

Serves 6

Baked Semolina Pasta with Garlic Mayonnaise

Pasta was first introduced to Spain by the Moors in the eighth century. In Catalonia and Valencia, fishermen traditionally made fideus *with thin one-inch lengths of pasta and the fish they could not sell.*

6 tablespoons olive oil
2 medium onions, chopped
Pinch of saffron
4 tomatoes, chopped, or 1½ cups canned
    Italian plum tomatoes, drained and
    chopped
4 garlic cloves, minced
Pinch of cayenne
¾ teaspoon paprika
1 tablespoon chopped fresh parsley
1 bay leaf
Pinch of dried thyme
½ cup dry white wine (Sauvignon Blanc)
3 pounds fish bones (see Note)
9 cups water
Salt and freshly ground pepper
12 ounces dry 100% semolina fidelini pasta
    (or linguine or fine spaghetti), broken
    into 1-inch lengths
1 recipe Spanish Garlic Mayonnaise (page
    275)

1 In a large skillet, heat 2 tablespoons oil and add the onions. Sauté over low heat for 40 minutes, uncovered, stirring occasionally, until the onions wilt and just begin to turn golden.

Heat the saffron in a small skillet over medium heat, shaking the pan frequently, for 1 minute. Add the saffron, tomatoes, garlic, cayenne, paprika, and parsley to the onions and continue to cook 10 minutes uncovered. Puree in a blender. Transfer to a stockpot. Add the bay leaf, thyme, wine, fish bones, and 6 cups water. Bring to a boil and simmer slowly, uncovered, for 35 minutes. During the cooking, crush the bones with a wooden spoon occasionally. Strain the fish stock and season with salt and pepper.

2 Heat the remaining 4 tablespoons olive oil in a 12-inch paella pan or shallow skillet until very hot and the oil is rippling, 1 minute. Remove from the heat and add the pasta, salt, and pepper and mix well. Place the pan back on medium heat and, stirring constantly, cook the pasta, uncovered, until light golden brown, 3 minutes.

3 Preheat the oven to 425°F.

4 In a saucepan, heat the fish stock to a low simmer. Stirring, gradually add the stock one cup at a time to the pasta, allowing the pasta to absorb stock after each addition. Add as much stock as needed until the pasta is almost cooked, about 10 minutes. Add the last cup of stock and continue to cook until the pasta is tender and still very, very moist, 5 minutes. Add additional water if needed.

This dish can be prepared 2 hours ahead of time to this point and kept at room temperature.

ʃ Place the pan in the oven, uncovered, and bake for 10 minutes, until the pasta is crusty on top but still tender and moist underneath. If the top is not crusty after 10 minutes, run it under the broiler for 10 to 20 seconds. Serve the pasta directly from the pan accompanied by a bowl of Spanish Garlic Mayonnaise.

Serves   6

NOTE: Use white fish like snapper, cod, grouper, perch, sole, trout, or pike. Remove the flippers, liver, gills, fat, skin, tail and any traces of blood.

TORTILLA DE CEBOLLAS A LA ANDALUZA

Caramelized Onion Omelette from Andalusia

Eggs are one of the most basic Spanish ingredients. The tortilla, a one-inch-thick egg pie—like a flat French omelette or a round Italian frittata—can be flavored with a variety of ingredients. Traditionally it was taken along to the fields and eaten at lunch by the farm workers. Today, the tortilla can be found in both fancy restaurants and country roadhouses. This one is common in Andalusia and is made sweet by cooking several pounds of onions until they have caramelized and almost melted.

3 pounds onions
8 tablespoons olive oil
6 eggs
Salt and freshly ground pepper

1 Finely chop the onions. Alternately, these can be chopped in the food processor by pulsing several times. In a skillet, heat 6 tablespoons olive oil, add the onions, and stir to combine. Cover and sauté 15 minutes over medium heat. Do not stir. Remove the cover, stir, and reduce the heat to low. Cover and continue to cook until the onion are very soft and golden, stirring occasionally. This will take 1¼ hours total, until the onions begin to almost melt. Remove from the heat and cool 10 minutes.

2 Beat the eggs with salt and pepper and add the onions. Let stand 15 minutes. In a 10-inch nonstick skillet, heat the remaining 2 tablespoons of oil until it just begins to smoke, 2 minutes. Pour the eggs into the pan and cook over moderate heat, using a spatula to loosen the edges, 10 to 15 minutes. When the tortilla is almost firm, put a plate over the top of the skillet. Invert the plate and skillet. Slide the tortilla back into the skillet, browned side up. Cook briefly until done. It should be slightly juicy inside.

3 Cut into wedges and serve hot or at room temperature.

Serves   6

NOTE: This can be prepared 1 day in advance. Bring to room temperature before serving.

Wild Mushroom and Roasted Garlic Flan

It is said that there are four mushroom hunters for every mushroom in Catalonia. This fiercely competitive sport has hunters hiding their bicycles along the side of the road, ducking behind trees and wearing camouflage clothing so as not to reveal their closely guarded "secret spot." Each fall, these warriors trudge through the forests in search of cèpes, chanterelles, and morels. To get the full effect of the Catalonian bounty, stop by Barcelona's Boqueria market in October and take a gander at the piles and piles of these rich, earthly delights. Stewed with game, simply oiled and grilled, or made into a flan, they are the gem of fall's harvest.

1 large head garlic
1 tablespoon olive oil
¼ ounce dried mushrooms
4 tablespoons butter
¼ cup minced onion
½ pound wild mushrooms, any variety or combination, thinly sliced
5 tablespoons medium-sweet Spanish sherry (Amontillado)
Salt and freshly ground pepper
3 egg yolks
3 whole eggs
1½ cups heavy cream
Small pinch of nutmeg
2½ cups chicken stock (page 272)
1 tablespoon chopped fresh parsley

1 Preheat the oven to 350°F.

2 Place the whole head of garlic in a small baking dish and drizzle with the olive oil and ¼ cup water. Cover with foil and bake in the oven until soft, 40 to 50 minutes. Press through a food mill or potato ricer to extract the pulp and reserve.

3 Pour ¾ cup boiling water over the dried mushrooms and soak 30 minutes. Drain, rinse, and finely chop the mushrooms. Reserve the soaking liquid and strain it through a layer of cheesecloth or a paper towel to remove the grit.

4 Heat 3 tablespoons butter in a skillet and sauté the onions until soft, 7 minutes. Add the sliced fresh mushrooms and sauté, uncovered, until the released juices have evaporated and the mushrooms are cooked, 10 to 15 minutes. Remove the mushrooms and reserve a quarter of them for garnish. Chop the remaining mushrooms and put them back in the pan with the reconstituted dried mushrooms and 3 tablespoons sherry, and simmer slowly 10 minutes, until dry. Season with salt and pepper. Remove from the pan and cool.

5 Whisk together the egg yolks, whole eggs, 1 cup heavy cream, garlic, nutmeg, ¼ teaspoon salt, and pepper. Add the mushrooms and mix well.

NOTE: These can be done up to one day ahead of time to this point. However, bring the custard mixture to room temperature before baking.

6 Butter six ⅔-cup ramekins with the remaining 1 tablespoon butter. Divide the flan mixture among the ramekins and place in a baking dish. Pour boiling water into the baking dish halfway up the sides of the ramekins. Bake in the oven 35 minutes, until the custards are firm in the center and brown on top.

7 Combine the chicken stock and the mushroom soaking liquid in a saucepan over medium-high heat and reduce by one-third, 10 minutes. In another saucepan, combine ½ cup cream and 2 tablespoons sherry over medium-high heat and reduce by one-half, 4 to 5 minutes. Combine the cream, stock, and reserved mushrooms. Stir well. Season with salt and pepper.

8 Cool the flans 5 minutes. Run a knife around the edge of the custards and turn onto a plate, browned side up. Pour the sauce around the custards and garnish with parsley.

Serves 6

Spanish Omelette, Gypsy-Style

*H*uevos a la Flamenca *originated in Seville, home of the flamenco dance. Just the word* flamenco *conjures up colorful dancers, gypsies, and robust guitar music. This vivacious dish is a whirl of red, green, orange, white, and yellow.*

3 tablespoons olive oil

1 medium onion, finely chopped

2 garlic cloves, minced

3 tomatoes, peeled, seeded, chopped and drained (page 278), or 1¼ cups canned Italian plum tomatoes, drained and chopped

1 teaspoon paprika

Salt and freshly ground pepper

⅓ cup chicken stock (page 272)

4 ounces Spanish ham, prosciutto, or Black Forest ham, cut into ¼-inch dice

4 ounces chorizo sausage, cut in ¼-inch slices

8 eggs

Pinch of cayenne

½ cup fresh or frozen peas, blanched

8 asparagus spears, cut into 1½-inch lengths and blanched

1 small red bell pepper, roasted (page 278)

2 tablespoons fresh chopped parsley

1 Preheat the oven to 400°F.

2 Heat 2 tablespoons oil in a skillet and sauté the onions until soft, 7 minutes. Add the garlic and sauté slowly 1 minute longer. Add the tomatoes, paprika, salt, and pepper and cook 2 to 3 minutes, stirring. Add the chicken stock, cover, and cook 5 minutes.

3 In another skillet, heat the remaining 1 tablespoon oil and sauté the ham and chorizo until golden, 5 minutes.

4 Pour the sauce into a 2-quart ovenproof baking dish. Break one egg at a time into a small bowl and slip into the sauce, distributing the eggs evenly in the tomato sauce. Season with cayenne, salt, and pepper. Arrange the ham, chorizo, peas, asparagus, and roasted pepper strips decoratively around and between the eggs. Season well with salt and pepper. Sprinkle with parsley.

5 Bake until the egg whites are lightly set and the yolks are still runny, 10 minutes. Garnish with parsley and serve immediately.

Serves 4 to 6

Tiny Spiced Meatballs with Tomatoes

I was invited for a simple dinner at the country house of my friend Beatriz Tamarit who lives outside Seville. I know Beatriz enough to know that anything she does is far from simple. On the long table she spread at least fifteen different tapas, *including these tiny succulent meatballs. I closed my eyes as I tasted one and was immediately transported to other parts of the Mediterranean. These highly spiced meatballs are also made in North Africa, the Middle East, Turkey, and Greece and are most frequently known there as* kefta. *In Spain, they are called* albondigas *and this is Beatriz's recipe.*

½ pound ground pork
½ pound ground beef
½ pound ground veal
1 cup dry bread crumbs
6 garlic cloves, minced
2 tablespoons chopped fresh parsley
1½ teaspoons ground coriander seeds
½ teaspoon nutmeg
½ teaspoon cumin
Pinch of cayenne
Salt and freshly ground pepper
3 tablespoons olive oil
1 medium onion, minced
1 cup dry white wine
3 cups (1 28-ounce can) Italian plum
    tomatoes, crushed

1 Preheat the oven to 350°F.

2 In a bowl, combine the pork, beef, veal, bread crumbs, 4 garlic cloves, parsley, ground coriander, nutmeg, cumin, cayenne, ¾ teaspoon salt, and ¼ teaspoon pepper. Form into 32 1-inch meatballs and place on a baking sheet. Bake for 10 to 12 minutes. Remove from the oven and reserve.

3 Heat the olive oil in a skillet. Add the onions and the remaining 2 garlic cloves and sauté 7 minutes, until soft. Add the wine and the tomatoes and simmer slowly 15 minutes. Add the meatballs, ½ teaspoon salt, and pepper and continue to simmer slowly 10 minutes.

4 Serve immediately or at room temperature.

Serves 6

NOTE: This recipe can be made completely up to 2 days ahead of time. Reheat before serving.

Pork Dumplings Wrapped in Cabbage Leaves

*F*arcel *in Catalan means" a little bundle" or "roll." This particular pork and cabbage dumpling is inspired by the cuisine of the Roussillon area, just over the French border. However, rolled or stuffed leaves, whether they are cabbage, grape, or lettuce, are found all over the Mediterranean.*

1 2- to 3-pound head green cabbage
2 slices white bread, crusts removed
⅓ cup milk
2 tablespoons olive oil
2 medium onions, finely chopped
3 garlic cloves, minced
1 pound ground pork
⅓ cup pine nuts, toasted (page 277)
¼ teaspoon crushed red pepper
2 tablespoons chopped fresh parsley
⅓ cup raisins
1 tablespoon sherry vinegar
2 eggs, lightly beaten
Salt and freshly ground pepper
1 28-ounce can chopped tomatoes
1 tablespoon tomato paste
1 teaspoon sugar
¾ cup dry white wine
Fresh parsley leaves, preferably Italian

1 Core the cabbage deeply by cutting into it 1½ to 2 inches. Fill a pot with water deep enough to submerge the cabbage and bring to a boil. Add the cabbage and turn every few min-utes until the leaves just begin to become trans-parent, 20 minutes. Remove the cabbage from the water and remove the loose outer leaves, which are soft. As soon as you reach leaves that are more firm, put the cabbage back into the water and repeat the process to yield 18 leaves. Trim the ribs on the larger leaves so they are not so thick. Continue to cook the center core until it is transparent. Remove from the water, cool, and finely chop the core.

2 In a large bowl, soak the bread in the milk. In a skillet, heat 2 tablespoons oil and sauté the onions until soft, about 7 minutes. Re-move half of the onions and reserve. Add the garlic and pork and cook slowly 12 minutes. Squeeze the bread, discard any excess milk, and return the bread to the bowl. With a slotted spoon, add the onions and pork to the bowl. Add ½ cup chopped cabbage, pine nuts, red pepper, parsley, raisins, vinegar, eggs, 1 teaspoon salt, and ½ teaspoon black pepper. Mix well.

3 Place 2 to 3 tablespoons filling in the cen-ter of each cabbage leaf. Fold up 2 sides of the cabbage leaf and roll to enclose the filling. Place the dumplings, seam side down, in a single layer in a baking dish.

4 Preheat the oven to 350°F.

5 Heat the remaining onions in a skillet. Add the tomatoes, tomato paste, sugar, and wine and simmer 15 minutes. Season with salt and pepper. Puree in a food processor or blender. Pour the sauce over the dumplings and bake until the leaves are soft, 1 to 1½ hours. Serve garnished with parsley leaves.

Serves 6

PINCHITOS MORUNOS

Spicy Pork Kebabs with Moorish Flavors

Pinchitos are heavily seasoned miniature meat kebabs grilled over a charcoal-fired hibachi or brazier. The spice mixture is of North African and Middle Eastern influence but the use of pork is not. Pork consumption is forbidden by the Muslim religion. In Spain, pork is favored but in North Africa, beef and lamb predominate.

2 garlic cloves, sliced
Salt and freshly ground pepper
1 teaspoon coriander seeds
¾ teaspoon paprika
¾ teaspoon cumin seeds
½ teaspoon dried thyme
¼ teaspoon crushed red pepper
1 teaspoon curry powder
4 tablespoons olive oil
1 tablespoon lemon juice
1 tablespoon chopped fresh parsley
1 pound lean pork, cut into ¾- to 1-inch cubes

1 In a mortar, pound the garlic with a pinch of salt to make a paste.

2 In a dry skillet, heat the coriander seeds, paprika, cumin seeds, thyme, crushed red pepper and curry powder until hot and aromatic, 30 seconds. Remove from the pan and put the mixture into a spice grinder or mortar and pestle. Grind to make a fine powder. In a bowl, combine the garlic, spices, olive oil, lemon juice, parsley, ¾ teaspoon salt, pepper, and pork cubes. Toss well to coat completely and let marinate several hours, mixing occasionally.

3 Skewer the pork. Broil or grill over coals, turning every 2 to 3 minutes, until well browned and still juicy, about 10 to 15 minutes. Baste occasionally with the marinade. Serve immediately.

Makes 12 skewers to serve 6

Pork Tenderloin Stuffed with Onion Marmalade

Because pork would not be used in a Muslim country, this is obviously a modern adaptation of a historical combination of Arabic ingredients— spices, raisins, citrus, caramelized onions—and meat. The outcome is a lusty blending of sweet, savory, and sour flavors, so prevalent in Morocco and other countries in North Africa. I tasted this dish in the hill town of Arcos de la Frontera in Andalusia, in the very south of Spain.

1 large (1 pound) pork tenderloin, trimmed
3 tablespoons olive oil
1 garlic clove, minced
Large pinch of paprika
Large pinch of cumin
Large pinch of cayenne
Large pinch of cloves
Freshly ground pepper
1 orange
3 tablespoons sultana or golden raisins
2 tablespoons sherry vinegar
1 medium onion, thinly sliced
1 teaspoon sugar
Salt
3 garlic cloves, peeled
3 sprigs of parsley
1 bay leaf
4 whole cloves
¼ cup dry white wine (Sauvignon Blanc)
1½ cups chicken stock (page 272)

1 Butterfly the pork by slitting lengthwise just far enough so it opens up to make a flat piece. Flatten slightly with a meat pounder. In a bowl, combine 1 tablespoon olive oil, the minced garlic, paprika, cumin, cayenne, cloves, and pepper. Rub the pork with the mixture, place in a baking dish, cover, and refrigerate overnight.

2 Using a vegetable peeler, zest one-quarter of the orange. Chop very fine. Juice the orange. In a small saucepan, combine the orange zest, orange juice, raisins, and sherry vinegar. Simmer very slowly, uncovered, for 10 minutes. Heat the remaining 2 tablespoons olive oil in a skillet, add the onions, and cook over medium heat until very soft, 20 minutes. Add the raisin mixture, sprinkle with sugar, and continue to sauté very slowly, covered, until very soft, 30 minutes. Add ¼ cup water and continue to sauté, uncovered, 20 minutes, until almost dry. Season with salt and pepper.

3 Flatten the pork on a work surface, cut side up. Season with salt and pepper. Spread the onion marmalade on the pork. Close to re-shape. Tie at 1-inch intervals with kitchen string.

This can be done 1 day ahead to this point.

4 Place the pork in a casserole with the peeled garlic, parsley, bay leaf, whole cloves, white wine, and chicken stock. Cover and bring to a boil. Turn down the heat to very low and simmer 30 minutes. Remove the pork and keep warm. Reduce the broth by one-half to thicken slightly, 10 to 15 minutes. Strain. Season with salt and pepper.

5 Remove the strings and slice the meat into ½-inch slices. Place on a platter with the sauce.

Serves 6

HABAS CON CHORIZO
Stewed Chick-Peas with Chorizo

The Phoenicians were known as the "traveling salesmen of the Mediterranean." In the south of Spain, they traded their glass, metal, and cloth for copper extracted from Spanish mines and salt from the coastal marshes. The Phoenicians also introduced chick-peas to the Spanish, who called them garbanzo beans. Chick-peas and other pulses remain a staple of Spanish cuisine, especially in Catalonia. The use of pulses eventually spread north to the Languedoc area of France where cassoulet, a dish of white beans, confit of duck, lamb, and sausage, is one of the most important dishes of southwestern France.

2 cups (12 ounces) dry chick-peas
1 small onion, quartered
⅛ teaspoon ground cloves
⅛ teaspoon cinnamon
1 bay leaf
Pinch of dried thyme
6 parsley stems
¼ cup extra virgin olive oil
1 medium onion, minced
3 garlic cloves, minced

3 chorizo (about 12 ounces total), pricked
    with a fork
Salt and freshly ground pepper

1 Pick over the chick-peas and discard any stones. Cover with water and soak overnight. The next day, drain and place in a saucepan with the quartered onion, ground cloves, cinnamon, bay leaf, thyme, parsley stems, and enough water to cover by 2-inches. Simmer, uncovered, until the skins just begin to crack and the beans are tender, about 30 to 45 minutes.

2 In a large skillet, heat the oil and sauté the onions, garlic, and chorizo until the onions are soft, 7 minutes. Add the chick-peas and their liquid and simmer slowly, uncovered, until the liquid is almost gone, 40 minutes. Season with salt and pepper.

3 Remove the chorizo from the pan and slice on the diagonal into thin slices. Return to the chick-peas and heat thoroughly.

Serves 6

NOTE: This recipe can be prepared completely ahead of time and reheated to serve.

Roasted Potatoes with Spicy Tomato Sauce

This simple, yet fiery dish is served all over Spain and its depth of spiciness depends upon the area where it is made. Often these roasted potatoes are accompanied by Spanish Garlic Mayonnaise (page 275).

3 pounds red potatoes, unpeeled and cut
    into ¾-inch cubes
4 tablespoons olive oil
Salt and freshly ground pepper
¼ cup minced onion
2 garlic cloves, minced
1 pound fresh tomatoes, cored and chopped
    (page 278), or 2 cups canned tomatoes,
    drained and chopped
1 tablespoon tomato paste
½ cup dry white wine
¼ teaspoon crushed red pepper flakes
½ teaspoon Tabasco sauce
1 bay leaf
2 tablespoons chopped fresh parsley
¼ teaspoon chopped thyme or ⅛ teaspoon
    dried thyme
Pinch of sugar
2 to 3 teaspoons red wine vinegar

1 Preheat the oven to 375°F.

2 Toss the potatoes, 2 tablespoons olive oil, salt, and pepper together in a baking dish. Arrange in a single layer and bake on the top shelf of the oven for 45 minutes, or until golden and cooked through.

3 Meanwhile, heat the remaining 2 tablespoons olive oil in a skillet and on medium-low heat, sauté the onion and garlic until soft, 10 minutes. Add the tomatoes, tomato paste, wine, 1 cup water, red pepper flakes, Tabasco, bay leaf, parsley, thyme, sugar, salt, and pepper. Simmer very slowly 20 minutes. Cool for 10 minutes. Remove the bay leaf and puree in a blender until smooth. Season with salt, pepper, and vinegar.

4 Place the warm potatoes on a serving dish and pour the sauce over the top.

Serves 6

Braised Spring Vegetables Stew from Alicante

In Italy, there is a mixed vegetable stew called ciamotta, *in France, the* garbure *and the familiar* ratatouille, *and in Greece, the* briam *and* lahanika yiahni. *In Spain,* menestra *is a colorful stewed hodgepodge of spring vegetables chosen from the* huerta, *or market garden, when they are at their prime.*

4 large fresh artichokes, cleaned (page 278)
5 tablespoons olive oil
6 small red potatoes
1¾ pounds fava beans in their pods or
    1 10-ounce package frozen fava beans
4 ounces thinly sliced Spanish ham,
    prosciutto, or Black Forest ham, cut into
    strips
1 medium onion, chopped
3 tomatoes, peeled, seeded, and chopped
    (page 278), or 1¼ cups canned Italian
    plum tomatoes, drained and chopped
2 small white turnips, peeled and cut into
    ¼-inch slices
2 carrots, peeled and cut into ¼-inch slices
2 cups green beans, trimmed and halved
1 cup fresh sweet peas, blanched, or frozen
    peas, unthawed
2 cups chicken stock (page 272)
10 spears asparagus, cut into 1½-inch
    lengths
Salt and freshly ground pepper
2 hard-boiled eggs, coarsely chopped
2 tablespoons chopped fresh parsley

1 Cut the artichoke hearts into quarters. Heat 2 tablespoons oil in a skillet and sauté the artichokes over low heat, covered, until almost soft, 15 minutes. Remove from the pan.

2 Cook the potatoes in boiling salted water until almost cooked, 15 minutes. Drain and cool. Cut in half. If using fresh fava beans, remove them from their pods. Boil the fava beans 30 seconds in boiling water. Remove the skins and discard. If using frozen beans, omit this step.

3 Heat the remaining 3 tablespoons olive oil in a skillet and sauté the ham until golden, 10 minutes. Remove from the pan with a slotted spoon and reserve. Add the onions and sauté until soft, 10 minutes. Add the tomatoes and simmer, uncovered, 10 minutes. Add the turnips, carrots, green beans, peas, potatoes, and artichokes and cook 5 minutes. Add the chicken stock, fava beans, and asparagus and simmer 10 minutes, uncovered, until all the vegetables are cooked. Season with salt and pepper.

4 Serve hot or at room temperature garnished with hardboiled eggs, ham, and parsley.

Serves 6

NOTE: If fava beans are unavailable, substitute 1 cup zucchini or summer squash, cut into ¼-inch slices. Add with the chicken stock and the asparagus.

Stuffed Eggplant with Oregano and Mint

Like the rest of the Mediterranean, Spain has an affinity for stuffed vegetables. This recipe is from the one-star restaurant called L'Ampurdan, a few miles north of the town of Figueras in Catalonia. Josep Mercader, the owner and chef, is considered to be the father of modern Catalan cuisine. He delved into the history of Catalonia and put together some wonderfully innovative, modern dishes that transcend time. He died in 1979, but his son-in-law Jaume Subiros now follows in his footsteps. If you go to his restaurant, ask him to make you his deep-fried anchovy spines. They are a must.

2 large eggplants
Salt and freshly ground pepper
7 tablespoons olive oil
6 garlic cloves, peeled and bruised
1 small onion, minced
3 tomatoes, peeled, seeded, and chopped (page 278), or 1 cup canned Italian plum tomatoes, drained and chopped
½ teaspoon sugar
1 teaspoon chopped fresh thyme
¾ teaspoon chopped fresh oregano
Large pinch of chopped fresh mint
8 anchovy fillets, soaked in cold water for 10 minutes and patted dry
½ cup fresh bread crumbs

3 tablespoons chopped fresh parsley
3 garlic cloves, minced

1 Halve the eggplants lengthwise and score the pulp of the eggplants with a knife, leaving the skin and a ½-inch border of the pulp intact and attached. Salt the eggplants and let them sit in a colander, cut side down, 30 minutes. Wash the salt off the eggplants and squeeze them dry.

2 Heat 2 tablespoons olive oil in a skillet over medium heat and fry the eggplants on all sides until golden, 35 minutes total. Remove and let sit until the eggplants are cool enough to handle. In the same skillet, add 1 tablespoon oil and sauté the garlic cloves until light golden brown, 4 to 5 minutes. Remove and discard the garlic. With a spoon, scoop out the pulp of the eggplants, leaving the skin and ½-inch of the pulp intact and attached. Do not pierce the skin. Chop the pulp very finely, return it to the skillet with the onions, and cook, uncovered, until soft, 15 minutes. Add the tomatoes, sugar, thyme, oregano, mint, anchovies, salt, and pepper and simmer slowly, uncovered, 30 minutes. Taste and season.

3 Preheat the oven to 375°F.

4 Fill the eggplant shells with the tomato-eggplant stuffing. Place in a greased 13 × 9-inch baking dish. Combine the bread crumbs, parsley, and garlic and sprinkle over the top. Drizzle with the remaining 4 tablespoons oil.

NOTE: This dish can be made ahead to this point. Cover with plastic wrap and place in the refrigerator. Bring to room temperature before baking.

♪ Bake 30 to 40 minutes, until the eggplants are soft and the tops are golden brown. Serve immediately.

Serves 6

ACELGAS CON PASAS, PINONES, Y MIGAS

Wilted Greens with Raisins, Pine Nuts, and Fried Bread

Wilted greens, pine nuts, raisins, and garlic are a common combination in Catalonia, Provence, Genoa, and Sicily. The combination can be seen on a pizza in northern Italy and in a tart in Provence. In Genoa and Sicily, it is also served as a side dish, or contorno. *Here in Catalonia, it is a first course but is mouth-watering when baked on* coca *dough, the equivalent of Catalan pizza.*

3 large bunches of spinach or Swiss chard
Salt and freshly ground pepper
¼ cup sultana or golden raisins
¼ cup dark raisins
¼ pound stale peasant bread, crusts
    removed
6 tablespoons extra virgin olive oil
6 garlic cloves
4 anchovy fillets, soaked in cold water for
    10 minutes and patted dry
½ cup pine nuts, toasted (page 277)

1 Remove all stems from the greens, wash, and dry well. Place in a skillet with 1 teaspoon water, salt, and pepper. Cover and cook over medium heat, tossing occasionally, until wilted. This will take 3 to 10 minutes, depending on whether it is spinach or Swiss chard. Drain.

2 Pour 1 cup boiling water over all the raisins and let stand 15 minutes. Drain.

3 Preheat the oven to 350°F.

4 Tear the bread into crouton-size pieces or cut into 1-inch cubes and place on a baking sheet. Heat 4 tablespoons olive oil in a skillet, add 4 minced garlic cloves, and turn off the heat immediately. Pour over the bread cubes and toss gently. Bake until golden and crisp, tossing occasionally, 10 to 15 minutes. Season with salt and pepper.

5 Heat the remaining 2 tablespoons olive oil in a large skillet over low heat and sauté the remaining 2 minced garlic cloves 1 minute. Mash the anchovies, add to the garlic, and stir until dissolved. Add the pine nuts, raisins, wilted greens, salt, and pepper. Toss together well and place on a platter. Garnish with the fried bread and serve warm.

Serves 6

Grilled Leeks and Scallions with Romesco

Romesco sauce hails from Tarragona, the old Roman capital of Spain. The word romesco *has three meanings: a seafood dish, the accompanying sauce, and the hot red pepper that grows here and is used to give the sauce its characteristic punch. Romesco, like rouille of Provence,* tarator *of Turkey, and* harissa *of Morocco, provides a good assault to the palate in an otherwise undistinguished dish. Romesco sauce differs from town to town and cook to cook, but is predominantly an emulsified sauce of olive oil, red pepper, bread, tomato, almonds, garlic, and vinegar.*

Sauce

3 tomatoes, peeled, cored, seeded, and
    chopped (page 278)
5 garlic cloves, unpeeled
2 dried sweet red peppers, such as ancho
    peppers (available at health food stores),
    or 2 teaspoons paprika
¼ teaspoon crushed red pepper
6 to 7 tablespoons red wine vinegar
6 to 7 tablespoons olive oil
1 slice white bread
15 whole almonds, skins removed
    (see Note)
15 whole hazelnuts, skins removed
    (see Note)
1 teaspoon paprika
Salt and freshly ground pepper

Vegetables

18 small leeks
18 large scallions
2 tablespoons butter, melted
2 tablespoons olive oil

1 Preheat the oven to 350°F.

2 Roast the tomatoes and garlic in an ungreased roasting pan for 30 minutes. Remove from the oven and peel, core, and seed the tomatoes. Peel the garlic and reserve both.

3 Place the dried red peppers and crushed red pepper in a saucepan with ¾ cup water and 4 tablespoons vinegar. Bring to a boil, cover, and simmer slowly 10 minutes. Turn the heat off and let steep 30 minutes. Strain the peppers, discard the seeds, and finely chop. (If using paprika, omit this step and add the two teaspoons of paprika and crushed red pepper in step 4 instead of the peppers.)

4 Heat 2 tablespoons oil in a small skillet and fry the bread until golden. Transfer to a food processor. In the same oil, fry the almonds and hazelnuts until golden and add to the processor with the peppers (or the two teaspoons paprika and the crushed red pepper), peeled garlic, and tomatoes. With the motor running, gradually pour in the remaining 4 to 5 tablespoons olive oil and 2 to 3 tablespoons vinegar, 1 teaspoon paprika, salt, and pepper. Strain through a coarse-mesh strainer. Let sit 2 hours.

5 Heat the grill until very hot.

6 In the meantime, trim the leeks and scallions and wash them well. Combine the butter and oil and brush the leeks and scallions with the mixture. When the grill is ready, place the leeks on the grill and cook, turning occasionally, about 15 minutes. When almost blackened, add the scallions and grill until golden, 5 minutes. Remove from the grill and wrap in newspaper. Allow to steam 10 minutes.

7 Remove the black skin from the leeks. Place the leeks and scallions on a serving plate with the *romesco* sauce.

Serves 6

NOTE: Alternatively, the leeks and scallions can be baked on the top shelf of a 450°F. oven, turning occasionally. The scallions will cook in 10 to 15 minutes and the leeks in 35 to 40 minutes.

To remove the almond skins, blanch the almonds in boiling water 1 minute. Puncture the skin and remove. Discard the skins.

To remove the hazelnut skins, place the hazelnuts on a baking sheet and spray with a light mist of water. Bake in a 325°F. oven 10 to 15 minutes. Cool slightly, wrap in a kitchen towel, and rub them together inside the towel to remove the skins.

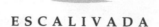

Warm Charcoal-Grilled Vegetable Salad

Escalivar is a Catalan word meaning "to cook in hot embers" or "to roast." As in the celebrated ratatouille of Provence, the vegetables are oiled and then grilled. With escalivada, however, they are removed from the grill and composed into a warm or room-temperature salad whereas in ratatouille, the vegetables are stewed together after they are taken from the grill. In both cases, grilling imparts a smoky flavor. Both dishes are best when made in the late summer or fall at the peak of the vegetable harvest.

1½ pounds eggplant, preferably long thin ones
5 small tomatoes
1 large red bell pepper
1 large green bell pepper
2 small onions, peeled
5 tablespoons extra virgin olive oil
2 garlic cloves, minced
Salt and freshly ground pepper
3 tablespoons chopped fresh parsley
18 cured black olives

1 Start a charcoal grill (See Note).

2 Preheat the oven to 350°F.

3 Wash and dry the vegetables. Do not peel. Grill the eggplant, tomatoes, peppers, and onions over a very hot fire, turning occasion-ally, until they are black on all sides, about 7 to 12 minutes, depending upon the size. Cut the tomatoes in half. Coat all the vegetables with 1 tablespoon oil. Place the vegetables in a roast-ing pan, with the tomatoes cut side up, and roast (tomatoes will cook in 20 minutes, pep-pers and eggplant in 45 minutes, and onions, 1 hour). As soon as they are done, remove them from the oven.

4 When the eggplant, tomatoes, peppers, and onions are done, place in a plastic bag and let stand 15 minutes. Core, seed, and peel the peppers. Slice into thin strips. Peel the eggplant and tear into thin strips. Slice the onions. Slip the tomatoes out of their skins and cut them into quarters.

5 Arrange the vegetables on a serving dish, alternating stripes of color. Season with salt and pepper and drizzle with the remaining 4 table-spoons olive oil. Combine the parsley and garlic and chop together until fine. Sprinkle over the vegetables. Garnish with the olives and serve.

Serves 6

NOTE: The vegetables can also be charred under the broiler, directly over the gas burners of the stove, or in a cast-iron pan. (See Red-Hot Smoked Tomato Relish, page 223.)

Fava Bean Salad with Fresh Mint

Beans and ham are a classic combination in Spain, the Languedoc, and all over Italy. This version, from L'Ampurdan, combines a time-honored favorite with a twist of newness, the mint. Another trademark of Josep Mercader, this salad is easy to make and quite addictive. If fresh fava beans are unavailable, do not substitute dry fava beans. Substitute 2 10-ounce packages frozen fava or lima beans. If fresh mint is unavailable, omit it completely.

3½ pounds fava beans in their pods or
    2 10-ounce packages frozen fava beans
3 sprigs of fresh mint
Salt and freshly ground pepper
4 ounces thinly sliced Spanish ham,
    prosciutto, or Black Forest ham
1 small head of romaine lettuce, washed
    and cut into thin strips
1 teaspoon Dijon mustard
⅓ cup extra virgin olive oil
2 tablespoons red wine vinegar

1 Peel the fava beans and discard the pods. Bring a pot of water to a boil. Add the fava beans and simmer 30 seconds. Remove the fava beans and cool. Peel.

2 Remove the leaves from the mint sprigs but reserve the sprigs. Pile the leaves one on top of the other and roll like a cigar. Cut into very thin strips and reserve. With the back of a knife, tap the mint sprigs several times to bring out the flavor. Bring 5 cups salted water and the mint sprigs to a boil. Add the fava beans and cook, uncovered, until tender, 3 minutes. Drain, discard the sprigs, and cool.

3 Cut the ham into thin strips. Combine the ham, lettuce, mint strips, and beans.

4 Whisk together the mustard, olive oil, and vinegar. Season with salt and pepper. Toss the vinaigrette with the bean mixture and serve immediately.

Serves 6

ESQUEIXADA

Shredded Cod Salad with Tomatoes, Peppers, and Onions

Spain began to import salt cod from the south of France in the fifteenth century. Today salt cod appears all over the Mediterranean; however, only in Catalonia is it eaten soaked but uncooked. Thus, it is imperative that the fish soak in many changes of cold water for a minimum of two to three days before use. Esqueixada (pronounced es-kwe-sada) is a popular and refreshing summer salad in Catalonia. The cod is torn or shredded (esqueixar) for this recipe. A knife must never be used.

¾ pound dry salt cod (see Note)
1 small red onion, thinly sliced
Salt and freshly ground pepper
3 medium tomatoes, peeled, seeded, and chopped (page 278)
1 red bell pepper, seeded and diced
2 garlic cloves, minced
6 tablespoons extra virgin olive oil
3 tablespoons red wine vinegar
24 cured black olives
12 slices rustic country-style bread, toasted

1 Soak the salt cod in cold water for 2 or 3 days, changing and replenishing the water a few times per day. Drain and press the cod with your hands to rid it of any excess water. Remove the skin and bones and discard. Tear the cod into thin strips with your fingers and place in a bowl.

2 Soak the onion in salted water 30 minutes. Drain and pat dry. Place in the bowl with the cod. Add the tomatoes to the cod. Add the peppers, garlic, oil, vinegar, and olives. Season with salt and pepper. Let marinate 2 to 3 hours.

3 Serve at room temperature. Place on a serving plate and serve with the toasted bread.

Serves 6

NOTE: Dry salt cod is available in fish markets or Italian or Spanish specialty shops.

Salt Cod Salad with Oranges and Olives

A Spanish friend told me that if I got to Granada in the south of Spain, I really must try this salad. I must admit that the combination of ingredients made me rather curious. So when I was in Granada, I scoured every restaurant menu until I found what I was looking for. The rustic little restaurant was tucked into a side street of bustling Granada and actually served two variations of the famed salad, (one with just olives, red onions, oranges, and sherry vinaigrette and this irresistible version with revived salt cod.)

1 pound dry salt cod (see Note, page 50)
3 cups milk
6 parsley stems
Pinch of thyme
1 bay leaf
1 garlic clove, peeled
1 tablespoon sherry vinegar
3 tablespoons white wine vinegar
3 tablespoons orange juice
½ cup extra virgin olive oil
Salt and freshly ground pepper
½ small red onion, thinly sliced
24 cured black olives
3 oranges, peeled and sectioned (page 279)
1 hard-boiled egg, peeled

1 Soak the salt cod in cold water for 2 or 3 days, changing and replenishing the water a few times per day. Drain and place in a saucepan with the milk, parsley stems, thyme, bay leaf, and enough cold water to cover. Over high heat, bring to just below the boiling point, cover, and turn off the heat. Let stand 10 minutes. Drain and chill immediately until completely cool. Remove and discard the skin and bones. Flake the fish and place in a bowl.

2 To make a vinaigrette, mash the garlic in a mortar and pestle. Mix together the garlic, sherry vinegar, white wine vinegar, olive oil, salt, and pepper. Marinate the cod in the vinaigrette 1 hour.

3 Add the onions, olives, and oranges to the cod and vinaigrette. Adjust the seasonings with salt, pepper, and vinegar. Place on a serving plate and garnish with the chopped egg.

Serves 6

Salad of Marinated Chicken, Pickled Vegetables, and Herbs

Escabeche comes from the Arabic word sikbaj, *which means "acid food" or "vinegar stew." The technique came to Spain by way of Persia and Arabia. A simple means of preservation that is easier than salting and drying, it always follows the same principles: First the fish, fowl, or vegetable is cooked in a vinegar solution and then it is allowed to marinate or pickle with a combination of flavorful aromatics like garlic, herbs, and spices for a period of time.*

1 3- to 3½-pound chicken
Salt and freshly ground pepper
½ cup olive oil
2 cups white wine vinegar
2 cups dry white wine
2 tablespoons peppercorns, lightly cracked
6 whole cloves
8 bay leaves
1½ teaspoons chopped fresh thyme
¾ teaspoon chopped fresh rosemary
2 bulbs garlic, cloves separated and peeled
12 ounces pearl onions, peeled
3 carrots, peeled and diagonally cut into
    ¼-inch slices
1 red bell pepper, roasted (page 278) and
    cut into thin strips
1 bunch of watercress, washed, dried, and
    trimmed

1 Cut the chicken into quarters and season with salt and pepper. Heat the oil in a large casserole. Sauté the chicken on all sides until golden, 15 minutes. Remove the chicken and reserve.

2 Add the vinegar, white wine, peppercorns, cloves, bay leaves, thyme, and rosemary to the casserole and bring to a boil. Return the chicken to the pot, lower the heat, and simmer slowly 30 minutes, covered. Add the garlic cloves and pearl onions and continue to simmer slowly 30 minutes, covered. Turn the chicken and vegetables. Add the carrots and continue to simmer 15 to 20 minutes, covered, until all the vegetables are done.

3 Remove and discard the skin and bones from the chicken and tear the meat into serving pieces. Place the chicken and vegetables in a glass baking dish or casserole. Place the peppers on top and pour the liquid from the casserole over the top. Cover and refrigerate at least 24 hours, up to 4 days.

4 Remove the fat from the top of the chicken and vegetables. Bring to room temperature. Arrange on a serving plate with the onions, carrots, and garlic cloves. Garnish with sprigs of watercress. Drizzle with marinade to moisten. Serve with crusty bread.

Serves 6

Clams Stewed with Tomatoes and Garlic

The tomato was introduced to Spain in the sixteenth century and from that time on it became the inspiration for a huge variety of dishes. Later the tomato migrated from Spain to Italy. Marineras is very similar to marinara sauce of the Campania area of southern Italy, both sauces based on tomatoes, olive oil, and garlic and originally made very quickly by fishermen who had only a few ingredients available to them.

4 tablespoons olive oil
1 medium onion, chopped
2 large tomatoes, peeled, seeded, and chopped (page 278), or ¾ cup canned Italian plum tomatoes, drained and chopped
1 tablespoon tomato paste
½ cup dry white wine (Sauvignon Blanc)
1 cup fish stock (page 272) or bottled clam juice
Salt and freshly ground pepper
1 large garlic clove, minced
2 tablespoons chopped fresh parsley
2 pounds fresh clams, washed

1 Heat 2 tablespoons olive oil in a skillet. Add the onions and sauté, uncovered, until they just begin to turn golden, 12 to 15 minutes. Add the tomatoes and tomato paste and continue to sauté 5 to 6 minutes. Add the wine and cook, uncovered, over medium heat, reducing by half, 5 minutes. Add the fish stock, turn up the heat, and simmer, uncovered, rapidly for 5 minutes. Cool 5 minutes. Transfer the sauce to a blender or food processor and puree until smooth. Season with salt and pepper.

2 Heat the remaining 2 tablespoons olive oil in a skillet large enough to hold the clams in one layer. Add the garlic, parsley, and clams. Cover and cook over high heat until the clams open, 5 to 10 minutes, depending upon their size. Discard any unopened clams.

3 With a slotted spoon, remove the clams and keep them warm. Add the tomato sauce to the skillet and reduce the sauce by one-quarter, uncovered, 3 to 4 minutes. Add the clams and mix well.

4 Serve immediately with crusty peasant bread.

Serves 6

Stuffed Mussels with Roasted Garlic Mayonnaise

As the waves rolled along the seaside in the little village of Sitges in Catalonia, I watched the waiters at Cal Pinxo restaurant set the tables outside with starched white tablecloths and candles, getting ready for a busy evening. Rumor filtered through that the chef here made a delicious version of stuffed mussels broiled with garlic mayonnaise. When I finally got my table under the stars and tasted the mussels, I realized why they were so famed. He used the freshest mussels, roasted garlic for the mayonnaise, and the perfect amount of Serrano ham, an excellent cured ham from the Spanish mountains.

Mayonnaise
    1 large head garlic
    10 tablespoons olive oil
    ½ teaspoon dried thyme
    1 bay leaf
    Salt and freshly ground pepper
    1 egg yolk
    1 to 2 teaspoons white wine vinegar

Mussels
    ¾ cup dry white wine
    1 small onion, minced
    6 parsley stems
    Pinch of thyme
    1 bay leaf
    36 large mussels (3 pounds), washed,
        beards removed

1 tablespoon olive oil
2 cups fresh spinach, washed and dried
3 tablespoons minced Spanish ham,
    prosciutto, or Black Forest ham
2 tablespoons butter
2 tablespoons all-purpose flour
¾ cup milk
Salt and freshly ground pepper

1 Preheat the oven to 350°F.

2 Place the garlic in a small baking dish and drizzle with 1 tablespoon olive oil, ¼ cup water, thyme, bay leaf, salt, and pepper. Cover and bake until soft, 30 to 40 minutes. Cool. Run the garlic through a food mill to extract the pulp. Reserve. Place the egg yolk and 1 tablespoon olive oil in a bowl. Whisk well to form an emulsion. Drop by drop, add the remaining 8 tablespoons oil to the egg yolk emulsion, whisking constantly until all the oil has been added. Add the roasted garlic puree, salt, pepper, and vinegar and mix well. Reserve.

3 Bring the white wine, ½ the onion, parsley stems, thyme, bay leaf, and mussels to a boil in a large covered saucepan. Steam, shaking the pan frequently, and remove the mussels as they open, discarding any unopened mussels. Cool the mussels. Reduce the cooking liquid to 2 tablespoons, strain, and reserve. Remove the mussels from their shells and save two-thirds of the shells. Separate each shell into 2 halves. Chop the mussels coarsely.

4 Heat the olive oil in a skillet. Sauté the remaining onion until soft, uncovered, 10 minutes. Finely chop the spinach. Add the ham and spinach, cover, and wilt 1 minute. Remove from the pan and place in a bowl with the mussels.

5 Preheat the broiler.

6 Heat the butter in a saucepan. Add the flour and cook slowly 2 minutes, stirring. Add

the milk and the reserved cooking liquid and cook until smooth and very thick. Add to the mussels and mix well. Season with salt and pepper.

7 Stuff the shells with the mixture. Spread the mayonnaise on top of the mussels and place on a baking sheet. Broil until hot and golden, watching closely, as they brown very quickly, 15 to 30 minutes. Serve immediately.

Serves 6

Shrimp and Green Onion Pancakes

An absolute must in Seville is Bodega La Albariza. While the patrons stand around old sherry barrels sipping fino, waiters scurry through the crowd delivering plates of alcaparrones *(giant capers from the Balearic Islands),* baskets of boquerones fritos *(golden deep-fried sardines), and these* tortillitas. *Tortillitas* are small tortas *made of tiny ½-inch shrimp, scallions, and chick-pea flour brought to Spain by the Moors.*

2 tablespoons olive oil
¾ cup minced scallions
¾ cup all-purpose flour
½ cup chick-pea flour (see Note)
½ teaspoon baking powder
Salt and freshly ground pepper
3 tablespoons minced fresh parsley
Large pinch of paprika
8 ounces small shrimp, shelled and finely
   chopped
1½ cups cold water
Olive oil for frying

1 Heat the olive oil in a small skillet over low heat. Add the scallions and cook, covered, until soft, 3 minutes. Cool slightly.

2 Combine the flours, baking powder, ½ teaspoon salt, and pepper. Add the scallions, parsley, paprika, shrimp, and water. Stir well. The batter should be the consistency of very heavy cream. Let rest 1 to 2 hours.

3 Heat the oil ¼ inch deep in a large skillet over medium-high heat. Drop 2 tablespoons batter at a time and spread it out to make a 2½-inch-diameter pancake. Repeat. Fry until golden, turning once, 2 minutes on each side. Drain on paper towels. Serve immediately.

Makes 18 pancakes to serve 6

NOTE: Chick-pea flour is available at any health food store. It is also called garbanzo flour.

Menorcan Lobster Stew

*A*lmost a Menorcan bouillabaisse, caldereta comes from the word caldero or cauldron, which is the cooking vessel used to make this simple masterpiece. Its main component is the langosta, the spiny lobster with five pairs of legs and no claws. The meat of the langosta—found primarily in its tail—is sweet but its texture is much coarser than the American lobster. Even though a Menorcan would gasp at the thought, American lobster is substituted without compromising the finished product significantly.

5 tablespoons extra virgin olive oil

4 garlic cloves, chopped

3 medium onions, finely chopped

2 pounds tomatoes, peeled, seeded, and chopped (page 278), or 1 28-ounce can Italian plum tomatoes, drained and chopped

1 large green bell pepper, seeded and chopped

6 sprigs of parsley

Salt and freshly ground pepper

2 1¼-pound lobsters

5 cups fish stock (page 272) (see Note)

12 slices French bread, cut ⅛ inch thick and lightly toasted

2 tablespoons chopped fresh parsley

1 In a skillet, heat 2 tablespoons oil and add the garlic, onions, tomatoes, green pepper, parsley sprigs, salt, and pepper. Simmer slowly 30 minutes.

2 In a soup pot, bring 2 cups lightly salted water to a boil. Add the lobsters and cook 4 minutes. Remove the lobsters and reserve the cooking water. Cut the lobster in two where the tail meets the body. Cut the tail into rings. Remove the claws from the body and crush slightly. Cut the head down the middle. Reserve the green tomalley and the coral. Discard the gill tissues and digestive tracts.

3 Heat 2 tablespoons oil in a soup pot and add the lobster pieces with the shells, a few at a time. Toss to cook lightly and remove after 1 minute. Discard the head pieces.

4 Place the tomato mixture in a blender or food processor. Blend until smooth and add to the soup pot. Add the fish stock and the reserved lobster water. Mix together the tomalley and coral and add to the soup. Simmer, uncovered, 20 minutes. Add the lobster pieces and simmer slowly 6 minutes. Taste and season with salt and pepper. If the flavors are light, remove 1 cup broth and place in a small saucepan. Reduce by three-quarters, about 5 to 10 minutes. Add back to the soup to concentrate flavors.

5 To serve, place 2 slices toast on the bottom of each bowl. Ladle the soup and lobster over the bread. Garnish with the parsley.

Serves 6

NOTE: Equal amounts of clam juice and water can be substituted.

Catalan Black Rice with Squid

There are many black ink dishes of the Mediterranean but this one is certainly one of the most extraordinary. Also known as "black paella" in Spain, it is made black with the ink from the cuttlefish or squid. Like risotto di seppioline *of Venice, it is an ingenious way to stain one's teeth and lips a briny black.*

2 pounds squid, cuttlefish, or calamari, cleaned, ink reserved (page 279)

1 teaspoon squid ink (see Note)

½ cup dry red wine

¼ cup olive oil

3 garlic cloves, peeled and crushed

1 medium onion, minced

1 small red bell pepper, seeded and finely diced

2 tomatoes, peeled, seeded, and chopped (page 278), or 1 cup canned Italian plum tomatoes, drained and chopped

1 tablespoon chopped fresh parsley

Pinch of cayenne

Salt and freshly ground pepper

2 cups short-grain white rice, preferably Spanish or Italian

4 to 5 cups fish stock (page 272) (see Note)

1 recipe Spanish Garlic Mayonnaise (page 275)

1 Clean the squid and reserve the ink. Combine 1 teaspoon squid ink, the ink extracted from the squid, and ¼ cup wine. Mix well and reserve. Slice the squid into thin rings and cut the tentacles into bite-size pieces. Wash well.

2 Heat the oil and garlic in a large oven-proof skillet and sauté until the garlic is golden brown, 4 to 5 minutes. Remove the garlic and discard. Add the onions, peppers, and the remaining ¼ cup wine and cook over medium-low heat until the onions are soft and the wine is evaporated, 12 minutes. Add the squid and sauté 10 minutes. Add the tomatoes, parsley, and cayenne and cook 3 minutes. Add the squid ink mixture, ½ teaspoon salt, pepper, and rice and stir well to coat the rice.

3 Preheat the oven to 300°F.

4 Bring the fish stock to a boil. Add it immediately to the rice and bring the mixture to a boil again. Reduce the heat to medium, stirring occasionally. Simmer 12 minutes. Cover and bake for 15 to 20 minutes, or until done. Remove from the oven, uncover, and let stand 10 minutes.

5 Serve with Spanish Garlic Mayonnaise.

Serves 6

NOTE: You will need to buy either 2 pounds extra squid to obtain the 1 teaspoon additional ink needed or 2 4-gram packages squid extract (1 teaspoon). Commercially packaged squid ink is more concentrated and it is now available in specialty food stores.

Grilled Tuna with Green Olive Relish

Spain is the world's largest producer of olive oil. It is the first country to have established a strict grading system, Spanish Denominacion de Origen. Almost all of the table olives, mainly the Manzanilla variety, come from Andalusia. Other olives grown here are the Gordal, Hojiblanca, Arbequina, and the Blanguetas. In the following recipe for tuna with green olive relish, the amount of olive oil in the relish can be reduced and the result spread on grilled bread. This relish then resembles tapenade *of Provence, France, and* garum *of Lazio, Italy.*

1 lemon

1 pound fresh tuna, cut into ¾-inch chunks

8 tablespoons extra virgin olive oil

2 garlic cloves, peeled and crushed

Salt and freshly ground pepper

2 anchovy fillets, soaked in cold water
    10 minutes and patted dry (optional)

½ cup pitted and finely chopped green
    olives (page 279)

1 garlic clove, minced

½ cup chopped fresh parsley

1 tablespoon white wine vinegar

4 lemon wedges

Fresh parsley leaves, preferably Italian

1 Peel the lemon with a vegetable peeler into long pieces, avoiding the pith. Marinate the tuna with the lemon peel, 2 tablespoons olive oil, crushed garlic, salt, and pepper for 2 hours or overnight.

2 Mash the anchovies and place in a small bowl. Add the olives, minced garlic, parsley, white wine vinegar, juice of ½ lemon, and the remaining 6 tablespoons of olive oil. Mix well. Season with salt, pepper, and additional lemon juice as needed.

3 Skewer the tuna. Broil or grill over coals, turning every 2 minutes, until cooked through and still juicy, about 5 to 6 minutes total.

4 Remove the tuna from skewers and toss with the relish. Serve warm or at room temperature garnished with the lemon wedges and parsley leaves.

Serves 6

Summer Tomato and Garlic Soup

Creamy Fennel and Oyster Soup
from the Languedoc

Baked Squash and
Toasted Bread Soup

Provençal Fish Soup with
Garlic Croutons and Spicy Hot
Garlic Mayonnaise

Anchovy Crusts

Croutons with Olive
and Tomato Tapenade

Grilled Bread
with Eggplant Caviar

Pan-Fried Garlic Bread with
Wild Mushrooms

Chick-Pea, Olive Oil,
and Cumin Pancakes

Rustic Goat Cheese Galette

Warm Olives with Wild Herbs

Cream Tart with Herbs
from the South of France

Short Crust Tart Shell

Onion, Tomato, and Anchovy Pie

Pasta with Scallops, Red Wine,
and Tomato Vinegar

Rich Egg Pasta

Corsican Cannelloni with
Farm Cheese and Herbs

Fresh Herb Pasta

Gnocchi with Roquefort Cream

Caramelized Onion and
Goat Cheese Soufflé
Baked in Ten Minutes

Layered Gratin of Eggplant,
Zucchini, Tomatoes,
and Chick-Peas

Stuffed Tomatoes Magaly

Basil Omelette

Provençal Roasted Summer
Vegetable Ragout

Southern France

Braised Artichokes Stuffed with
Sausage and Mushrooms

Salad of Roasted Peppers,
Anchovies, and Basil La Merenda

Layered Summer Salade Niçoise
with Fresh Grilled Tuna

Warm Beans with
Cherry Tomatoes, Basil,
and Garlic Mayonnaise

Garden Salad with Pears and
Roquefort Croutons

Toasted Goat Cheese Salad with
Smoked Bacon

Auberge d'Aillane Chick-pea
Salad with Provençal Herbs
and Olives

Salt Cod, Garlic, and
Potato Gratin

Mussels in the Style
of the Camargue

Shellfish Fritters with
Spicy Hot Garlic Mayonnaise

Ragout of Clams, Sausage, and
Garlic Confit à La Provençal

In the South of France, Provence, Languedoc, and Roussillon rim the azure Mediterranean, and the island of Corsica sits in the sea not far away. This land is magnetic. Groves of citrus and olives are juxtaposed against vineyards and rolling herb-scented hillsides dotted with terra-cotta–roofed farmhouses of various pastel shades of color: ocher, mauve, amber, and viridian. These bleached-out houses are faint in the translucent haze that hangs over the landscape and the quality of light is compelling. It is no wonder this enchanted land attracted painters like Renoir, Cézanne, and Matisse.

In the south, the sun blazes relentlessly and saturates the land. It penetrates deeply into the simple, sensate lives of the people who live and work here. During the day, the hard work in the fields is interrupted while families gather to share the midday meal. Seeking shade under arbors full of vine leaves and clusters of grapes, men come in from their work and children from school or play. A table will be covered with a flowered oilcloth and platters of hors d'oeuvres and entrées. Women will dash back and forth from the kitchen through strings of beads hung to keep out flies, symbols of the indoor-outdoor life lived here. For the next couple of hours, appetite-arousing foods are consumed, stories exchanged, and bodies and minds revived. And

then it is back to work or play for the afternoon hours.

As the workday ends and the sun begins to relax and settle into the skyline, the arbor is again frequented. Men and women with wide smiles and well-tanned faces from long, hot hours in the sun relax and contemplate their arduous day and the bounty set before them. Small plates of well-seasoned hors d'oeuvres and entrées are served with slightly chilled rosé, light red or white wine, or pastis, a favored licorice-flavored liqueur. These first courses are meant to tease and please the appetite and take the edge off the sweltering day. In this region of sunburned beauty, full-flavored hors d'oeuvres and entrées reflect the strong clarity of the sunshine, the bold character of the inland landscape contrasted with the gentleness of the Mediterranean Sea.

In France, first courses go by two names: hors d'oeuvre and entrée. Hors d'oeuvres, literally translated, means "out of, saved from, or apart from work." Hors d'oeuvres are simple bites of food that require little preparation and are served to amuse the palate before the meal. Entrée means "to enter," specifically, to enter the meal. The distinction between hors d'oeuvres and entrées is subtle, as both refer to the wide range of starters served before the main course. These include soups, crudités, or raw vegetables, charcuterie, salads, savory pies, egg dishes, fish dishes both raw and cooked, grilled breads with various toppings, and even pasta. Hors d'oeuvres and entrées can be as light as a few raw vegetables served with an anchovy and olive oil sauce or as hearty as a robust vegetable and bean soup served over a crust of olive oil–doused bread. They can be as simple as a saucer of tiny jet-black Niçoise olives marinated in herbaceous olive oil or as complex as a *galette,* a thin pie filled with goat cheese and wild thyme from the hillsides. These are not foods to pass over the tongue quickly but foods to pause upon and savor.

Whether the foods of Provence, Languedoc, and Roussillon are light or substantial, simple or complex, the joys of the table are an integral part of everyday life and first courses are a feast of color, creativity, and spirit. The French love to extend their time at the table and are not beyond serving several different hors d'oeuvres spread about the table to start and then serving an individual entrée before the main course. A meal has not really begun until at least one first course has been consumed while seated at the table.

In Provence, Languedoc, and Roussillon, hors d'oeuvres and entrées center around two major themes: flavor and simplicity. The first produces foods that are bold, assertive, and forthright—sour, bitter, spicy, and salty—accomplished with aromatics like wild herbs, tender garlic, salt-packed anchovies, lemons, and pungent golden olive oil. The second theme compels cooks to take the excellent

ingredients from the land and sea and prepare them in a way that accentuates their natural state: freshly shucked oysters on the half shell garnished with a wedge or two of lemon and thin slices of rye bread spread with sweet butter, or a salad of sweet grilled peppers with anchovies and briny black Niçoise olives.

Hors d'oeuvres and entrées are today very much a part of everyday life in southern France, but their roots go back many civilizations. Probably the Greeks and the Phoenicians were the first to travel to this region, sailing across the Mediterranean to the old port of Massalia (Marseilles today) in the seventh century B.C. to set up trade settlements. They brought olive trees and grapevines, matchless gifts, as it turned out. And they introduced the custom of *mezethes,* or spreading the table with an array of first plates. Five hundred years later, the Romans were summoned to help the Greeks in defending "their" land from the Celts and Ligurians. The Romans came and stayed, later settling parts of Provence as well as Languedoc. Their endowment too was tremendous: architecture, engineering, culture, and food traditions. The Romans refined the table and reiterated the value of first courses, incorporating legumes, anchovies, herbs, and perhaps dried orange peel into various dishes.

The Arabs and North Africans arrived in Languedoc in the eighth century A.D. to set up trade colonies, and their legacy can still be seen: piles of spices in the market and even Arabic-derived street signs. In Languedoc, Arabic and North African influences can be seen with the rich use of spices, rice, eggplant, legumes, citrus, almonds, and sweet-and-sour flavor combinations.

The Spanish were also very influential in southern France, particularly in Roussillon, the province that borders Spain and was once part of Catalonia. Roussillon did not become part of France until 1659, and the roots of Spanish and Catalan culture are still very deep: red pimientos, cayenne pepper, green olives, ham, sausage, snails, anchovies, bitter orange peel, eggplant, tomatoes, garlic, and the liberal use of olive oil. A favorite first course in Roussillon is a slice of grilled bread rubbed with whole garlic cloves, doused with coarse salt and olive oil, and rubbed with ripe tomato. In Roussillon, it is called *pain Catalan* and in Catalonia, it is called *pan con tomate*.

Provence, Languedoc, and Roussillon are all distinctive for the abundance of their produce, the bounty from the sea, and the traditions of their cooking techniques. The trinity of olives, tomatoes, and garlic, synonymous with the cooking of Provence, offers numerous combinations to entice the palate. Olive oil is the main cooking medium throughout the south. The Provençal, Languedoc, and Roussillon cook uses garlic liberally, but due to the strong sun and fiery summer climate, the garlic doesn't have the same harshness: It

tends to be sweeter and doesn't linger with the senses after it has been consumed. Artichokes are ubiquitous and are served more than most other vegetables. Other common vegetables are asparagus, onions, broad beans, green beans, eggplant, peppers, wild fennel and mushrooms, tomatoes, squash, and cardoon. Mesclun is a traditional Niçoise salad mix of small leaves of rocket or arugula, dandelion greens, chervil, mâche or lamb's lettuce, wild chicory, and purslane or oak leaf lettuce. These greens, which vary beautifully in color, texture, and flavor, are both grown together and picked together. The climate in Provence is perfect for a profusion of wild herbs and the array is endless: mint, chervil, savory, lavender, rosemary, thyme, tarragon, chives, basil, marjoram, oregano, and sage. A specific combination of herbs called herbes de Provence—thyme, rosemary, bay, basil, savory, and lavender—is sold in colorful sachets in the market and used to enhance many dishes.

The Mediterranean, from Nice to the Spanish border, has more than fifty different species of fish. Most cities along the sea feature outdoor fish markets with their own specialty, but Marseilles is the place where one can sample the widest variety. Wander down to the Vieux Port and try a plate of *coquillage* as an appetizer, an intriguing array of bivalves: impeccably fresh Bouzigues oysters, shiny black mussels—violets or the leathery little sea-floor creature—and *oursin*, or sea urchin, a golf ball–size delicacy with a tough, hairy, repellent exterior that when opened exposes a sweet, salmon-colored coral. There are all kinds of clams like *clovisses* and large praires. Sardines are grilled, stuffed, or served raw doused with good virgin olive oil. *Poutargue,* a specialty from the Etang de Berre, is compressed salted roe from the gray mullet and is considered to be a real treat, a poor man's caviar.

Aioli, garlic-flavored mayonnaise similar to Spanish *allioli,* is Provence's most popular sauce. In addition to its use as a garnish for seafood soup, aioli is the centerpiece of a favorite dish, also known as aioli, that is served on Fridays: a large bowl of silky smooth aioli surrounded by an assortment of hard-cooked eggs, freshened salt cod, snails, Jerusalem artichokes, beetroot, chick-peas, small red potatoes, carrots, green beans, artichokes, and olives. When roasted red pepper, cayenne, and fish stock are added to aioli, it becomes rouille (French for "rust") and is used as a garnish for bouillabaisse.

Favored cooking techniques in Provence, Languedoc, and Roussillon are spit-roasting, grilling, and slow simmering. Most kitchens are equipped with a fireplace or grill and can turn out first courses as delectable and simple as a plate of grilled sardines brushed with a fennel branch dipped in fruity virgin olive oil. Soups and stews hold a time-honored place in the kitchen—*aigo boulido,* a garlic broth with

olive oil–doused crusts of bread; ratatouille, a mélange of squash, onions, garlic, bell peppers, eggplant, tomatoes, and herbs; or *tian,* unique to the area, a casserole of leftover ingredients cooked slowly in olive oil.

The mortar and pestle, brought to France by the Romans, are fundamental implements in the southern French kitchen. They are essential in making *pistou*—a Provençal mix of basil, garlic, olive oil, and cheese pounded into a paste—which can be swirled into a minestrone-style soup or served as a sauce for gnocchi and pasta, Italian dishes made in the area. *Pistou* resembles pesto, made just over the Italian border in Genoa, except that it contains no nuts. The mortar and pestle is also used to make *tapenade*—an aromatic spread of olives, capers, garlic, anchovies, and lemon—and *anchoïade*—made of anchovies, garlic, parsley, and olive oil. Both are spread on grilled bread. With the addition of warm olive oil, *anchoïade*—becomes *bagna cauda,* a dipping sauce for vegetables. *Brandade de morue* is dried salt cod, boiled potatoes, olive oil, and plenty of garlic ground into a creamy spread. It is much favored by people in Provence and Languedoc.

The southern French are avid cheese makers. Most Provençal cheeses are made from goat's milk, but those of the Languedoc are made of ewe's milk, including the world-renowned Roquefort. These cheeses are aromatic and can be cooked into various dishes or served on their own, especially goat cheese marinated in herbes de Provence and olive oil. They are used in a variety of other ways: salads, tarts, and sauce for gnocchi and pasta.

Corsica is a dramatic island that seems to jump out of the Mediterranean Sea with great force. It is extremely diverse with lovely sand beaches on the coast and rugged mountains in the interior. Lying between France and Italy, Corsica has been owned by France since the middle of the eighteenth century, though it is closer to Italy geographically in its traditions. The island's traditions also reflect the influences of fifty different invaders. Strong and intriguing flavors are combined to create a simple country fare: pasta, minestrone, risotto, and polenta from Italy; bouillabaisse or *ziminu, anchoiade,* stuffed vegetables, and gar-

lic sauces from the south of France; pimiento and salt cod from Spain; and *galettes,* or flat pies, and the aromatic use of spices from North Africa. Their charcuterie and *brocciu,* a ricottalike cheese, are most prized in the Mediterranean.

In comparison to the cuisine of northern France the food of the south rarely aspires to the same classical principles and formal presentation. In fact, the food of southern France has more in common with the cuisines of its Mediterranean neighbors than it does with, say, the cuisines of Normandy or Alsace-Lorraine. If you asked a Parisian his feelings about the food of the south he might turn up his nose a bit. But he probably spends his summer holiday in Nice enjoying a nice slice of *pissaladière.*

Summer Tomato and Garlic Soup

Pastel-colored cities with a thousand-year patina dot the hillsides one after the other along the coastline. Oftentimes, a village balances on the very edge of the cliff, looking as though the next wisp of air might send it plummeting down into the broad blue depths of the Mediterranean. This is how I found Antibes, a town steeped in history, art, and sumptuous food. I tasted this soup in Antibes, at the height of summer, when the tomatoes were brilliant red, herbs covered the hills, and the garlic was still slightly green and sweet.

3 tablespoons olive oil
½ pound garlic, peeled, each clove halved
1 small onion, minced
1½ pounds tomatoes, peeled, seeded, and
    chopped (page 278), or 2½ cups canned
    Italian plum tomatoes, drained and
    chopped
3 cups chicken stock (page 272)
1 cup water
2 ounces dry 100% semolina spaghetti or
    linguine, broken into 1-inch pieces
2 tablespoons mixed chopped fresh herbs,
    such as parsley, thyme, savory, chives,
    oregano, and marjoram
Salt and freshly ground pepper
1 tablespoon red wine vinegar
¼ cup fruity red wine (Côtes du Rhône,
    Zinfandel)

1 Heat the olive oil in a soup pot and add the garlic and onions. Sauté over very low heat, uncovered, for 15 minutes.

2 Add the tomatoes, chicken stock, and water and simmer, uncovered, 10 minutes. Add the pasta and herbs and continue to simmer, uncovered, 10 minutes.

3 Season with salt, pepper, red wine vinegar, and red wine. Simmer 2 minutes and serve.

Serves 6

Creamy Fennel and Oyster Soup from the Languedoc

The southern French usually have an eye to-ward economy, but a tight-fisted hand will yield to perfectly ripe vegetables and fruits, sea-sweet fish and shellfish, and free-range chickens. Then culinary abandon takes over. This can be seen in the outdoor market when tender young bulbs of fennel are piled high next to the fishmonger selling plump, briny Bouzigues oysters. Somehow nothing else matters. This classic combination of oysters and fennel tastes wonderful together and is worth every cent.

1½ dozen small live oysters
5 bulbs fennel with stalks and greens
3 tablespoons olive oil
1 medium onion, coarsely chopped
3 cups fish stock or clam juice
3 cups water
⅓ cup heavy cream or milk
Salt and freshly ground pepper
2 to 3 teaspoons Pernod or pastis (optional)
1 to 2 teaspoons lemon juice

1 Open the oysters and reserve the oysters and oyster liqueur separately.

2 Clean the fennel bulbs by cutting off the base and any outside leaves that are damaged. Reserve the tops for garnish. Chop 4 fennel bulbs coarsely. Reserve the remaining bulb for garnish.

3 Heat 2 tablespoons oil in a soup pot, add the onion, and sauté until soft, 10 minutes. Add the coarsely chopped fennel, fish stock, water, and oyster liqueur. Simmer until the fennel gets very soft, 30 to 35 minutes. Cool slightly. Puree one-third of the soup in a blender on top speed until very smooth, 3 minutes. Repeat with the remaining soup. Strain through a fine strainer. Add the cream and stir well. Season with salt and pepper.

4 Slice the remaining fennel bulb into paper-thin slices. Heat the remaining 1 table-spoon oil in a skillet and sauté the fennel, covered, over low heat, until soft but still slightly crisp, 5 to 7 minutes. Season with salt and pepper.

5 Heat the soup and add the oysters and sautéed fennel. Simmer slowly 1 minute. Flavor with Pernod and lemon juice. Ladle the soup into bowls and serve immediately garnished with chopped fennel greens.

Serves 6

Baked Squash and Toasted Bread Soup

This very old soup preparation provides substance and sustenance, and with its stock, vegetables, and leftover bread it is an ingenious way to use up any extras you might have on hand. Baked in layers, it resembles a gratin and is particularly good served as a hearty winter soup.

3 tablespoons rendered duck fat or olive oil
3 pounds red onions, sliced
Salt and freshly ground pepper
Large pinch of chopped fresh rosemary
Large pinch of chopped fresh sage
Large pinch of chopped fresh thyme
1½ pounds butternut, acorn, or turban
    squash, peeled, halved and seeded
6 cups chicken stock (page 272)
¾ cup fruity red wine (Côtes du Rhône,
    Zinfandel, Beaujolais)
6 slices rustic country-style bread, toasted
2 whole garlic cloves
½ cup grated Parmesan cheese
Chopped fresh parsley, preferably Italian

1 Heat the duck fat in a heavy skillet and add the onions, salt, pepper, and herbs. Sauté the onions over medium-low heat, covered, stirring occasionally, for 40 minutes. Remove the cover and sauté until very soft and lightly golden, 20 minutes.

2 Slice the squash into ¼-inch slices. Bring the chicken stock to a boil. Add the squash and simmer slowly until almost soft yet still crisp, 8 to 10 minutes. Remove the squash with a slotted spoon and reserve the broth.

3 When the onions have cooked 1 hour, increase the heat to high, add the wine, and deglaze, stirring, 2 minutes. Add the stock, salt, and pepper.

4 Preheat the oven to 350°F.

5 Rub the toasted bread with garlic. Break the toast into rough pieces and place half on the bottom of a 13 × 9-inch baking dish. With a slotted spoon, cover the bread with half of the onions and half of the squash. Ladle 1 cup stock over the squash and sprinkle with half the cheese. Repeat the layering with the remaining bread, vegetables, 1 cup stock, and cheese. Reserve the remaining stock for later when serving the soup. Bake, uncovered, until nearly all of the stock has been absorbed and the top is golden, 1 to 1 ¼ hours.

6 With a large spoon, scoop a portion of the gratin into the soup bowls. Heat the reserved broth and distribute evenly. Garnish with the parsley and serve immediately.

Serves 6 to 8

Provençal Fish Soup with Garlic Croutons and Spicy Hot Garlic Mayonnaise

Seafood soups of all sorts are made on every shore of the Mediterranean: kakavia *and* psarosoupa *from Greece;* caldo de perro, sopa de pescadores, suquet, sarsuela, *and* caldereta *from Spain;* shorabit semak *from Egypt;* balik corbasi *from Turkey;* caciucco, zuppa di pesce, *and* brodetto *from Italy;* cassola *from Sardinia; and* bouillabaisse, bourride; *and* soupe de poissons *from France. The following recipe is the closest you can get to* soupe de poissons *without buying a plane ticket to Nice.*

¼ cup olive oil
1 large onion, chopped
2 leeks, white only, coarsely chopped and
　　washed
1 small bulb fennel, coarsely chopped
1 carrot, peeled and coarsely chopped
3 large tomatoes, cut in 1-inch dice, or 1 ½
　　cups Italian plum tomatoes, drained and
　　coarsely chopped
3 garlic cloves, chopped
Bouquet garni (6 parsley stems, pinch of
　　thyme, 1 bay leaf)
1 3-inch piece orange peel
Pinch of cayenne

5 cups water
1 cup dry white wine (Sauvignon Blanc)
3 pounds assorted meaty white fish bones
　　(sea bass, flounder, red snapper,
　　grouper, perch, sole, pike, haddock, cod)
　　(see Note)
¼ pound dry 100% semolina pasta (spaghetti
　　or linguine), broken into 1-inch pieces
Salt and freshly ground pepper
Large pinch of saffron threads
1 baguette, cut into thin slices on the
　　diagonal, toasted
2 large whole garlic cloves, peeled
½ recipe Spicy Hot Garlic Mayonnaise
　　(page 274)

1 Heat the olive oil in a large soup pot. Add the onions, leeks, fennel, and carrots and sauté over low heat, uncovered, until soft, 15 minutes. Add the tomatoes, garlic, bouquet garni, orange peel, cayenne, water, and white wine and stir to mix. Bring to a rapid boil. Place the fish bones on top and continue to boil, uncovered, for 25 minutes, crushing the bones with a wooden spoon from time to time. Strain the soup through a coarse strainer using the back of a spoon to extract all the liquid from the solids. Strain the broth through a fine strainer back into the soup pot. Discard the bones and vegetables.

2 Bring the soup to a boil. Add the pasta and continue to simmer until the pasta is al dente, 6 to 8 minutes. Add salt, pepper, and saffron and cook 3 minutes.

3 To serve, rub the toasted baguette slices with the whole garlic cloves and spread with Spicy Hot Garlic Mayonnaise. Float them in the soup. Serve immediately.

Serves   6

NOTE: Remove the fins, liver, gills, fat, skin, tail, and any traces of blood from the fish bones. Wash well.

ANCHOIADE

Anchovy Crusts

If you are an anchovy lover, you will be delighted with this recipe. If anchovies are not a particularly favorite food of yours, please read on. The anchovies are soaked in cold water for 10 minutes and patted dry. The flavor of the anchovy is further tempered by the pungency of the garlic, red wine vinegar, and parsley. This Provençal classic is simple and very flavorful, so give it a try. I have changed many a mind.

2 2-ounce cans or 4 ounces flat anchovy
　　fillets, soaked in cold water 10 minutes
　　and patted dry
2 shallots, minced
3 tablespoons extra virgin olive oil
1 tablespoon red wine vinegar
4 garlic cloves, minced
⅓ cup chopped fresh parsley
Freshly ground black pepper
1 baguette, cut diagonally into ¼-inch slices
　　and toasted

Lemon wedges
Radishes
Black olives

1 Finely chop the anchovies. Add the shallots and the extra virgin olive oil and continue to chop until the anchovies, shallots, and oil are very fine and mixed well. Place in bowl. Add the vinegar, garlic, and parsley. Season with pepper and mix well.

2 Spread the *anchoïade* on the toasts and broil for about 1 minute, just until warm. Place the croutons on a platter and garnish with lemon slices, radishes, or olives. Serve immediately.

Serves 6

Croutons with Olive and Tomato Tapenade

*T*apenade *comes from the word* tapeno *meaning "caper"; originally this olive spread contained more capers than it does today. This recipe varies from the classic* tapenade *recipe with its inclusion of chopped sun-dried tomatoes. It is a natural on grilled bread or pizza, or as a stuffing for chicken breasts. Grill the stuffed chicken breasts, slice thinly on the diagonal, and use them in a salad or on an assorted hors d'oeuvres platter.*

1 cup pitted black Niçoise or Kalamata
 olives (page 279)
2 garlic cloves, minced
3 anchovy fillets, soaked in cold water 10
 minutes and patted dry
3 tablespoons chopped capers
¼ teaspoon grated lemon zest
½ teaspoon herbes de Provence
Freshly ground pepper
1 to 2 tablespoons lemon juice
½ cup sun-dried tomatoes in oil, tomatoes
 finely chopped, oil drained and reserved
 (see Note)
12 slices rustic country-style bread, cut in
 half on the diagonal
Lemon wedges
Whole leaves of Italian parsley

1 Place the olives, garlic, anchovies, capers, lemon zest, and herbes de Provence in the bowl of a food processor. Pulse a few times until the mixture becomes a rough paste. Remove the mixture from the work bowl and place in a mixing bowl. Add the pepper, lemon juice, tomatoes, and 2 tablespoons of the reserved oil.

This can be prepared up to this point 1 week ahead of time and stored in the refrigerator until ready to use. Bring to room temperature before using.

2 Toast the bread or grill over a charcoal fire. Spread with the *tapenade*. Place on a platter and garnish with the lemon wedges and parsley. Serve immediately.

Makes about 1 ½ cups tapenade to serve 8

NOTE: Sun-dried tomatoes are available both packed in oil and plain. I recommend purchasing the ones from Italy packed in oil as they are sweeter and have more flavor. They can be used straight from the jar. The plain dried ones can be revived by being placed in a bowl, covered with boiling water, and drained immediately. Both kinds of sun-dried tomatoes are available at most grocery stores and specialty food stores.

Grilled Bread with Eggplant Caviar

There is no need to salt the eggplant here as its acidity will further enhance the robust flavor of this spread. Garnished with black olives, lemon wedges, and whole parsley leaves, these croutons are irresistible served on their own or as a garnish to a garden salad or cold slices of roast leg of lamb as a main course.

1 1- to 1½-pound eggplant
3 to 4 garlic cloves, minced
3 shallots, minced
1½ tablespoons chopped capers
5 anchovy fillets, soaked in cold water 10
    minutes, patted dry, and mashed
1 tablespoon extra virgin olive oil
2 tablespoons chopped fresh parsley
2 to 3 tablespoons lemon juice
Salt and freshly ground pepper
1 baguette, sliced diagonally into ¼-inch
    slices

1 Preheat the oven to 350°F.

2 Puncture the eggplant several times with a fork, place it on a baking sheet, and bake it until it can be easily skewered with a knife, about 35 to 40 minutes. Remove from the oven and cool.

3 Peel the eggplant and discard the skin. Mash the pulp in a mixing bowl. Add the garlic, shallots, capers, mashed anchovies, olive oil, and parsley. Season with lemon juice, salt, and pepper.

4 Toast or grill the bread slices. Spread the toasted bread with the eggplant puree. Serve immediately.

Serves 6 to 8

Pan-Fried Garlic Bread with Wild Mushrooms

These pan-fried garlic croutons are as habit-forming as potato chips. Combine the garlic fried bread with savory wild mushrooms and persillade, *a Provençal concoction of chopped parsley and garlic added toward the end of the cooking time, and the result is a real winner.*

2 tablespoons chopped fresh parsley
2 garlic cloves, minced
6 slices rustic country-style bread
4 tablespoons extra virgin olive oil
2 tablespoons butter
2 whole garlic cloves, peeled
¾ pound wild mushrooms (field, morels,
    chanterelles, cèpes), brushed clean and
    cut into large pieces not bigger than
    1 inch
½ pound button mushrooms, brushed clean
    and cut in half
1 cup chicken stock (page 272)
Salt and freshly ground pepper

1 Combine the parsley and garlic and chop together until fine. Set aside.

2 Cut the bread slices in half on the diagonal. Heat 1 tablespoon oil and the butter in a large skillet. Place the bread in the skillet to coat each side lightly with the oil and butter. Sauté the bread, uncovered, until golden on each side, 5 minutes. Remove from the pan and rub with the whole garlic cloves.

3 Heat the remaining 3 tablespoons oil in a large skillet over medium-high heat. Add the mushrooms and sauté, uncovered, until golden and cooked through, 5 to 8 minutes. Increase the heat to high, add the chicken stock, and reduce by half, 5 minutes. Season with salt, pepper, and the reserved chopped parsley and garlic.

4 Place the bread on serving plates and distribute the mushrooms and sauce evenly on top. Serve immediately.

Serves 6

Chick-Pea, Olive Oil, and Cumin Pancakes

Theresa runs the small vending cart that travels from one market to another along the Azure Coast in southern France. You can't miss her in Antibes or Nice: Her name is painted on the side of the cart in big yellow letters. She is an expert at baking these Arabic-influenced chick-pea pancakes on a twenty-inch-diameter pizza pan over a metal drum filled with slowly burning olive wood. Cut into half-moons and placed on wax paper, they are doused with shimmering virgin olive oil and coarsely cracked pepper. Be careful. These are delicious and deceptively habit-forming.

1¾ cups chick-pea flour
   (see Note, page 56)
¾ teaspoon salt
¾ teaspoon cumin
1½ cups water
8 tablespoons extra virgin olive oil
2 tablespoons olive oil
Coarsely cracked black pepper

1 In a bowl, combine the dry ingredients. In another bowl, combine the water and 5 tablespoons extra virgin olive oil. Sift the dry ingredients into the wet ingredients, whisking constantly. Let stand at room temperature for 1 hour.

2 Preheat the oven to 425°F.

3 Oil three 9-inch round cake pans with the 2 tablespoons olive oil and pour one-third of the batter in each one so that it coats the bottom of the pan with ¼ inch of the batter. Bake them in the upper third of the oven until golden brown on top and crisp, 25 to 30 minutes.

4 Remove the pancakes from the pan with a spatula and cut into wedges. Drizzle with the remaining 3 tablespoons extra virgin olive oil and sprinkle with black pepper. Serve immediately.

Makes three 9-inch socca to serve 6

Rustic Goat Cheese Galette

Nearly two-thirds of the world's goat cheese comes from France. When sold fresh, these cheeses are sweet and moist; when aged, they develop a stronger, more pungent flavor. In France, chèvre *is the generic term for the many varieties of goat's milk cheese. By law, cheeses described as* chèvre *are made entirely of goat's milk and contain 45 percent fat. One of my favorites is Banon, a creamy, nutty-flavored four-ounce disk of goat's or ewe's milk cheese, wrapped in eau-de-vie-soaked chestnut leaves and tied with raffia. They are stored for a few months in earthenware jars before eating. Banon is the most prized cheese from the mountains of northern Provence. In this recipe for* galette, *or flat pie, just about any goat's milk cheese can be used.*

Pastry

1½ cups all-purpose flour, chilled in the freezer 1 hour

¼ teaspoon salt

9 tablespoons butter, cut into ½-inch pieces and chilled in the freezer 1 hour

⅓ to ½ cup ice water

Filling

5 ounces goat cheese

4 ounces ricotta or fresh farm cheese

3 ounces mozzarella, coarsely grated

¼ cup *crème fraîche* (page 275) or sour cream

3 tablespoons grated Parmesan cheese

Salt and freshly ground pepper

½ recipe Warm Olives with Wild Herbs (recipe follows)

1 Place the flour and salt on a cold work surface. With a pastry scraper, cut the butter into the flour and salt until half is the size of peas and the other half a little larger. Make a well in the center and add half of the water. Push together with your fingertips and set aside any dough that holds together. Add the rest of the water and repeat. Form the mixture into a rough ball. Alternatively, this can be made in an electric mixer using the same technique. Roll the dough on a well-floured surface into a 14- to 15-inch circle. Trim the edges. Place on a large sheet pan in the refrigerator.

2 Mix together the goat cheese, ricotta, mozzarella, *crème fraîche*, and Parmesan. Mix well and season with salt and pepper.

3 Preheat the oven to 350°F.

4 Remove the pastry from the refrigerator. Spread the cheese over the pastry, leaving a 2½-inch border around the edge uncovered. Fold the uncovered edge of the pastry over the cheese, pleating it to make it fit. There will be an open hole in the center.

5 Bake the *galette* in the oven for 35 to 40 minutes, until golden brown. Let cool 5 minutes, then slide the *galette* off the pan and onto a serving plate. Serve hot, warm, or at room temperature garnished with warm olives.

Serves 6

Warm Olives with Wild Herbs

Olive trees were introduced to Marseilles by the Greeks 2,500 years ago and they have proliferated there ever since. Ancient olive groves, with their twisted and gnarled trunks and limbs and burnished-silver leaves, cover much of this area. Today thirty different types of olives are grown here, mellow green Picholine and small briny black Niçoise olives being the most common. These two types of olive dominate this simple recipe, which I always have on hand to serve with a glass of wine or sherry.

4 ounces small black Niçoise olives
4 ounces green Picholine olives or other
   green olives with pits
2 ounces brined or Kalamata olives
¾ cup extra virgin olive oil
Several sprigs of fresh rosemary, thyme,
   and savory
Small pinch of crushed red pepper
¼ teaspoon lemon zest

1 Heat all the ingredients until warm. Let sit at room temperature for 6 hours.

2 Before serving, discard any herbs that have turned brown and replenish with fresh herbs if desired. Reheat the olives to serve.

Makes 1¼ cups

NOTE: These can be made several months in advance and the flavor will improve with age. Reheat the olives before serving.

Cream Tart with Herbs from the South of France

When you taste this tart, you will experience the best of France right there on your plate. The filling for this tart was inspired by Madeleine Kamman when I studied with her many years ago at the Modern Gourmet Cooking School in Newton Centre, Massachusetts.

½ cup *crème fraîche* (page 275) or sour cream
½ cup heavy cream
½ cup cream cheese, at room temperature
2 eggs, lightly beaten
¼ cup snipped fresh chives
¼ cup assorted chopped fresh herbs, such as thyme, basil, parsley, marjoram, oregano, and savory
Salt and freshly ground pepper
1 prebaked 9-inch short crust tart shell (recipe follows)

1 Preheat the oven to 425°F.

2 Combine the *crème fraîche*, heavy cream, and cream cheese. Add the eggs and herbs and mix thoroughly. Season with salt and pepper. Pour the cream and herbs into the prebaked tart shell.

3 Place the tart in the oven and immediately turn the oven down to 375F°. Bake the tart until golden and firm to the touch, 35 to 40 minutes. Let rest 20 minutes before serving.

Serves 6

Short Crust Tart Shell

6 tablespoons butter
1⅛ cups all-purpose flour
2 tablespoons vegetable shortening
⅛ teaspoon salt
1 to 3 tablespoons ice water

1 Cut the butter into 1-inch pieces. Using the paddle attachment on an electric mixer, blend the butter and flour at low speed until it resembles coarse meal. Alternatively, this can be done in a food processor by pulsing several times. It can also be done with a pastry blender: Add the shortening and cut it into the flour and butter until the pieces are a little larger than coarse meal. Now mix the salt and water together and add to the flour mixture a little at a time until it holds together. Blend only until the dough comes together. Cover with plastic wrap and let it rest in the refrigerator for at least 30 minutes.

2 With a floured rolling pin, roll out the pastry into a 10-inch circle on a floured surface. Place in a 9-inch tart pan. Crimp the edges and prick the bottom of the pastry. Place in the freezer for 30 minutes.

3 Preheat the oven to 350°F.

4 Completely line the bottom and sides of the pastry with parchment or aluminum foil. Fill the lining, up to the top of the rim, with dried beans or metal pie weights. Bake in the middle of the oven for 25 minutes, or until the top of the crust is golden brown. Remove the beans or pie weights and remove the lining. If the bottom of the pastry is still moist and pale, return it unlined to the oven for a few minutes more until it is fully cooked.

5 Remove from the oven and cool completely.

Makes a 9-inch crust

Onion, Tomato, and Anchovy Pie

A pissaladière *is best when baked directly on a pizza brick or unglazed quarry tiles set on the bottom shelf of the oven covering an area of at least 10 × 12 inches. Heat the oven to its hottest temperature 30 minutes prior to baking the pizza. The results will closely resemble what you will find in Provençal bakeries using wood-fired ovens.*

1 recipe Pizza Dough (page 276)
5 tablespoons extra virgin olive oil
3 pounds or 6 medium onions, thinly sliced
3 garlic cloves, chopped
1 teaspoon chopped fresh thyme
½ teaspoon chopped fresh rosemary
2 large tomatoes, peeled, seeded, and
    chopped (page 278), or 1 cup Italian
    plum tomatoes, drained and chopped
Salt and freshly ground pepper
1 2-ounce can flat anchovy fillets, soaked in
    cold water 10 minutes, patted dry, and
    cut in half lengthwise
½ cup pitted Niçoise olives (page 279)

1 Prepare the dough according to the recipe and let rise in a warm place (75°F.), for 1 hour.

2 Place the pizza brick or tiles on the bottom shelf of the oven and preheat the oven to 500°F.

3 Heat 3 tablespoons oil in a skillet and add the onions, garlic, thyme, and rosemary and sauté over low heat, until the onions are soft and golden, stirring often, 50 to 60 minutes. Add the tomatoes and continue to simmer slowly, until almost dry, 20 minutes. Season with salt and pepper and cool.

4 On a floured surface, roll the dough to a large rectangle, ¼ inch thick. Place the dough on a well-floured pizza peel. Cover the dough to within ½ inch of the edge with the onions and tomatoes. Arrange the anchovy fillets in a lattice fashion on top and place a pitted olive in the middle of each section. Drizzle with the 2 additional tablespoons of olive oil. Transfer the pizza onto the brick and bake for approximately 8 to 10 minutes, or until the crust is golden and the bottom is crisp.

Makes 1 large rectangular pizza to serve 6

Pasta with Scallops, Red Wine, and Tomato Vinegar

*R*aito *is a Provençal sauce made of onions, red wine, garlic, thyme, parsley, and tomatoes. Brought to Marseilles by the Phoenicians, it was traditionally served with fish before mass on Christmas Eve for the grand celebration supper. It continues to be served today but much more regularly. In this recipe,* raito *is served with pasta and scallops in an updated version.*

4 tablespoons extra virgin olive oil
1 large onion, chopped
5 garlic cloves, chopped
8 medium tomatoes, coarsely chopped, or 1 28-ounce can Italian plum tomatoes, drained and chopped
3 cups sturdy red wine (Côtes du Rhône, Cabernet Sauvignon)
1 cup water
5 tablespoons assorted chopped fresh herbs, such as parsley, savory, thyme, rosemary, tarragon, and oregano
3 bay leaves
4 whole cloves
Salt and freshly ground pepper
1 to 2 tablespoons red wine vinegar
½ cup black pitted and chopped Niçoise or Kalamata olives (page 279)
¼ cup capers
1½ pounds scallops, white muscle on side of scallop removed

1 recipe Rich Egg Pasta (recipe follows) cut into wide noodles or fettuccine, or 1 pound dry 100% semolina pasta
Whole parsley leaves, preferably Italian

1 Heat 2 tablespoons oil in a skillet and sauté the onion over low heat until soft, 10 minutes. Add the garlic and continue to sauté 1 minute. Add the tomatoes, wine, water, herbs, bay leaves, and cloves. Cook, uncovered, over medium heat until the sauce is thick, 1 hour. Discard the cloves and bay leaves. Pass the mixture through a food mill or puree in a blender. If using a blender, strain through a fine strainer. Season with salt, pepper, and red wine vinegar.

2 Heat 1 tablespoon olive oil in another skillet. Add the olives and capers and sauté until heated. Remove and reserve.

3 Add the remaining 1 tablespoon olive oil to the skillet and sauté the scallops until almost firm to the touch, 2 to 3 minutes. Add the scallops to the tomato sauce.

4 Bring a large pot of boiling salted water to a boil. Cook the pasta until al dente (for homemade fettucini, 3 to 4 minutes; for dry pasta, 10 to 12 minutes). Heat the sauce gently. Drain the pasta, toss with the sauce, and place on a serving platter. Garnish with the olives, capers, and parsley. Serve immediately.

Serves 6

Rich Egg Pasta

Rice flour is an excellent medium for rolling out pasta dough, absorbing excess moisture without making the pasta dough gummy. Sometimes I use a mixture of half all-purpose and half rice flour, which also works very well.

2½ cups all-purpose flour
¾ teaspoon salt
3 whole eggs (see Note)
3 egg yolks (see Note)
White rice flour to roll out the pasta

1 Place the flour and salt on a work surface and toss to mix. Beat the eggs and egg yolks together in a bowl.

2 Make a well in the center of the flour and add the eggs into the well. Beat with a fork or your thumb and first finger, bringing the flour in from the sides until the mixture thickens. After this, use a pastry scraper to combine all of the flour and liquid. It should be a fairly dry mixture. Knead for 2 minutes to form into a ball. Cover with plastic wrap and let it rest for 30 minutes.

3 Roll the pasta to a thickness of ⅟₁₆ inch (see page 134). Use rice flour to facilitate the rolling. To check the thickness, when you hold the pasta up, you should just be able to see your hand through it.

4 Cut the pasta into ½-inch-wide noodles or use the fettuccine cutter attached to a pasta machine.

Makes 1 pound

NOTE: The total egg volume should be ¾ to ⅞ cup. Water or olive oil can be substituted for any part of this liquid. Eggs, however, yield a much richer, more supple and tender dough.

Corsican Cannelloni with Farm Cheese and Herbs

My friend, Josie, first made these cannelloni for me at her restaurant Chez Josie in Porto Vecchio on the island of Corsica in the early fall, when the tomatoes were sweet and ripe. I asked her to tell me about the sauce. She bent over and whispered in my ear, "I can't let the village people know my secret. I put a splash of cream into the tomato sauce. It brings out the sweetness." Josie is right.

Filling

1 pound spinach, washed and spun dry

1 pound ricotta, drained overnight in a
    cheesecloth-lined strainer

2 eggs

¼ teaspoon chopped fresh mint

¼ teaspoon chopped fresh oregano

¼ teaspoon chopped fresh thyme

¼ teaspoon chopped fresh rosemary

¼ teaspoon chopped fresh savory (optional)

Salt and freshly ground pepper

¼ cup grated Parmesan cheese

Sauce

5 tablespoons olive oil

1 small onion, chopped

5 garlic cloves, chopped

4 pounds ripe plum tomatoes, peeled,
    seeded, and chopped (page 278), or
    2 28-ounce cans Italian plum tomatoes,
    drained and chopped

⅓ cup heavy cream

Salt and freshly ground pepper

Pasta

1 recipe Fresh Herb Pasta (recipe follows)

Whole parsley leaves, preferably Italian

1 Heat the spinach in a dry pan over medium heat, covered, until wilted, 2 to 3 minutes. Squeeze out all of the excess moisture in paper towels.

2 Combine the spinach with the ricotta, eggs, mint, oregano, thyme, rosemary, savory, ¾ teaspoon salt, pepper, and Parmesan cheese. Reserve.

3 Heat 4 tablespoons olive oil in a large skillet and sauté the onions until soft, 7 minutes. Add the garlic and sauté 2 minutes. Add the tomatoes and cook until the sauce is thick and the liquid has reduced by about half, 20 to 30 minutes. Puree the sauce in a blender or put it through a food mill fit with the smallest holes. Add the cream and season with salt and pepper.

4 Make the pasta and roll it out until it is ¹⁄₁₆ inch thick and the outline of your hand is just visible (see page 134). Use rice flour to facilitate the rolling. Cut the pasta into 5-inch squares. (You should have at least two squares for each person.) Blanch the squares in boiling salted water 30 seconds. Immediately remove and place in a bowl containing ice water and 2 tablespoons olive oil. Drain on slightly dampened kitchen towels. Cover well.

5 Preheat the oven to 350°F.

6 Divide the filling into as many portions as you have squares of pasta. Put 2 heaping tablespoons of filling in the center of each square of pasta and roll the pasta over the filling in a tube fashion. Oil a 13 × 9-inch baking dish with 1 tablespoon oil. Place a small ladle of sauce on the bottom of the dish. Place the cannelloni next to each other in a single layer in the dish. Pour the sauce on top and bake until hot and bubbling around the edge, 20 to 30 minutes.

7 To serve, place 2 cannelloni on each plate and garnish with whole parsley leaves.

Serves 6 to 8

Fresh Herb Pasta

If the herbs are eliminated from this recipe, the result will be an excellent basic pasta that can be used for all kinds of recipes.

1¼ cups all-purpose flour
¼ teaspoon salt
¼ cup assorted chopped fresh herbs, such as
    rosemary, thyme, chives, parsley, basil,
    and mint
1 whole egg
1 egg yolk
1 tablespoon water
3 tablespoons olive oil
White rice flour to roll out the pasta

1 Place the flour, salt, and herbs on a work surface and toss to mix. Beat the egg, yolk, water, and oil in a bowl.

2 Make a well in the center of the flour mixture and add the liquid into the well. Beat with a fork or your thumb and first finger, bringing the flour in from the sides until the mixture thickens. After this, use a pastry scraper to combine all of the flour and liquid. It should be a fairly dry mixture. Knead for 2 minutes to form into a ball. Cover with plastic wrap and let rest for 30 minutes.

3 At this point, roll out the pasta according to the recipe you are making, using the rice flour to facilitate the rolling.

Makes ¹/₂ pound

Gnocchi with Roquefort Cream

This recipe is one of the traditional methods for making gnocchi in France. It is basically like making a choux paste or cream puff dough. The finished gnocchi are featherlight and irresistible.

1⅔ cups milk
¾ cup (1½ sticks) butter
Salt and freshly ground pepper
1⅓ cups all-purpose flour
6 eggs
2 cups heavy cream
6 ounces Roquefort cheese, crumbled
¼ cup grated Parmesan cheese

1 Bring a large pot of salted water to a boil. Reduce the heat to a simmer.

2 Bring the milk, butter, and ¾ teaspoon salt to a boil. As soon as it comes to a boil, take the pan off the heat and add the flour all at once. Mix vigorously with a wooden spoon until it forms a ball. Place the dough in a mixing bowl. While still warm, add the eggs one at a time, beating well with a wooden spoon after each addition. The mixture should be very thick and smooth.

3 Fit a large pastry bag with a ¾- to 1-inch plain round tip. Fill the pastry bag with dough.

Into the simmering water, squeeze out 1-inch pieces of dough, cutting them off with a knife. Do not overcrowd the pan. Simmer the gnocchi slowly until they begin to puff slightly and are slightly firm, 5 to 10 minutes. Remove the gnocchi from the water with a slotted spoon, drain well, and cool.

NOTE: The gnocchi will keep for up to 2 days in the refrigerator at this stage. They can also be frozen. Make sure that they are at room temperature before proceeding to the next step.

4 Preheat the oven to 425°F.

5 In a large saucepan, bring the cream, Roquefort, salt, and pepper to a boil. Simmer on low heat to reduce the cream by one-quarter, or until it thickens slightly, 5 to 10 minutes. Add the Roquefort cream to the gnocchi and mix carefully. Place the gnocchi and sauce in a 13 × 9-inch baking dish. They will form a very full single layer. Sprinkle with Parmesan cheese and bake until the gnocchi puff and are golden brown, 10 minutes. If the gnocchi have not turned golden, run them under the broiler.

6 Serve immediately.

Serves 6 to 8

Caramelized Onion and Goat Cheese Soufflé Baked in Ten Minutes

This soufflé base is like any other and can be made ahead up to the point of whipping the egg whites to stiff peaks. What makes it different is that it is baked on a large ovenproof platter on the top shelf of a hot oven, resulting in a soufflé that is about two inches high.

3 tablespoons olive oil

3 medium onions (1½ pounds), thinly sliced

Salt and freshly ground pepper

1 teaspoon chopped fresh thyme

6 tablespoons plus 2 teaspoons butter

6 tablespoons all-purpose flour

1 cup milk

1 cup heavy cream

5 egg yolks

1¼ cups or 5 ounces crumbled goat cheese

6 egg whites

½ cup grated Parmesan cheese

1 Heat the olive oil in a skillet and add the onions, salt, pepper, and ½ teaspoon thyme. Sauté the onions over medium-low heat, covered, stirring occasionally, for 30 minutes. Uncover and sauté until very soft and light golden, 30 minutes. Remove the onions with a slotted spoon and place them in a strainer set over a bowl to drain. Reserve.

2 Butter a large 10 × 18-inch ovenproof platter with 2 teaspoons butter.

3 Preheat the oven to 450°F.

4 Meanwhile, melt the remaining 6 tablespoons butter in a saucepan over low heat and add the flour. Stir with a whisk to combine and let the mixture bubble for 2 minutes. Add the milk and cream to the flour-butter mixture, stirring rapidly with a whisk. Cook for 2 to 3 minutes, until very thick and smooth. Transfer to a bowl and add the drained onions. Mix well. Add the yolks, one at a time, stirring well after each addition. Add the goat cheese and mix well. Season with salt and pepper.

5 Beat the whites until stiff. Add half of them to the base and fold well. Fold in the remaining whites. Pour this onto the prepared platter. Sprinkle with the Parmesan cheese and the remaining ½ teaspoon thyme and bake on the top shelf of the oven for 10 to 14 minutes, until well browned.

6 Serve immediately.

Serves 6 to 8

Layered Gratin of Eggplant, Zucchini, Tomatoes, and Chick-peas

The name tian *is derived from the earthenware terrine in which this Provençal gratin is cooked. The* tian's *defining characteristic is the process of slowly cooking the ingredients in olive oil, with herbs and spices. Tians are usually made in the home, often using leftovers. They are a snap to make and pack a lot of Provençal flavor like this savory one with thyme, allspice, and crushed red pepper.*

1 cup dry chick-peas
Bouquet garni (6 parsley stems, pinch of
    thyme, 1 bay leaf)
1 1½-pound eggplant, unpeeled
Salt and freshly ground pepper
5 tablespoons plus 1 teaspoon olive oil
1 medium onion, minced
2 garlic cloves, minced
2 tablespoons chopped fresh parsley
½ teaspoon chopped fresh thyme
6 tomatoes, peeled, seeded, and chopped
    (page 278), or 1 28-ounce can Italian
    plum tomatoes, drained and chopped
½ teaspoon ground allspice
½ teaspoon crushed red pepper flakes
12 to 15 torn fresh basil leaves
½ cup grated Parmesan cheese

1 Pick over the chick-peas and discard any stones. Cover with water and soak overnight. The next day, drain and place them in a sauce-pan with enough water to cover by 2 inches and the bouquet garni. Simmer, uncovered, until the skins begin to crack and the beans are tender, 45 to 60 minutes.

2 Cut the eggplant into 1-inch cubes. Set the cubes in a colander and lightly salt them. Leave to drain for 30 minutes. Rinse and pat very dry with paper towels.

3 Heat 3 tablespoons olive oil in a large skillet and sauté the eggplant over moderately high heat until lightly browned on all sides, 15 minutes. Remove the eggplant and place in a bowl. Add 2 tablespoons olive oil to the pan and sauté the onion until soft, 10 minutes. Add the garlic, parsley, and thyme and sauté 2 minutes. Add the tomatoes and cook, uncovered, until the liquid has disappeared, 15 to 20 minutes.

4 Preheat the oven to 375°F.

5 Combine the eggplant, tomato sauce, all-spice, red pepper, basil, and chick-peas. Season with salt and pepper.

6 Oil a large shallow gratin dish with the re-maining 1 teaspoon oil. Place the mixture in the dish and sprinkle the top with Parmesan cheese. Bake until hot and golden, 40 to 45 minutes.

Serves 6 to 8

Stuffed Tomatoes Magaly

Magaly and Raymond Fabre are the proprietors of Domaine du Mont Redon, producing the finest Châteauneuf du Pape wines. The first time I met Magaly, she invited me to lunch and recommended that I arrive at 9:00 in the morning. I spent the early morning with Raymond at the winery and later cooking lunch and talking with Magaly. We grilled croutons on the hearth to be served with anchoïade; *we stuffed tomatoes and sliced truffles for salad. Finally we were finished. Magaly, Raymond, and I sat at the table for the next several hours eating lunch, drinking their wine, and talking. As the sun began to set we left the table and gathered around the fireplace. Raymond brought out a bottle of their exquisite house-made Marc de Châteauneuf du Pape, 1945. The bottle was covered with a layer of dust and Raymond had a sly smile as he opened it. While we sipped, Magaly wrote out for me this excellent recipe, which we had eaten hours earlier.*

6 large, ripe red tomatoes, cored
Salt and freshly ground pepper
2 tablespoons olive oil
½ medium onion, minced
¾ pound fresh pork sausage
½ cup milk, scalded
1 cup fresh white bread crumbs
1 egg, whisked
4 tablespoons chopped fresh parsley
¼ teaspoon chopped fresh thyme

½ teaspoon chopped fresh savory or ¼ teaspoon dried savory
2 garlic cloves, minced
1 tablespoon butter
Whole sprigs of thyme, Italian parsley, or savory

1 With the cored side up, cut the tomatoes in half horizontally and press just slightly to remove any excess moisture. Sprinkle the interior of the tomatoes with salt and place them, cut side down, on paper towels for at least 1 hour to drain.

2 Preheat the oven to 350°F.

3 Heat 1 tablespoon olive oil in a skillet on medium heat and add the tomato halves, 6 at a time, cut side down. Cook, uncovered, 5 minutes. Season them with salt and pepper and carefully turn them over and cook for 3 additional minutes. Remove the tomatoes from the skillet.

4 Oil a 13 × 9-inch baking dish with 1 tablespoon oil and place the tomatoes, cut side up, side by side in the dish. Add the onions to the skillet and sauté until the onions are soft, 10 minutes. Add the crumbled sausage and cook over medium heat, uncovered, 5 minutes. With a slotted spoon, transfer the sausage and onions to a mixing bowl. Add the scalded milk and bread crumbs. Cool slightly. Add the egg, 2 tablespoons parsley, thyme, and savory. Season with salt and pepper.

5 Divide the stuffing among the tomatoes. Bake the tomatoes 10 minutes. In the meantime, chop the remaining 2 tablespoons parsley and the garlic together. Remove the tomatoes from the oven. Heat the broiler. Sprinkle the parsley and the garlic on top of the tomatoes. Dot with butter and broil until golden brown.

6 Garnish with some whole sprigs of thyme, Italian parsley, or savory and serve hot, warm, or at room temperature.

Serves 6

OMELETTE AU PISTOU
Basil Omelette

Pistou is the cousin of Italian pesto, the only difference being that pistou *does not include pine nuts. Pistou is made in the vicinity of Nice, where basil fills the hillsides and garlic perfumes the air. Most often,* pistou *is a sauce used as a garnish for thick vegetable and pasta soups, but here it is used as a delightful flavoring for an omelette.*

3 garlic cloves, chopped
1 cup fresh basil leaves, washed and dried
Salt and freshly ground pepper
4 tablespoons olive oil
1 cup grated Parmesan cheese
8 eggs
1 tablespoon water

1 Put the garlic, basil, salt, pepper, and 3 tablespoons oil in a mortar and pestle, blender, or food processor and process until smooth. Add the cheese, a little at a time, until a very stiff paste is formed. Set aside.

2 Whisk the eggs with salt, pepper, and water until foamy. Heat the remaining 1 tablespoon oil in a large omelette pan until very hot and the oil is rippling. Add the egg mixture and let it cook 5 seconds. As the eggs begin to set, with a fork lift the outer edges of the omelette and let the liquid run underneath. Continue until it is almost set but still slightly soft inside, a total of 30 seconds. Quickly spread the eggs with the *pistou*.

3 To serve, fold the omelette onto a serving plate to form a slight roll. Serve immediately.

Makes 2 small or 1 large omelette to serve 6

RATATOUILLE

Provençal Roasted Summer Vegetable Ragout

Throughout Provence there are as many variations of ratatouille as there are vegetable stew recipes made in the countries bordering the Mediterranean Sea. In this version, the vegetables are sautéed separately first and later stewed together, thus maintaining their brilliant colors.

1 1½- to 2-pounds eggplant, cut into 1-inch
    cubes
Salt and freshly ground pepper
6 tablespoons olive oil
3 yellow or red bell peppers, seeded, cut
    into 1-inch strips, and the strips halved
4 small zucchini, trimmed and cut into
    ¾-inch slices
2 medium onions, cut into quarters and the
    quarters halved
4 garlic cloves, minced
5 tomatoes, peeled, seeded, and cut into
    1-inch cubes
2 bay leaves
4 tablespoons chopped fresh parsley
½ teaspoon chopped fresh thyme
1 to 2 tablespoons red wine vinegar
20 fresh basil leaves, cut into thin strips

1 Place the eggplant in a colander and salt lightly. Leave to drain for 30 minutes. Wash the eggplant and pat dry with paper towels.

2 Heat 3 tablespoons olive oil in a large heavy casserole. Add the eggplant and brown on all sides, 15 minutes. Remove with a slotted spoon and reserve. Add 1 tablespoon oil to the pan and add the bell peppers. Sauté until they begin to wilt, 5 to 7 minutes. Remove with a slotted spoon and reserve with the eggplant. Add the zucchini and sauté until lightly browned, 3 to 4 minutes. Remove and reserve with the other vegetables. Add 2 tablespoons olive oil, onions, and garlic and sauté until the onions are soft, 7 to 10 minutes. Add the tomatoes, bay leaves, parsley, thyme, and pepper and simmer slowly 20 minutes. Add the reserved vegetables to the pan and cook, stirring occasionally, 15 minutes. Season as needed with salt, pepper, and red wine vinegar.

3 Place the ratatouille on a platter and garnish with the basil.

Serves 6

NOTE: Ratatouille can be served hot, warm, or at room temperature. It can be prepared 1 day in advance. Bring to room temperature or heat slightly to serve.

Braised Artichokes Stuffed with Sausage and Mushrooms

Some have big hearts, some have a distinct purple hue, some are so small they can be eaten whole, and some so tender they can be eaten raw. Artichokes are one of the favored vegetables grown in the south of France and a multitude of dishes are created around it. Jean-Noel Escudier, the father of the Provençal table, described the artichoke as "a petaled cone that started as a thistle and was cultivated into a classic vegetable." This dish is an old, yet beloved classic.

6 medium artichokes, trimmed (page 278)
4 tablespoons olive oil
¼ cup chopped onion
¼ pound mushrooms, brushed clean and
  thinly sliced
½ pound lean pork sausage, crumbled
4 garlic cloves, minced
¼ cup chopped fresh parsley
½ teaspoon chopped fresh thyme
10 fresh basil leaves
4 ounces country-style ham (Westphalian,
  Black Forest, Virginia, Smithfield,
  prosciutto, Serrano), finely diced
Salt and freshly ground pepper
3 medium onions, thinly sliced
2 small carrots, peeled and thinly sliced
Bouquet garni (6 parsley stems, pinch of
  thyme, 1 bay leaf)
1¼ cups dry white wine (Sauvignon Blanc)

1 Blanch the artichoke hearts in boiling salted water for 8 minutes. Cool and reserve.

2 For the stuffing, heat 2 tablespoons olive oil in a sauté pan over medium heat. Add the chopped onions, mushrooms, and sausage and sauté until soft, 10 minutes. Chop the garlic, parsley, thyme, and basil leaves together and add to the onions with the diced ham. Mix well. Season with salt and pepper. Stuff the centers and between the leaves of the artichokes with the stuffing mixture.

3 In a small flameproof casserole just large enough to hold the artichokes, heat the remaining 2 tablespoons olive oil over medium heat. Add the sliced onions, carrots, salt, pepper, and bouquet garni and sauté 2 minutes. Place the artichokes on top, stuffing side up. Saute for 6 to 8 minutes, or until the vegetables start to brown. Turn the heat to high, add the white wine, and reduce for 1 minute. Turn the heat to low, cover the pan, and cook slowly, 45 minutes. Check to see that they don't dry out. Uncover the artichokes, raise the heat to high, and boil down the broth until you have a syrupy sauce.

4 To serve, place the onions and carrots on a serving plate with the artichokes on top. Spoon the juices over the top and serve warm.

Serves 6

Salad of Roasted Peppers, Anchovies, and Basil La Merenda

My only complaint is how uncomfortable the little leather woven stools are at La Merenda, the bistro tucked in an alley just steps from the Cours Selaya market in Nice. If it's any indication of how much I like the place, though, I have been known to eat there three nights in a row when I'm in Nice. It is down-home and rustic, right up my alley. The menu, delivered on a chalkboard, changes nightly depending upon what is available in the market. One of my favorites that Jean Guisti, the chef, makes is this pungent salad of roasted sweet peppers, anchovies, and basil leaves.

3 red bell peppers, roasted (page 278)
3 yellow bell peppers, roasted (page 278)
1 2-ounce can flat anchovy fillets, soaked in
    cold water 10 minutes and patted dry
1 garlic clove, mashed with a mortar and
    pestle
1 teaspoon red wine vinegar
5 tablespoons extra virgin olive oil
Salt and freshly ground pepper
½ teaspoon chopped fresh oregano
⅓ cup small black olives, preferably Niçoise
20 to 25 fresh basil leaves

1 Cut the peppers into 1-inch strips. Toss with the anchovies, garlic, vinegar, olive oil, salt, and pepper. Let marinate 30 minutes.

2 Place the peppers on a serving plate and sprinkle oregano over the top. Garnish with the olives and basil leaves and serve immediately.

Serves 6

Layered Summer Salade Niçoise with Fresh Grilled Tuna

This colorful salad is best made during the summer months when the vegetables are at their peak. If fresh tuna is unavailable, substitute canned, water-packed albacore tuna.

3 garlic cloves, minced

¼ cup red wine vinegar

½ cup plus 2 tablespoons extra virgin olive oil

Salt and freshly ground pepper

1 pound fresh tuna or 2 6-ounce cans water-packed albacore tuna, drained

¾ pound small, new red potatoes

¾ pound green beans, ends trimmed

1 medium head of crisp romaine, washed, spun dry, and torn into large pieces

1 small red onion, peeled and thinly sliced

1 small red bell pepper, seeded and thinly sliced

4 small ripe tomatoes, cored and cut into wedges

½ cup black olives, preferably Niçoise or Kalamata

2 hard-cooked eggs, peeled and quartered

1 2-ounce can flat anchovy fillets, soaked in cold water 10 minutes, drained, and patted dry

3 tablespoons mixed minced fresh herbs, such as thyme, parsley, basil chervil, tarragon, and chives

1 Whisk the garlic and vinegar together in a bowl. Whisk in ½ cup oil slowly and season with salt and pepper. Reserve.

2 Marinate the fresh tuna in 1 tablespoon oil, salt, and pepper. Either grill the tuna on a barbecue or sauté it in 1 tablespoon oil in a sauté pan until it is still slightly pink inside, 3 to 4 minutes per side. Remove and let cool. (If using canned tuna, omit this step.) Break the tuna into large bite-size pieces and toss with one-quarter of the vinaigrette, salt, and pepper.

3 Boil the potatoes in salted water until tender, 10 to 15 minutes. Drain and cool. Cut into thin slices. Boil the green beans in salted water until tender, 4 to 6 minutes. Rinse under cold water and cut into large bite-size pieces.

4 Layer the salad in a large glass bowl in this order: the greens, potatoes, beans, onions, peppers, tomatoes, tuna, olives, eggs, anchovies, and herbs. At the table, season the salad with salt and pepper and add the vinaigrette, tossing carefully. Serve immediately.

Serves 6

Warm Beans with Cherry Tomatoes, Basil, and Garlic Mayonnaise

In Provence, aïl *is garlic and* oli *is the local dialect for oil. Aioli is the butter of Provence. This sauce dominates along the Mediterranean, spreading through Languedoc where it is called* aïllade *and is often thickened with blanched and ground walnuts. Heading farther west to Roussillon and later Spain,* allioli, *a similar sauce, is made. In the following recipe, the Provençal version of aioli literally melts over the warm beans and imparts the heady flavors of garlic. Be sure to serve plenty of bread to mop up the delicious juices.*

1 recipe Provençal Garlic Mayonnaise
   (page 273)
2 to 3 tablespoons warm water
1½ cups fresh shell beans (flageolets,
   black-eyed peas, cranberry beans, limas,
   cannellini, or a combination)
5 tablespoons red wine vinegar
5 tablespoons extra virgin olive oil
Salt and freshly ground pepper
¾ pound green beans, ends removed
¾ pound yellow beans, ends removed
½ pound assorted cherry tomatoes
   (red, yellow, pear-shaped)
20 fresh basil leaves

1 Whisk the aioli with the water to lighten the texture and to make a barely fluid sauce.

2 Cover the shell beans with water by 2 inches. Bring to a boil and cook until tender, 20 to 25 minutes. Drain and toss with 4 tablespoons vinegar, 5 tablespoons extra virgin olive oil, salt, and pepper. Keep warm.

3 Blanch the green and yellow beans in boiling salted water until they are tender but still slightly crisp, 5 to 8 minutes. Drain. Add to the shell beans and toss together. Keep warm.

4 Halve the cherry tomatoes and season with salt, pepper, and the remaining 1 tablespoon vinegar. Toss together.

5 Place the various beans on a platter and top with the tomatoes and a spoonful of aioli. Garnish with basil and serve immediately.

Serves 6

Garden Salad with Pears and Roquefort Croutons

There are many imitations of Roquefort, the French equivalent of Italian Gorgonzola. This ewe's milk cheese, with its distinctive blue veins, comes from the underground caves of Roquefort-sur-Soulzon, a small town devoted to making Roquefort. Roquefort has gained a world reputation with the memorable flavors that are displayed in this salad of pears and Roquefort croutons.

Vinaigrette

2½ tablespoons red wine vinegar
1 shallot, minced
1 tablespoon walnut or other nut oil
3 tablespoons olive oil
¼ cup extra virgin olive oil
Salt and freshly ground pepper

Croutons

3 tablespoons butter, at room temperature
4 ounces Roquefort cheese, at room temperature
2 ounces cream cheese, at room temperature
1 tablespoon chopped fresh parsley
2 scallions, white and green, thinly sliced
2 tablespoons finely chopped walnuts, toasted (page 277)
6 large slices rustic country-style bread, cut in half on the diagonal and lightly toasted

Salad

2 or 3 small heads of salad greens (oak leaf lettuce, *frisée*, mizuna, radicchio, arugula, and watercress)
2 pears or apples, peeled and thinly sliced
⅓ cup walnuts or pecans, toasted (page 277)

1 To make the vinaigrette, place the vinegar and shallots in a small bowl and let sit 10 minutes. Combine the oils and whisk into the vinegar. Season with salt and pepper and set aside.

2 Preheat the oven to 400°F.

3 In a bowl, mash the butter, Roquefort cheese, cream cheese, parsley, scallions, and walnuts together or place in a food processor and pulse until the ingredients are mixed. Season with salt and pepper. Spread the mixture on the toasted bread. Place the bread on a baking sheet and toast on the top shelf of the oven until golden around the edges, 30 to 45 seconds.

4 Trim the heads of the salad greens. Discard any outside leaves that may be damaged. Tear the leaves into the appropriate size for a salad, wash them, and spin dry. Season the greens with salt and pepper. Toss the greens, pears, and walnuts with the vinaigrette. Divide among 6 plates. Garnish each salad with 2 Roquefort croutons and serve immediately.

Serves 6

Toasted Goat Cheese Salad with Smoked Bacon

Around Banon, in the Haute Provence in summer, the goats graze in herb-filled pastures, giving their milk and cheese an herbaceous quality. Storing summer's sweet creamy goat cheese in local olive oil and herbs for eating in the cold winter months is an ancient way of preserving its goodness. In this recipe, the preserved goat cheese is rolled in bread crumbs, baked, and served with smoked bacon and croutons. What a combination!

½ cup olive oil

½ cup extra virgin olive oil

3 large sprigs of fresh thyme

2 large sprigs of fresh oregano

1 large sprig of rosemary

1 large sprig of savory (optional)

8 peppercorns, coarsely cracked

8 whole coriander seeds, coarsely cracked

¾ pound fresh goat cheese, cut into 3 small round disks, 1 inch thick × 2½ inches in diameter and cut in half horizontally to make 6 pieces

6 ounces thickly sliced smoked bacon, cut into ½-inch dice

4 thick slices rustic country-style bread, cut or torn into ½-inch cubes

½ teaspoon Dijon mustard

1 garlic clove, minced

2 tablespoons red wine vinegar

Salt and freshly ground pepper

4 large handfuls of mesclun or mixed salad greens (red leaf, radicchio, butter, mustard green, mizuna, arugula, and oak leaf)

1½ cups fine dry bread crumbs

1 Combine the olive oils in a saucepan and heat until warm. With the back of your chef's knife, tap the sprigs of herbs to bruise the stems to release the flavor. Add the herbs, peppercorns, and coriander seeds to the oil and remove from the heat. Let the oil cool. Pour two-thirds of the oil over the goat cheese rounds. Reserve the remaining oil. Let the goat cheese marinate in the refrigerator for 2 hours or up to 1 month (see Note).

2 Preheat the oven to 325°F.

3 Combine the bacon and bread cubes and place on a baking sheet. Bake, tossing occasionally, until both the bread and bacon are golden, 10 to 12 minutes. Leave the oven on.

4 Combine the mustard, garlic, and red wine vinegar. Drizzle in the reserved oil. Season with salt and pepper.

5 Tear the greens into salad-size pieces. Wash well and spin dry.

6 Season the bread cubes with salt and pepper. Remove the goat cheese from the oil and coat with the bread crumbs. Place on a baking sheet and bake until the cheese is slightly bubbling around the edges, 4 to 6 minutes.

7 Toss the vinaigrette with the greens. Arrange the greens on a salad plate and place the cheese in the center. Surround the cheese with the croutons and bacon.

Serves 6

NOTE: This cheese is best when marinated at least 1 week before using. The oil can be used again.

SALADE DE L'AUBERGE D'AILLANE

Auberge d'Aillane Chick-pea Salad with Provençal Herbs and Olives

We had been in the market all morning and by the time we left Aix-en-Provence I was already starving and couldn't wait for lunch. Auberge d'Aillane is set in the middle of an industrial park on the outskirts of Aix, rather tricky to find, but well worth the trip. After many wrong turns, we finally arrived, about one hour later than our reservation. We ran through the gardens and into the front door. The place was empty. Out from the kitchen came one of the daughters of the proprietor. I explained our plight. With a sympathetic look, she agreed to make us lunch, but only if she could plan our menu. This was the first dish she brought and I was delighted.

1 cup (6 ounces) dry chick-peas
4 to 5 tablespoons red wine vinegar
4 garlic cloves, minced
½ cup extra virgin olive oil
Salt and freshly ground pepper
3 tablespoons mixed chopped fresh herbs,
    such as mint, thyme, rosemary, tarragon,
    oregano, and basil
2 tablespoons chopped fresh parsley

⅓ cup pitted black olives, preferably
    Niçoise (page 279)
1 small red onion, cut into ¼-inch dice

1 Pick over the chick-peas and discard any stones. Cover with water and soak overnight. The next day, drain and place in a saucepan with enough water to cover by 2 inches. Simmer, uncovered, until the skins begin to crack and the beans are tender, 45 to 60 minutes. Drain and cool.

2 In a large bowl, whisk together 4 tablespoons vinegar, garlic, and olive oil. Season with salt and pepper.

3 Add the herbs, chick-peas, olives, and onion to the vinaigrette. Toss well. Season with salt, pepper, and more vinegar, if needed.

This salad can be prepared 1 day in advance and stored in the refrigerator. Bring to room temperature before serving.

4 Place on a platter and serve at room temperature.

Serves 6

Salt Cod, Garlic, and Potato Gratin

Along the Mediterranean coast of France, fresh fish is plentiful, but inland fresh fish is an impossibility, especially in the little town of Lourmarin. At Feurie, a small restaurant on a side street, I had a brandade *that was extraordinarily creamy and rich. Here is the recipe as Reine, the chef, gave it to me.*

1¼ pounds dry salt cod (see Note, page 50)
½ pound peeled boiling potatoes, cut into
    small chunks
1 cup cold milk
1 small onion stuck with 4 cloves
1 bay leaf
4 parsley sprigs tied together
Pinch of fresh or dried thyme
¾ cup heavy cream
¼ cup extra virgin olive oil
½ cup plus 1 tablespoon olive oil
4 to 5 garlic cloves, minced
Salt and freshly ground pepper
¼ to ½ teaspoon freshly grated nutmeg
1 baguette, thinly sliced and toasted

1 Soak the cod in water for 48 hours, changing the water a few times each day.

2 Bring a pot of salted water to a boil and cook the potatoes until soft, 10 to 15 minutes. Drain and discard the water.

3 Clean the cod of all bones and skin. Place it in a saucepan with ½ cup milk, the onion, bay leaf, parsley sprigs, thyme, and just enough cold water to cover. Place it on medium heat and just as it begins to simmer, remove it from the heat and let it cool 30 minutes. Drain the salt cod and discard the parsley and bay leaf. Discard any additional bones and skin from the cod.

4 Preheat the oven to 375°F.

5 Heat the additional ½ cup milk, heavy cream, and all but 1 tablespoon of the olive oils. Place the garlic and potatoes in a blender or food processor and mix at low speed. Flake the fish and add to the blender alternately with one-third of the warm milk-cream-olive oil mixture. Process for 1 minute and scrape down the sides of the blender. Process 3 more minutes. Add the remaining warm milk-cream-olive oil mixture a little at a time, stopping from time to time to scrape down the sides of the blender. The blending process should last for 8 minutes. Turn the speed to high and process until the mixture is light, 2 minutes. Season with salt, pepper, and nutmeg.

This can be prepared 1 day ahead of time to this point. Bring to room temperature before the final baking.

6 Oil a shallow 2-quart baking dish with the remaining 1 tablespoon olive oil. Spread the *brandade* in the dish and bake 15 minutes, until hot. Serve with warm croutons.

Serves 6 to 8

Mussels in the Style of the Camargue

The Camargue is the half-ranch, half-quagmire stretch of mysterious land that juts into the Mediterranean and divides Provence and Languedoc. It is the land of Provençal cowboys, pink flamingos, and wild horses. From this area also comes the little thumbnail-size clams called tellines, *that are so delicious when steamed open and doused with an astringent parsley vinaigrette. In this recipe, I have substituted mussels and the result is superb.*

3 pounds extremely fresh medium mussels, washed, beards removed
1 small onion, chopped
1 leek, white and 1 inch of green, chopped
3 garlic cloves, coarsely chopped
Bouquet garni (6 parsley stems, pinch of thyme, 1 bay leaf)
½ cup dry white wine (Sauvignon Blanc)
3 to 4 tablespoons lemon juice
¼ cup olive oil
¼ cup extra virgin olive oil
2 garlic cloves, minced
Salt and freshly ground pepper
⅓ cup chopped fresh parsley, preferably Italian
6 lemon wedges
Crusty bread

1 Discard any mussels that are broken or cracked. Soak in a generous quantity of salted water for 15 to 20 minutes.

2 Place the mussels in a large pan with the onions, leeks, 3 garlic cloves, bouquet garni, and wine. Cover and steam for 3 to 6 minutes over high heat, shaking the pan periodically until they open. Remove the mussels from the pan as they open and spread them, in their shells, on a baking sheet to cool. Reserve the cooking liquids and strain through several layers of cheesecloth or a coffee filter. Reduce the cooking liquids by two-thirds, 4 to 5 minutes, and reserve.

3 Mix the lemon juice, olive oils, and 2 garlic cloves together. Add the reduced cooking liquids and season with pepper.

4 Toss the mussels with the vinaigrette and parsley and place on a platter. Garnish with lemon wedges and serve immediately with crusty bread.

Serves 6

Shellfish Fritters with Spicy Hot Garlic Mayonnaise

Beignets, croquettes, *croquetas, bunyols, bunelos, fritto misto, and* crokettes *are a few of the names given to the wide variety of deep-fried fritters of fish, meat, and vegetables served around the northern Mediterranean Sea. This irresistible recipe is addictive.*

1 cup all-purpose flour
Salt and freshly ground pepper
2 eggs, separated
2 tablespoons olive oil
¾ cup warm beer
¼ cup water
1 pound clams, washed well, in their shells
1 pound mussels, washed well, beards removed, in their shells
¼ pound scallops, white muscle on side removed from shell
¼ pound medium shrimp, peeled
12 oysters, shucked
1 quart corn or peanut oil for deep-frying
Lemon wedges
1 recipe Spicy Hot Garlic Mayonnaise (page 274)

1 Sift the flour and ½ teaspoon salt together in a bowl and make a well in the center. In another bowl, whisk together the egg yolks, olive oil, and beer and pour into the well. Mix together just until mixed. Let it rest for 1 hour at room temperature.

2 Bring the water to a boil in a skillet. Add the clams and cover. Cook until the clams open and remove them immediately. Remove the clams from their shells and place in a bowl. Discard the shells. Repeat with the mussels. Reduce the heat to medium and add the scallops and more water if necessary. Cover and cook 1 minute. Cut into ¼-inch pieces. Add to the clams and mussels. Add the shrimp, cover, and cook 1 minute. Remove and cut them in half. Add to the other shellfish with the raw oysters. Season with salt and pepper and reserve in the refrigerator.

3 Heat the corn or peanut oil in a deep pan until it sizzles on contact with a drop of the batter (375°F.)

4 Beat the egg whites until stiff peaks form. Fold the whites into the batter and fold the batter into the shellfish.

5 Using a heaping tablespoon of batter, deep-fry a few fritters until they are golden brown, 3 to 4 minutes. Do not overload the pan. Garnish with a lemon wedge and serve with Spicy Hot Garlic Mayonnaise.

Makes 24 to 30 fritters to serve 8

Ragout of Clams, Sausage, and Garlic Confit à la Provençal

The word ragout *dates from the 1600s and is a classic term used to describe a stew concocted of meat, poultry, game, fish, and vegetables flavored with herbs and seasonings. The verb* ragouter *means "to bring forth someone's appetite." The term may be a classic one but this first course is a modern version of an old theme: clams and sausage stewed together with sweet garlic. New or old, it will definitely stimulate your taste buds as a first course. It is one of my favorites.*

¼ pound spicy pork sausage, pricked with a
    fork
3 tablespoons extra virgin olive oil
1 medium onion, thinly sliced
½ cup whole large garlic cloves, peeled
½ cup chicken stock (page 272)
1 cup dry white wine (Sauvignon Blanc)
5 medium tomatoes, peeled, seeded, and
    chopped (page 278), or 2 cups Italian
    plum tomatoes, drained and chopped
2 pounds clams, washed well
Salt and freshly ground pepper
3 tablespoons chopped fresh parsley
Crusty bread

1 Heat ¼ cup water in a skillet and cook the sausage, uncovered, 5 to 7 minutes. Remove and slice the sausage on the diagonal into ½-inch-thick slices. Reserve.

2 Heat the olive oil in a large skillet over low heat. Add the onions and garlic and sauté, uncovered, until the onions are soft, 8 minutes. Add the chicken stock, cover, and simmer slowly, 3 minutes. Add the wine and simmer, uncovered, until the liquid has reduced by one-half, 8 to 10 minutes. Add the tomatoes, cover, and simmer until the garlic is soft, 8 to 10 minutes. Add the clams, increase the heat to medium, cover, and cook until the clams open, 3 to 4 minutes. Simmer, uncovered, until the sauce has thickened slightly, 5 minutes. Season with salt and pepper.

3 Place the ragout on a serving platter. Garnish with the parsley and serve immediately with crusty bread.

Serves 6

Tuscan Three-Onion Soup
with Grilled Bread
and Shaved Parmesan

Summer Vegetable Soup with
Basil and Mint Pesto

Smoked Eggplant Soup with
Red Pepper Cream

Shellfish Soup with
Couscous from Trapani

Grilled Bread Salad
with Lemon Anchovy Vinaigrette

Grilled Bread with
Wild Mushrooms, Fontina,
and Gorgonzola

Grilled Bread with Beans
and Bitter Greens

Grilled Bread with
Sweet-Sour Chicken Livers

Layered Torte with Greens,
Ricotta, and Italian Meats

Crepes

Baked Crepes with Creamy Wild
Mushrooms and Prosciutto

Garlic Flat Bread with
Smoked Mozzarella
and Tomato Vinaigrette

Pizza with Fresh Herb, Olive,
and Pecorino Salad

Flat Bread with Gorgonzola,
Pine Nuts, and Red Onions

Calzone with Escarole, Olives,
Capers, and Toasted Pine Nuts

Pizza with Sun-Dried Tomato
Paste, Roasted Eggplant,
and Basil

Pasta with Pancetta, Tomatoes,
and Hot Red Pepper

Farfalle with Shellfish, Tomatoes,
and Arugula

"Little Ears" with Sicilian Pesto

Lemon and Herb Pansoti
with Wilted Greens

Italy

Spinach Pasta Dough

Potato Gnocchi with Tomatoes
and Fresh Milk Mozzarella

Pepper Pasta with Tuna and
Orange Puttanesca

Black and Red Pepper
Pasta Dough

Crispy Polenta Gratin with
Gorgonzola and Mascarpone

Fried Polenta Sticks with Sweet
and Hot Roasted Pepper Sauce

Gorgonzola Sauce

Risotto with Fennel Sausage,
Leeks, and Red Peppers

Risotto with Spring Vegetables

Frittata with
Roasted Sweet Peppers

Risotto Croquettes with
Smoked Ham and Mozzarella

Rolled Eggplant with
Prosciutto and Herbs

Fennel, Prosciutto, and Parsley
Salad with Shaved Parmesan

Salad of Radicchio, Arugula,
Blood Oranges, Raisins,
and Pine Nuts

White Bean Salad with
Gremolata and Grilled Tuna

Seafood Salad with
Garden Herb Sauce

Tuscan Bread Salad with
Tomatoes and Basil

Lit by a silver slice of moon, the piazza is full of spirit and exhilaration, the Italian air heavy with perfumed citrus. In the distance, cicadas serenade and olive trees whisper their announcement of summer when most meals are taken outside or "al fresco." The Mediterranean's warm breezes rustle the faded checked tablecloths at outdoor trattorias, or cafés, that line the streets and frame the corners. In homes upstairs, doors open to flower-laden balconies, and inside families gather around the table for the daily ritual they so enjoy. Carafes and plain glass tumblers filled with robust red wine vie for space on tables crowded with first courses. Everyone talks at the same time with gesturing arms and songlike Italian words as they assemble to celebrate the highlight of their day, eating. At home and in the local trattorias, fires of brush from the undergrowth and fruit and nut woods burn in the brick ovens baking flat breads made of wheat and other grains. Hearths are raised for grilling fresh fish, meat, and vegetables. At the tables, course after course arrives, none overpowering or overshadowing the others. The meal has been carefully scripted, almost like theater. Each course plays its part in the whole composition or experience, the first courses setting the stage for those that follow. In Italy, the joys of the table are unparalleled and food holds center stage in everyday life.

The drama begins. The opening act is the antipasto, the singular form of antipasti, which means "before the meal" and is meant to prepare the stomach for the courses to follow. Antipasti can be as informal as a relish platter of sliced meats like salami and mortadella, pickled peppers, olives, a morsel of cheese, and a few radishes. In the home, antipasto focuses on freshness, availability, and simplicity: a few slices of prosciutto with perfectly ripe figs or juicy melon, or *bruschetta*—garlic and olive oil toast. At the trattoria, the scope is often enormous. Several antipasti are strategically placed inside the entrance of the trattoria to tempt the already hungry restaurant client with their elaborate and varied display. The range is limitless: deep-fried polenta sticks, aromatic white bean salads with fresh herbs and grilled fish, caponata or stewed vegetables, pungent eggplant sandwiches, golden-fried calamari or artichokes, rustic layered pies, or *torte,* and savory *crostini* topped with everything under the sun.

Antipasto platters reward the palate with a variety of tastes and surprises and are made up of a subtle blend of colors and textures. They are meant to stimulate the imagination and whet the appetite; antipasti are to be savored rather than gobbled, a fan for the appetite, not an extinguisher. Most times, hot antipasti are served before a light meal and cold antipasti before a more substantial meal. They are usually served on plates at the table and eaten with forks, though it is not uncommon for them to be served at cocktail parties where one might have to juggle an antipasto in one hand and a drink in the other while standing.

The roots of antipasto can be traced back to the opulent feasts of the Roman Empire when lengthy banquets of gustatory excess are rumored to have lasted for hours and hours, sometimes even days. Elaborate presentations of oysters, caviar, piles of mussels and fried snails, three-dimensional displays of pickled vegetables, sausages, and eggs were served on silver trays, presented one after the other. These beginning courses were called *gustus* or *gustatio* and much later, antipasto. Antipasti may not have had their present name, but they had as prominent a place at the table then as they do today.

The next act after antipasti is *primi piatti,* or "first plates" and helps develop the theme of the dinner or play. This course sets the tempo and mood for the rest of the drama to follow. With an abundance of luscious raw materials, the *primi piatti* repertoire is immense: hundreds of soups and a wealth of polenta, risotto, and of course, pasta dishes, the king of the Italian table. *Primi piatti* are most often served in a wide flat bowl and can be called *minestra,* or "wet course," since they usually contain a sauce or some liquid.

Primi piatti are a filling course, consisting of some sort of starch or carbohydrate, a way to provide sustenance in a country where economic circumstances have been marginal at times. Steaming bowls of hearty fare provide the solution: spicy pasta puttanesca with olives, capers, garlic, and anchovies; pasta carbonara with pancetta, egg yolks, garlic, and red pepper; lasagne with veal meatballs and tomatoes; flavorful risottos with artichokes and shrimp, spring vegetables, or Barolo wine; comforting polenta layered with cheeses and greens or wild mushrooms; legumes stewed with pasta and vegetables. And what a fantastic way to use leftover bits of meats or the daily catch of fish that cannot be sold, vegetables and herbs picked from the family garden, and local cheeses—all go into creating a substantial and flavorful dish in times when there are few pennies to spare. But if the garden produces an overabundance of artichokes for two straight months, it is the cook's task to create different artichoke preparations every night. Depending upon one's creativity and financial resources, *primi piatti* can be very distinctive, and they are always comforting and flavorful. Whether simple or complex, *primi piatti* are a real favorite and a tough act to follow (which explains the traditional simpler main and dessert courses).

These present-day traditions have their roots deep in Italy's past. Waves of invasion stirred Italy for 3,000 years, the Greeks, Etruscans, and Arabs leaving the most profound effects. The Greeks were a strong force in the Mediterranean before the first millennium, overpowering southern Italy and Sicily for several hundred years. Their legacy was tremendous: They planted wheat and olive and almond trees; showed the southern Italians how to make wine and honey, and introduced spit roasting. The Arabs, who had settled in North Africa and the eastern Mediterranean, migrated to southern Italy in the ninth century and superimposed their influences on the Greeks. They brought rice, nuts, saffron and other spices, flaky pastry, couscous, and citrus. Not having as pronounced an effect as the Greeks or the Arabs, the Etruscans in 500 B.C. occupied northern Italy and introduced *pulmentum,* or polenta, which served as sustenance for the Roman Empire's survival and later, as today, as an important and integral part of the Italian diet. And much later, in the sixteenth century, tomatoes, peppers, and various squash and beans were introduced to Italy from the New World. These ingredients have played a crucial role in the formation of its present-day cuisine.

Geographically, Italy juts out into the Mediterranean in the shape of a boot giving a swift kick toward Sicily and North Africa. Only seven hundred miles from north to south and never wider than three hundred miles at any one point, Italy is nevertheless a land of varied geography, culture, people, and food. Twenty different regions can be identified,

each region so different from the other that a single distinct Italian cuisine is impossible to classify. And then, not only is each region unique, but each town and village is a world unto its own. The same dish might be prepared in northern and southern Italy, but it will vary dramatically with respect to ingredients and technique, though it still has the same name. For example, in Naples in the south, the soup *pasta e fagioli* is made with beans, pasta, garlic, celery, tomatoes, parsley, oregano, and crushed red pepper; in Bologna in the north, it is made with beans, pasta, garlic, onions, prosciutto, and sage. Each area gives the soup the same name but the ingredients vary, sometimes significantly.

The north is well irrigated and more lush for grazing cattle, and the food reflects this richness through the use of cream, eggs, and butter. The provinces of northern Italy have made a substantial donation to the culinary network that runs through Italy: prosciutto or cured ham, Reggiano Parmesan, pancetta—a peppered and brined bacon—and Balsamic vinegar from Emilia-Romagna, Gorgonzola—a very flavorful blue-veined cheese—polenta, arborio rice—a short-grained rice perfect for risotto making—basil from the hillsides of Liguria, Tuscan olive oil, excellent beef, truffles, wild mushrooms, Pecorino cheese, and tremendous amounts of fish.

The rural south by contrast with the prosperous north, is sun-parched and barren.

The terrain is rugged and mountainous, unsuitable for farming because of the poor soil conditions that have left this area ravaged by economic hardship over the years. The cooking medium is olive oil and pork is the dominant meat at the table. Just a hint of crushed red pepper appears in many dishes. This is a holdover from times when black pepper prices were so high that southern Italians grew hot red pepper, which could be easily grown, to substitute in their dishes and acquired a taste for it. Pasta reigns supreme on the southern table and is often factory-made of 100 percent semolina or freshly made of water and/or olive oil, but never eggs. Buffalo milk mozzarella is made here from the milk of water buffalos grazing in the mountains above Sorrento. Sweet red tomatoes are present in many dishes and large sheets of tomato concentrate can be seen drying on many Neapolitan balconies. And in the bustling city of Naples, pizza and calzone are sold on every corner. Antipasti are not as important in the south as the north but the enjoyment of *primi piatti* is every bit as strong as its counterpart.

Sicily is a kingdom unto its own. This broadly triangular island is the largest in the Mediterranean. It is not as barren as southern Italy and the cultivated countryside is carefully plotted in rows of abundant color producing fantastic produce—fennel, eggplant, tomatoes, and artichokes. Citrus trees grow in profusion and caper bushes grow wild along the shores. North Africa is just ninety miles southwest of Sicily and its influence can be tasted in sweet-and-sour dishes, spices, raisins, pine nuts, and couscous. Anchovies and sardines are a favored accent to many dishes; again the cooking medium is olive oil. Sardinia, the second largest island in the Mediterranean, makes excellent Pecorino or sheep's milk cheese. Here, hunting game is a sport of necessity, and blackbird and wild boar are presented in a variety of guises. Bread replaces pasta as the starch of choice. Sardinia has been invaded and colonized over and over by a multitude of forces for centuries, driving its people from the coasts into the central mountains where they have become farmers and shepherds rather than fishermen. This move has been so complete that fish is rarely served in the home in Sardinia. The last invasion on Sardinia was mounted by the Italians just one hundred years ago. Their influence has not been felt nearly as strongly as that of the Spanish, French, and North Africans who dominated Sardinia's early history. Only time will tell its future.

Italian cuisine has taken thousands of years to develop, drawing from three distinct culinary heritages. *Cucina alto-borghese*, or the cuisine of the upper classes, courts, or merchant families, with its refined principles and ingredients, was developed during the Roman Empire and prospered throughout the Middle Ages, flourishing in the Renaissance. Court cuisine contributed a refinement to today's Italian kitchen. *Cucina povera*, or the poor cuisine, has been cooked by a large percentage of the population of Italy for centuries out of sheer necessity for lack of money and other resources. *Cucina casalinga* is a common term in Italy used to describe the cuisine of the home, which is more informal, down-to-earth, and unadulterated, where bold and concentrated flavors are vital constituents to the success of the meal. Somewhere in the middle, these three different styles have merged to create a rich, varied, and well-respected world cuisine, utilizing excellent local ingredients, a true peasant-style set of recipes, simple preparations, assertive flavors, and sound theory and practices as seen here in these antipasto and *primo piatto* recipes.

Tuscan Three-Onion Soup with Grilled Bread and Shaved Parmesan

This soup is made with three onions—white onions, leeks, and garlic. Leeks are an extremely flavorful aromatic vegetable readily available in just about every grocery store. One problem is washing them. The dirt gets lodged inside as they grow and it is virtually impossible to clean them when they are whole. The trick is to chop the leeks first, place them in a bowl of cold water, and rinse them well. Drain them well before using.

4 large white onions

4 medium leeks

4 ounces pancetta in 1 piece

¼ cup extra virgin olive oil

6 cups chicken stock (page 272)

3 to 4 tablespoons Balsamic vinegar

¾ to 1 cup fruity red wine (Chianti,
      Beaujolais, Zinfandel)

Salt and freshly ground pepper

6 slices rustic country-style bread

2 garlic cloves, peeled

1 6-ounce chunk of Parmesan cheese

2 tablespoons chopped fresh parsley

1 Peel the onions and cut them in half. Slice into thin slices. Trim the leeks and cut in half lengthwise. Slice the leeks across into ¼-inch slices, using 3 inches of green. Place in a bowl of cold water and rinse out the dirt. Drain and reserve.

2 Unroll the pancetta and slice into ¼-inch slices.

3 Heat the olive oil in a soup pot. Add the pancetta and cook until some of the fat has been rendered, 5 minutes. Add the onions and leeks and continue to sauté 20 minutes. Add the stock and simmer 30 minutes.

This soup can be prepared 1 day in advance to this point.

4 Just before serving the soup, season with the vinegar, red wine, salt, and pepper. Toast the bread slices and rub with the peeled garlic cloves. Float the croutons in the soup. Pare 4 or 5 shavings of the Parmesan on top of each serving of soup. Garnish with the chopped parsley and serve immediately.

Serves 6

Summer Vegetable Soup with Basil and Mint Pesto

Pesto comes from the Liguria region of Italy. Just over the border in Provence, a similar version called pistou *is made with the same ingredients, excluding pine nuts.*

Soup

1¼ cups dry navy beans

1 small bunch of Swiss chard, washed, stems removed

½ small head of savoy cabbage

Salt and freshly ground pepper

¼ cup olive oil

3 ounces pancetta, chopped

¼ cup chopped fresh parsley

2 garlic cloves, minced

2 stalk celery, trimmed and cut into ¼-inch dice

1 carrot, peeled and cut into ¼-inch dice

1 medium onion, cut into ¼-inch dice

1 medium potato, cut into ¼-inch dice

½ cup green beans, trimmed and cut into ½-inch lengths

1 small zucchini, halved and cut into ¼-inch half circles

3 tomatoes, peeled, seeded, and chopped (page 278)

1 tablespoon tomato paste

7 cups chicken stock (page 272)

⅓ cup Italian arborio rice

Pesto

5 garlic cloves, minced

1 packed cup fresh mint leaves, washed and dried

1¼ packed cup fresh basil leaves, washed and dried

1 cup grated Parmesan cheese

½ cup olive oil

5 tablespoons pine nuts, toasted (page 277)

1 Soak the dry beans in water overnight. Drain and put in a large pot with 5 cups water. Bring to a boil, turn the heat down, and simmer slowly until almost tender, 40 minutes. Turn off the heat and let the beans sit in the cooking liquid.

2 Wash the chard and cabbage and cut into thin strips. Place in a saucepan with a large pinch of salt and ¼ cup water. Cover and simmer slowly until the leaves are wilted, 15 minutes. Drain and set aside.

3 Heat a stockpot and add the olive oil and pancetta and sauté slowly until it renders its fat and just begins to turn golden, 10 minutes. Add the parsley and garlic and sauté slowly for 2 minutes. Add the celery, carrots, onions, potatoes, green beans, and zucchini and sauté for 5 minutes. Add the navy beans with their water to the stockpot. Add the Swiss chard, cabbage, tomatoes, and tomato paste. Add 6 cups chicken stock to cover the vegetables. Simmer slowly for 40 minutes.

4 Bring the remaining 1 cup stock to a simmer. Add the rice and simmer 10 minutes. Turn off the heat.

5 In the meantime, place the garlic, mint, basil, salt, and pepper in a blender or food processor. Process until a rough paste is formed. Add half the cheese and oil and process until the paste is smoother. Add the pine nuts and continue to add the Parmesan and oil until a stiff paste is obtained. Season with salt and pepper.

6 Ten minutes before the soup is finished, add the rice and simmer until it is cooked. Season with salt and pepper.

7 Ladle the soup into soup bowls and place a large tablespoon of pesto on top. Garnish with the remaining Parmesan and serve immediately.

Serves 6 to 8

ZUPPA DI MELANZANE

Smoked Eggplant Soup with Red Pepper Cream

Soup also doubles as a main course in many homes in Italy. Coupled with a loaf of bread, a salad, and a glass of wine, a bowl of soup makes an easy, comforting, and satisfying meal.

2 1½-pound eggplants, smoked (page 277)
3 tablespoons olive oil
2 medium onions, chopped
4 garlic cloves, minced
6 cups chicken stock (page 272)
1 to 2 tablespoons lemon juice
Salt and freshly ground pepper
1 red bell pepper
¼ cup heavy cream
Pinch of cayenne
Whole parsley leaves, preferably Italian

1 Preheat the oven to 375°F.

2 Place the eggplants on a baking sheet and bake until they can be easily skewered, 20 to 30 minutes depending upon the size. Cool. Discard the skin and stem and reserve the pulp.

3 In a soup pot, heat the olive oil. Add the onions and garlic and sauté over low heat until the onions are soft, 10 minutes. Add the eggplant and sauté for 15 minutes, uncovered. Add the chicken stock and simmer 30 minutes, uncovered. Puree the soup well in a blender. Season with lemon juice, salt, and pepper. If it is too thick, correct with additional chicken stock or water.

4 Roast the red pepper either under the broiler or directly on a gas jet until the skin is completely black. Steam in a plastic bag for 10 minutes. Remove the black skin, seeds, and stem. Puree to make a very smooth paste in a blender or food processor. Whip the cream with a whisk until very soft peaks form. Add the roasted red pepper puree and a pinch of cayenne. Season with salt and pepper.

5 Ladle the soup into bowls. Garnish with the red pepper cream and a few leaves of parsley.

Serves 6

Shellfish Soup with Couscous from Trapani

Just ninety miles of blue Mediterranean water stand between Sicily and North Africa, making the two countries' relationship an ancient one. Several hundred years ago, soldiers were recruited from Tunisia to conquer Sicily. Tucked away in the soldiers' bags were not only arms but also the golden grains of semolina they loved and couldn't leave behind. Semolina is durum wheat, the hardest kind of wheat grown. It is used in making couscous, a process of coating the semolina grains with flour. The Tunisians introduced couscous to Sicily and it took hold. This North African–influenced dish can be seen in a small pocket of western Sicily, from Marsala to Trapani. When buying couscous, there are two types, instant and regular. Do not purchase instant couscous, which is precooked and of inferior quality. Instead buy regular couscous and enjoy the uniqueness of this dish.

¾ cup couscous
2½ cups fish stock (page 272) or bottled clam juice
½ cup water
Salt and freshly ground pepper
2 pounds assorted shellfish (mussels, clams, shrimp, and scallops)
3 tablespoons olive oil
1 small onion, minced
3 garlic cloves, minced

Small pinch of crushed red pepper
1 cup dry red wine
2 bay leaves
3 large tomatoes, peeled, seeded, and chopped (page 278), or 1¼ cups canned Italian plum tomatoes, drained and chopped
1 teaspoon red wine vinegar
3 tablespoons chopped fresh parsley
Large pinch of saffron
Chopped fresh parsley

1 Wash the couscous in cold water and drain immediately. Lift and rake the grains with your fingertips to separate them. Let rest 10 minutes.

2 Heat the fish stock in the bottom of a large soup pot fitted with a steamer on top. Line the steamer with 3 layers of cheesecloth. Add the couscous to the steamer and steam slowly for 20 minutes, uncovered, fluffing the grains halfway through the cooking. Remove from the steamer and dump the couscous into a baking pan. Combine ½ cup water and ¼ teaspoon salt. Sprinkle the couscous with the salt water. Lift and rake the grains with your fingertips to separate them. Let rest 10 minutes.

3 Heat the fish stock to a simmer. Wash the shellfish. Add the mussels to the soup pot, cover, and cook until they open, 2 to 5 minutes. Remove the mussels from the pan with a slotted spoon as they open, place in a large bowl, and cover with foil. Add the clams to the soup pot, cover, and cook until they open, 2 to 5 minutes. Remove the clams from the pan with a slotted spoon as they open and add to the mussels. Strain the cooking broth and reserve. Peel the shrimp and add the raw shrimp to the cooked shellfish. Remove the muscle from the side of the scallops. Add the raw scallops to the cooked shellfish. Reserve.

4 Heat the olive oil in the soup pot. Add the onions and sauté until soft, 7 minutes. Add the garlic and crushed red pepper and sauté 1 minute. Turn the heat to high and immediately add the wine. Reduce by one-half, 2 minutes. Add the bay leaves, tomatoes, vinegar, reserved shellfish broth, and pepper. Bring to a boil, then reduce the heat to a slow simmer. Place the steamer back on the top of the soup pot and place the couscous in the cheesecloth-lined steamer. Simmer slowly, uncovered, 15 minutes, until the couscous is hot to the touch on top. Remove the steamer and couscous.

5 Add the parsley, saffron, and shellfish to the soup pot and simmer slowly 2 minutes. Turn off the heat and let sit 3 minutes. Stir the soup well and season with salt and pepper. Divide the couscous among 6 bowls. Ladle the soup over the couscous, garnish with the parsley, and serve immediately.

Serves 6

Grilled Bread Salad with Lemon Anchovy Vinaigrette

Mozzarella is the second most popular cheese in Italy after Parmesan. There are several types of mozzarella but the most common variety in the United States is firm enough that if you drop it, it almost bounces. What this cheese lacks in flavor, it makes up for in texture when melted. On the opposite end of the spectrum is the prized buffalo milk mozzarella, a specialty of Naples. Mozzarella di bufala has a mild distinctive farm flavor, is extremely expensive, and is best served fresh, perhaps with a salad of ripe tomatoes and basil. Fresh cow's milk mozzarella is somewhere in between the two; it is stringy when melted, with more flavor than the former but less expensive than the latter. It makes a perfect addition to this recipe.

6 large slices rustic, firm, country-style
    bread
2 garlic cloves, peeled
¼ cup lemon juice
6 anchovy fillets, soaked in cold water 10
    minutes, patted dry, and mashed
1 shallot, minced
½ cup extra virgin olive oil
Salt and freshly ground pepper
¾ pound fresh milk or buffalo milk
    mozzarella, thinly sliced

6 lemon wedges
The following garnishes:
    Small radishes with young green tops
    Grilled Japanese eggplant slices
    Black or green olives
    Marinated artichoke hearts
    Roasted red or yellow bell peppers

1 Cut each slice of bread on the diagonal into 2 pieces. Toast or grill the bread until golden and rub each side with garlic.

2 In a small bowl, whisk together the lemon juice, anchovies, shallots, and extra virgin olive oil. Season with salt and pepper.

3 Preheat the oven to 400°F.

4 Place the grilled bread on a baking sheet and place the mozzarella on top, distributing it evenly. Bake on the top shelf of the oven until the mozzarella begins to melt, 1 to 2 minutes

5 To serve, place 2 pieces of grilled bread on each plate. Drizzle a spoonful of the lemon anchovy vinaigrette on top. Garnish with lemon wedges, radishes, eggplant, olives, artichokes, and roasted peppers. Serve the remaining sauce on the side in a small bowl.

Serves 6

Grilled Bread with Wild Mushrooms, Fontina, and Gorgonzola

In Italy, mushrooms mean wild mushrooms and in most cases, this means the highly prized porcini mushrooms, named for their supposed likeness to pudgy little piglets, or porca. *Porcini gathering is a national autumn pasttime and during mushroom season, the marketplace is not to be missed. Huge piles of creamy golden brown porcini mushrooms fill the tables, and ladies doing their daily marketing pick and choose these beauties with a very discerning eye.*

1 tablespoon extra virgin olive oil
1 tablespoon butter
½ pound wild mushrooms (porcini, chanterelles, shiitake, morels) cleaned with a brush and thinly sliced (see Note)
½ pound button or field mushrooms, cleaned with a brush and thinly sliced
1 teaspoon mixed chopped fresh herbs, such as sage, rosemary, and thyme
Large pinch of chopped fresh mint
1 tablespoon chopped fresh parsley
Salt and freshly ground pepper
12 slices country bread, toasted
2 garlic cloves, peeled
4 ounces fontina cheese, coarsely grated
2 ounces Gorgonzola cheese, crumbled
Juice of ½ lemon
Whole parsley leaves, preferably Italian

1 Heat the olive oil and butter in a large skillet over medium high heat. Add the mushrooms and continue to cook until the liquid has evaporated and the mushrooms are dry, 10 minutes. Add the herbs and toss together. Season well with salt and pepper. Remove from the heat.

2 Rub each side of the toast lightly with the garlic cloves. Distribute the warm mushrooms on top of the toast. Combine the two cheeses and sprinkle them evenly on top of the mushrooms. Place the mushroom toasts under the broiler until the cheese melts, 30 to 60 seconds. Place on a platter and drizzle with the lemon juice.

3 Serve immediately, garnished with parsley leaves.

Serves 6

NOTE: If fresh wild mushrooms are unavailable for this recipe, an equivalent amount of button or field mushrooms can be substituted along with ¼ ounce dried porcini mushrooms soaked in hot water for 30 minutes.

Grilled Bread with Beans and Bitter Greens

My favorite way to serve crostini *or grilled bread, is to make an assortment and serve them together on one platter. I call it* crostini misti *or mixed grilled bread. Not only is it a surprising mixture of colors and flavors, but it is also unique and everyone will want to taste them all. Put this delicious combination of beans and bitter greens with Grilled Bread with Wild Mushrooms, Fontina, and Gorgonzola (page 115), Grilled Bread with Sweet-Sour Chicken Livers (page 117), or maybe even grilled bread with sun-dried tomato puree.*

¾ cup (5 ounces) dry white, cannellini, or
  navy beans (see Note)
1 bay leaf
Large pinch of dried thyme
3 tablespoons extra virgin olive oil
2 teaspoons chopped fresh sage
4 garlic cloves, minced
Salt and freshly ground pepper
1 small bunch of Swiss chard, escarole, or
  beet or turnip greens
½ small onion, minced
¼ teaspoon crushed red pepper
2 teaspoons red wine vinegar
6 to 8 large slices country bread, toasted or
  grilled
2 garlic cloves, peeled

1 Pick over the beans and discard any stones. Cover with water and soak overnight. The next day, drain the beans and place them in a saucepan with the bay leaf, thyme, and enough water to cover by 2 inches. Simmer, uncovered, until the skins crack and the beans are tender, 45 to 60 minutes. Drain the beans, reserving ½ cup of the cooking liquid.

2 Heat 2 tablespoons olive oil in a skillet. Add the beans, sage, half of the garlic, and the reserved cooking liquid. Cook together, mashing occasionally, until the moisture evaporates and the mixture forms a paste, 5 to 10 minutes. Season with salt and pepper.

3 Wash the greens well and spin dry. Remove the stems and cut into 1-inch pieces. Heat the remaining 1 tablespoon olive oil in a skillet over low heat and sauté the onions until soft, 7 minutes. Add the greens and the remaining garlic and cook until wilted, stirring occasionally, 3 minutes. Season with salt, pepper, red pepper, and vinegar.

4 Rub each side of the toast with the garlic cloves. Spread the beans on the toasted bread and top with the greens. Serve immediately.

Serves 6 to 8

NOTE: This can also be made with 2 cups canned cooked beans.

Grilled Bread with Sweet-Sour Chicken Livers

Bruschetta, fettunta, and crostini are three different types of grilled bread used as a tonic for a ferocious appetite. Indigenous to southern Italy, bruschetta celebrates the olive harvest with thick slices of rustic bread grilled over an open fire, rubbed with garlic, and brushed with green-gold olive oil and maybe a sprinkling of coarse salt. Fettunta of northern Italy means "oiled slice" and is basically the same thing as bruschetta. Crostini is sliced thinner than bruschetta and can be topped with all kinds of flavorful combinations of ingredients: anchovies, olives, and capers; roasted eggplant with garlic and olive oil; chopped tomatoes with red wine vinegar, garlic, and herbs; and this sweet-sour chicken liver paste.

1 tablespoon olive oil

2 ounces pancetta, finely chopped

¼ cup minced onion

1 teaspoon mixed chopped fresh herbs, such as sage, thyme, and rosemary

2 tablespoons dry Marsala or white wine

1 tablespoon extra virgin olive oil

1 tablespoon butter

½ pound chicken livers, trimmed of veins and fat

Salt and freshly ground pepper

1 garlic clove, mashed in a mortar and pestle

2 anchovy fillets, soaked in cold water 10 minutes, patted dry, and mashed

1 tablespoon chopped capers

2 to 3 teaspoons Balsamic vinegar

6 large slices country bread, cut ¼ inch thick and each slice cut in half

1 In a skillet over medium heat, heat the olive oil. Sauté the pancetta, onions and herbs until the onions are soft, 10 minutes. Add the Marsala and simmer until the moisture evaporates. Remove from the pan, place on a work surface, and chop together until fine. Reserve.

2 In the same pan, heat the olive oil and butter over low heat. Place the livers in the pan side by side and cook for 2 to 3 minutes, turning them a few times. Season with salt and pepper. As soon as they are firm yet still pink on the inside, remove them from the pan and let cool. Chop the livers coarsely and combine them in a bowl with the onions. Add the garlic, anchovies, capers, and vinegar to taste. Season with salt and pepper.

3 Toast or grill the bread until golden on each side. Spread the liver paste on the warm crostini and serve immediately.

Makes 12 crostini to serve 6

Layered Torte with Greens, Ricotta, and Italian Meats

One of the most memorable meals I have had in the south of Italy was in the heel of the boot in Apulia. Alberobello is a village known for its curious beehive-shaped houses made of mortarless stone that nestle together among the vines and olive trees. This is the home of Franco Lippolis, the chef of the Dei Trulli, the only hotel and restaurant housed in one of these historical buildings. Franco planned a special meal for me that lasted for hours. The flavors were sensational and this colorful pie was one of my favorites.

D o u g h

    1¼ teaspoons dry yeast
    1¼ cups warm water (115°F.)
    3¼ cups all-purpose flour
    1 teaspoon salt
    ¼ cup olive oil

F i l l i n g

    1½ pounds greens (Swiss chard, spinach, mustard greens, escarole, beet greens), stems removed, washed well, and spun dry
    4 tablespoons plus 1 teaspoon olive oil
    1 pound mushrooms, thinly sliced
    4 garlic cloves, minced
    Salt and freshly ground pepper
    2 red bell peppers, cored, seeded, and thinly sliced
    2 medium onions, thinly sliced

1 pound ricotta, drained in a cheesecloth-lined strainer 2 hours
1 egg, lightly beaten
¾ pound mozzarella, grated
½ pound fontina, grated
¾ pound assorted Italian sliced meats, such as prosciutto, salami, soppressata, capocollo, and mortadella

1 To make the dough, place the yeast in a bowl with ¼ cup warm water. Dissolve and let proof until it bubbles, 10 minutes. Add the rest of the dough ingredients to the bowl and stir to mix. Place on a work surface and knead for 7 to 10 minutes, until soft and smooth. This can also be done in a food processor or electric mixer: Process the yeast, flour, and salt in a food processor. With the motor on, add 1¼ cups warm water within 15 seconds. Quickly add the olive oil and process until the dough is smooth and evenly soft, about 45 seconds. If the dough is dry and rough and doesn't form a ball, add a tablespoon or two of water.

2 Place the dough in an oiled bowl and turn to coat with oil. Cover tightly with plastic wrap and set aside in a warm place until doubled in volume, 1 hour.

3 To make the filling, heat a large skillet and sauté the greens until wilted. Squeeze in a towel to remove excess moisture. Chop coarsely and set aside. Heat 2 tablespoons olive oil in a skillet and sauté the mushrooms and garlic until the liquid has completely evaporated, 15 minutes. Season with salt and pepper. Set aside, drained on paper towels. Add 2 tablespoons oil and sauté the peppers and onions until soft, 15 minutes. Set aside. In a bowl, mix the ricotta, egg, and greens. Season with salt and pepper. Set aside. Combine the mozzarella and fontina cheeses.

4 To assemble, place a 10-inch springform pan on a baking sheet and brush the inside with the remaining 1 teaspoon olive oil. Punch down the dough and divide in 2 pieces, three-quarters and one-quarter. Roll the larger piece into a 16-inch circle. Transfer to the pan and line the bottom and sides so that it comes up and over the edges.

5 Preheat the oven to 400°F.

6 Place one-quarter of the meat on the bot-

tom and one-quarter of the combined cheeses on top. Next, layer one-half of the mushrooms and one-half of the onions and peppers on top of the cheese. Sprinkle with one-quarter of the combined cheeses. Place another layer of the meat on top. Spread the greens mixture over the meat, repeating the layering sequence again, ending with the cheese.

7 Roll the remaining dough into a 10-inch circle. Brush the overhanging crust lightly with water, cover with the top crust, and pinch the crusts together. Make two ½-inch vents in the middle of the top. Bake on the lowest rack of the oven 1¼ hours. Cool 30 to 45 minutes before slicing.

Serves 10

NOTE: If the top gets too dark during baking, place a piece of foil over it.

CRESPELLE

Crepes

2 cups all-purpose flour
¼ teaspoon salt
1¾ cups milk
4 eggs
4 to 5 tablespoons butter

1 Put the flour and salt in a bowl and add the milk slowly, a little at a time, mixing vigorously with a fork to avoid lumps. Add 1 egg at a time, beating rapidly with a fork after each addition. Let the batter rest 30 minutes.

2 Grease the bottom of an 8-inch crepe pan with 1 teaspoon butter to start. Place the pan over medium heat. Stir the batter, pour ⅓ cup into the pan, and rotate to completely cover the bottom of the pan. As soon as the batter has set, loosen the crepe with a spatula and flip the crepe. When the other side is firm, remove the crepe and place it on a plate. Repeat with the rest of the batter, stirring the batter occasionally and regreasing the pan as needed. Crepes can be stacked on top of one another until ready to use.

Makes 12 crepes

Baked Crepes with Creamy Wild Mushrooms and Prosciutto

Crespelle *are the same as French crepes. Supposedly, they were introduced to Naples by the French courts.* Crespelle *are popular mainly on the Campania coast of the Mediterranean and in the south of Italy and a few other scattered pockets throughout the country.*

½ ounce dried wild mushrooms
2 cups boiling water
6 tablespoons butter
1 medium onion, finely chopped
½ pound fresh button mushrooms, very thinly sliced
6 ounces very thinly sliced prosciutto, cut into thin strips
2 tablespoons all-purpose flour
2 cups milk
¾ cup grated Parmesan cheese
Salt and freshly ground pepper
1 recipe Crespelle or Crepes (page 119)
2 tablespoons fine dry bread crumbs

1 Soak the dried mushrooms in the boiling water 30 minutes. Drain well and reserve the water. Chop the mushrooms coarsely. Filter the mushroom water through a paper towel–lined strainer and reserve.

2 Heat 2 tablespoons butter in a sauté pan and add the onions. Cook over medium heat until the onions are soft, 10 minutes. Add the fresh mushrooms and continue to sauté until the mushrooms have evaporated their liquid, 10 minutes. Add the chopped soaked wild mushrooms and continue to sauté 1 minute. Add the mushroom water, turn the heat to high, and simmer, stirring constantly, until almost dry, 10 minutes. Turn the heat to medium, add the prosciutto, and continue to sauté 2 minutes.

3 Melt 3 tablespoons butter in a saucepan over low heat. Stirring constantly, add the flour and stir 2 minutes. Add the milk, stirring constantly, and cook until the mixture thickens, 2 to 3 minutes. Add the mushroom mixture and mix well. Add ½ cup grated cheese and season with salt and pepper.

4 Preheat the oven to 425°F. Butter the bottom and sides of a 9 × 12-inch baking dish.

5 Place a crepe flat on the work surface. Spread half of it with a few tablespoons filling. Fold in half, then quarters. Stand the triangles in a baking dish, overlapping one another with the curved side up. Repeat. Melt the remaining 1 tablespoon butter and brush on the tops of the crepes. Combine the remaining ¼ cup grated Parmesan and the bread crumbs. Sprinkle over the top. Bake the crepes for 20 minutes, or until golden on top. Allow the crepes to cool for 10 minutes before serving.

Makes 12 crepes to serve 6

Garlic Flat Bread with Smoked Mozzarella and Tomato Vinaigrette

Hearth bread or focaccia derives its name from the Latin word focus, *meaning "hearth."*

Dough

1 package (7 grams) dry yeast
1 cup lukewarm water (110°F.)
¼ cup whole wheat flour
3 tablespoons extra virgin olive oil
½ cup water
1¾ cups all-purpose flour
¾ teaspoon salt

Topping

4 garlic cloves, sliced paper-thin
6 tablespoons extra virgin olive oil
¼ cup Balsamic vinegar
1 garlic clove, minced
Salt and freshly ground pepper
¼ pound yellow cherry tomatoes, cut in half
¼ pound red cherry tomatoes, cut in half
6 ounces smoked mozzarella or Scamorza
   cheese, coarsely grated
¼ cup fresh basil leaves, loosely packed,
   cut into thin strips

1 To make a sponge, combine the yeast, lukewarm water, and whole wheat flour in a bowl. Let stand for 10 minutes, then add the remaining dough ingredients. Mix the dough thoroughly. Knead on a floured board for 10 minutes, until it is soft yet still moist. Place in an oiled bowl, turning once. Cover the bowl with a towel and put in a warm place (75°F.). Let the dough rise for 1 hour, or until doubled in size.

2 Preheat the oven to 450°F. and place a pizza brick or tiles on the bottom shelf of the oven.

3 On a floured surface, divide the dough into 2 pieces and roll each piece into an 8-inch circle, ½ inch thick. Transfer to a well-floured pizza peel or paddle. Sprinkle the sliced garlic on top and press into the dough. Transfer the dough from the peel onto the heated brick in the oven. Bake until golden and crisp, 8 to 10 minutes. Remove from the oven and let rest on a cooling rack.

4 In a bowl, whisk together the oil, vinegar, and minced garlic. Season with the salt and pepper. Add the cherry tomatoes and toss together. Leave at room temperature.

The recipe can be prepared several hours ahead to this point.

5 Heat the oven broiler.

6 Place half of the cheese on top of each flat bread. Place under the broiler and broil until the cheese is melted and the crust is golden, 1 to 2 minutes. Remove from the oven and place on a platter. Top each flat bread with half of the tomatoes, vinaigrette, and basil. Serve immediately.

Makes two 8-inch flat breads to serve 6

Pizza with Fresh Herb, Olive, and Pecorino Salad

This is not a traditional Neapolitan pizza. Rather it is adapted from Chez Panisse where I worked for a few years. At the restaurant, we topped a hot pizza with a parsley and shaved Parmesan salad. Here the pizza is topped with a salad of parsley, basil, chives, mint, olives, and shaved Pecorino. The combination may sound odd, but once you have made it, you will understand why it has become a Chez Panisse favorite.

3 garlic cloves, minced

3 tablespoons olive oil

2 to 3 cups parsley leaves, preferably Italian

1 cup fresh basil leaves, loosely packed

3 tablespoons snipped fresh chives

2 tablespoons very coarsely chopped fresh mint

¼ cup pitted and coarsely chopped Italian black olives (page 279)

5 tablespoons extra virgin olive oil

3 to 4 tablespoons lemon juice

Salt and freshly ground pepper

1 recipe Pizza Dough (page 276)

¾ cup (3 ounces) grated mozzarella cheese

¾ cup (3 ounces) grated fontina cheese

1 3-ounce chunk of Pecorino cheese

1 Combine the garlic and olive oil and let stand for 30 minutes.

2 Preheat the oven to 500°F. and place a pizza brick or tiles on the bottom shelf of the oven.

3 Pick the parsley and basil leaves from the stems and discard the stems. Wash the parsley and basil leaves and spin dry. Tear the basil leaves into pieces about the same size as the parsley. Combine the parsley, basil, chives, mint, and olives.

4 In a small bowl, whisk together the olive oil and lemon juice. Add one-quarter of the reserved garlic mixture and mix well. Season with salt and pepper.

5 On a floured surface roll half of the dough into a 9-inch circle, ¼-inch thick. Transfer to a well-floured pizza peel or paddle. Brush the dough to within ½ inch of the edge with the garlic oil. Sprinkle the combined mozzarella and fontina cheeses over the dough. Transfer the dough from the peel directly onto the heated brick. Bake until golden and crisp, 8 to 10 minutes.

6 Toss the herbs and olives with the vinaigrette. Place half of the salad on top of the pizza. With a cheese shaver or vegetable peeler, slice as many paper-thin slices of Pecorino on top as desired. Serve immediately. Repeat with the other pizza dough.

Makes two 9-inch pizzas

Flat Bread with Gorgonzola, Pine Nuts, and Red Onions

Marietta told me the trick to making this focaccia. Her great aunt, who lives in Monza in the north of Italy, very close to the home of Gorgonzola cheese (the prized cow's milk cheese with its distinctive blue veins), knew a secret trick for making the cheese melt and ooze in a way uncharacteristic of Gorgonzola. She simply mashed a few tablespoons of butter with the Gorgonzola. See for yourself . . . it really is a treat.

3 tablespoons warm water (115°F.)

1 teaspoon dry yeast

1½ cups plus 4 tablespoons all-purpose flour

⅓ cup water

½ teaspoon salt

2 tablespoons olive oil

3 ounces Gorgonzola cheese, at room temperature

2 tablespoons butter, at room temperature

1 ½ tablespoons pine nuts, toasted (page 277)

¼ small red onion, very thinly sliced

1 Combine 3 tablespoons warm water, yeast, and 4 tablespoons flour in a small bowl. Let stand for 20 minutes until it gets foamy. Add ⅓ cup water, salt, olive oil, and the remaining 1½ cups flour. Mix the dough well. Knead on a floured surface for 10 minutes until it is smooth, elastic, and still moist. Place in an oiled bowl, turning once. Cover the bowl with plastic wrap and put in a warm place (75°F.). Let it rise for 1 hour or until doubled.

2 Place a pizza brick or tiles on the bottom shelf of the oven. Heat the oven for at least 30 minutes to its hottest temperature.

3 Divide the dough into 2 pieces. On a well-floured surface, roll 1 piece of dough into a 10 × 12-inch rectangle, ⅛ inch thick. Transfer to a pizza peel or paddle and arrange so that the longer side is parallel to your body and your work space. Mash the Gorgonzola, butter, and pine nuts together. Spread half the cheese mixture on the right half of the dough, leaving a 1-inch border around the edge. Spray or brush the edges of the dough lightly with water. Fold the empty half of the dough over the Gorgonzola-butter-pine nuts mixture. Press the edges together and trim them with a sharp knife close to the edge, enclosing the cheese. Score the top of the dough in 3 or 4 places with 1-inch slits. Place a few slices of onion on the top of the flat bread. Repeat with the other piece of dough.

4 Transfer the flat bread to the pizza brick or tiles and bake until lightly golden, 5 to 7 minutes. Remove from the oven and serve immediately.

Makes 2 flat breads to serve 6

Calzone with Escarole, Olives, Capers, and Toasted Pine Nuts

Calzone is a bit of a mystery, the name meaning "pant leg." Originally a calzone dough was rolled out, stuffed, and folded into a square, which could possibly resemble a folded pant leg. Today, calzone is a bulbous turnover that looks as though someone inflated it with an air pump. The "pumping" happens during the baking process when the steam is trapped inside the dough, and the dough rises and expands. When the calzone is taken from the oven and cut into, it does reveal a gaping air pocket but it also oozes with various melted cheeses, vegetables, herbs, and bits of meat.

4 garlic cloves, minced

2 tablespoons olive oil

5 anchovy fillets, soaked in cold water 10 minutes, patted dry, and mashed

¼ cup whole capers

½ cup pitted and chopped Italian black olives (page 279)

6 cups (2 bunches) escarole leaves, stems removed, washed, spun dry, and roughly chopped

Pinch of crushed red pepper

1 tablespoon Balsamic vinegar

Salt and freshly ground pepper

¼ cup pine nuts, toasted (page 277)

1 recipe Calzone Dough (recipe follows)

1½ cups (6 ounces) grated fontina cheese

1½ cups (6 ounces) grated mozzarella cheese

1 Preheat the oven to 500°F. and place a pizza brick or tiles on the bottom shelf of the oven.

2 Combine the garlic and olive oil and let stand for 30 minutes.

3 Heat half of the reserved garlic oil in a skillet. Add the anchovies, capers, olives, escarole, and red pepper. Toss together and sauté, covered, until the escarole begins to wilt, 5 minutes. Uncover and continue to sauté until the escarole is completely wilted, 5 minutes. Increase the heat to high, add the Balsamic vinegar, and cook until almost dry, 1 minute. Turn off the heat. Season with salt and pepper. Add the pine nuts and toss together.

4 On a floured surface, roll half of the dough into a 12-inch circle, about ¼ inch thick, and place it on a well-floured pizza peel. Brush the dough lightly to within 1 inch of the edge with the reserved garlic oil. Combine the fontina and mozzarella cheeses and spread half of the cheese mixture on half of the dough, leaving a 1-inch border. Arrange half of the wilted greens over the cheese.

5 With a pastry brush, moisten the bottom edges of the dough lightly with water and fold the dough over the filling so that the bottom edge is showing a bit more. Fold the bottom edge up over the top, crimping as you go so you have a tight seal.

6 Slide the calzone onto the stone and bake until golden and crisp, 12 to 15 minutes. Remove from the oven and let cool 10 minutes before serving.

Makes 2 large or 4 small individual calzone

CALZONE DOUGH

1 package (7 grams) dry yeast
Pinch of sugar
¼ cup warm water (110°F.)
2¾ cups all-purpose flour
1 teaspoon salt
3 tablespoons olive oil
¾ cup water

1 By hand, combine the yeast, sugar, ¼ cup warm water, and ¼ cup flour in a large bowl. Let proof for 10 minutes.

2 Add the remaining 2½ cups flour, salt, olive oil, and ¾ cup water and mix well with a wooden spoon. Turn out onto a work surface and knead 7 to 10 minutes, until smooth and elastic. It should feel moist to the touch. (Alternatively, this can be made in an electric mixer: In the mixer bowl, combine the yeast, sugar, ¼ cup lukewarm water, and ¼ cup flour. Let proof 10 minutes. Add the remaining 2½ cups flour, salt, olive oil, and ¾ cup water. On low speed, using the dough hook, mix for 5 to 7 minutes, until smooth and elastic. It should feel moist to the touch. You can also make this dough in a food processor; process the dough for one minute.)

3 Place the dough in an oiled bowl and turn over to coat the top with oil. Cover with plastic wrap and let rise in a warm place (75°F.), for 1 to 1½ hours, until doubled in volume. It is now ready to use.

NOTE: If you make the dough one day and will not roll it out until the next, store the dough in the freezer or it will turn gray. Defrost and bring to room temperature before rolling.

Pizza with Sun-Dried Tomato Paste, Roasted Eggplant, and Basil

The making of pizza originated in Naples during Roman times. For hundreds of years, it has been a favorite Neapolitan street food. As its popularity spread throughout Italy, each area added a bit of its own flavor and nuance to create a pizza of its own. Ultimately, pizza has managed to be transported from Italy across mountains and oceans to be consumed in almost every country throughout the world.

5 garlic cloves, minced
5 tablespoons extra virgin olive oil
½ cup sun-dried tomatoes in oil, coarsely chopped, oil reserved
½ small red onion, chopped
½ cup water
2 teaspoons Balsamic vinegar
Salt and freshly ground black pepper
2 small long thin eggplants
1 recipe Pizza Dough (page 276)
¾ cup (3 ounces) grated fontina cheese
¾ cup (3 ounces) grated mozzarella cheese
⅓ to ½ cup fresh basil leaves, cut into thin strips

1 Combine half of the garlic and 2 tablespoons olive oil and let stand for 30 minutes.

2 Preheat the oven to 400°F. and place a pizza brick or tiles on the bottom shelf of the oven.

3 Heat 2 tablespoons of the oil from the tomatoes in a small saucepan. Add the onions and the remaining garlic. Sauté over medium heat until the onions are soft, 7 minutes. Add the tomatoes and water and simmer over low heat until the tomatoes are soft, 10 minutes. Add more water if needed. Remove the onions and tomatoes from the pan and puree in a food processor or blender to obtain a smooth paste. Add 1 teaspoon vinegar, salt, and pepper.

4 Slice the eggplants on the diagonal into ¼-inch slices. Brush a baking sheet lightly with some of the remaining 3 tablespoons oil. Place the eggplant on the oiled baking sheet and brush the tops with oil. Turning occasionally, bake on the top shelf of the oven until very lightly golden, 10 to 15 minutes. Toss with 1 teaspoon minced garlic from the reserved garlic oil, the remaining 1 teaspoon vinegar, salt, and pepper.

5 Increase the oven temperature to 500°F.

6 Roll the dough into a 9-inch circle, ¼ inch thick, on a floured surface. Transfer to a well-floured pizza peel or paddle. Brush the dough to within ½ inch of the edge with the garlic oil. Spread 4 tablespoons tomato paste on the oil. Reserve the extra tomato paste for another use (see Note). Sprinkle half of the combined fontina and mozzarella cheeses on top of the tomato. Distribute half of the eggplant on the cheese. Transfer the dough from the peel directly onto the heated brick in the oven. Bake until golden and crisp, 8 to 10 minutes. Repeat with the other dough.

7 Remove from the oven and sprinkle the basil leaves on top.

Makes two 9-inch pizzas to serve 6 to 8

NOTE: The sun-dried tomato puree is another flavorful topping that can be spread on grilled or toasted bread or *crostini* and served with your mixed *crostini* platter (page 116).

PASTA ALL'AMATRICIANA

Pasta with Pancetta, Tomatoes, and Hot Red Pepper

Pasta all'Amatriciana (that is to say, Pasta from Amatrice) is really best made with good-quality, store-bought pasta. With its simple sauce, this dish could hardly be easier to prepare.

¼ cup extra virgin olive oil
8 ounces thinly sliced pancetta, cut into
    ½-inch pieces
¾ teaspoon crushed red pepper
4 garlic cloves, minced
1 cup dry white wine
1 large red onion, thinly sliced
2 ½ pounds fresh ripe tomatoes, peeled,
    seeded, and chopped (page 278), or
    1½ 28-ounce cans Italian plum tomatoes,
    drained and chopped
4 tablespoons chopped fresh parsley
Salt and freshly ground pepper
1 pound dry semolina vermicelli, spaghetti,
    or linguine
½ cup freshly grated Pecorino cheese
½ cup freshly grated Parmesan cheese

1 Heat the olive oil in a skillet over medium heat and sauté the pancetta until golden but still soft, 10 minutes. Add the red pepper and garlic and sauté 3 minutes. Add the wine and simmer until the wine evaporates, 5 minutes. Remove the pancetta with a slotted spoon and reserve. Add the onions to the pan and sauté until soft, 5 minutes. Pass the tomatoes through a food mill and add them and the parsley to the onions. Simmer 20 minutes. Season with salt and pepper. Add the pancetta and mix well.

NOTE: This can be prepared 1 day in advance to this point.

2 Bring a large pot of salted water to a boil. Cook the pasta until al dente. Drain and toss with the sauce. Place on a platter and garnish with the combined grated Pecorino and Parmesan cheeses.

Serves 6

Farfalle with Shellfish, Tomatoes, and Arugula

L'Antica Trattoria is a modest restaurant located on a small alley in Sorrento. It was highly touted to me as a restaurant that excelled in its first courses, so of course I was eager to make a visit. The antipasti were intriguing and delicious: deep-fried seaweed and late summer vegetables, and sfolino, *a puff pastry turnover. When we got to the* primi piatti *course, our friend Paolo emerged from the kitchen with one masterpiece after another, the range and flavor of which far exceeded my wildest dreams. This is a recipe for one of my absolute favorites. And so simple!*

3 tablespoons extra virgin olive oil
2 garlic cloves, minced
Large pinch of crushed red pepper
1 pound clams, washed
1 pound mussels, washed, beards removed
2 pounds tomatoes, peeled, seeded, and
    chopped (page 278), or 1 28-ounce can
    Italian plum tomatoes, drained, juice
    discarded, and chopped
½ pound farfalle or bow ties
2 bunches of arugula, washed and spun dry
Salt and freshly ground pepper

1 Heat the olive oil in a large skillet over medium heat. Add the garlic and red pepper and cook slowly for 1 minute. Add the clams and cover. Cook, shaking the pan periodically, until the clams open, 2 to 5 minutes, depending upon the size of the clams. Remove the clams from the pan with a slotted spoon and keep warm in a bowl. Add the mussels, cover, and cook, shaking the pan periodically, until the mussels open, 2 to 3 minutes. Remove the mussels from the pan with a slotted spoon and add to the clams.

2 With a food mill or blender, pulverize the tomatoes and add to the skillet. Simmer over high heat, uncovered, until the liquid begins to evaporate and the sauce thickens slightly, 4 to 5 minutes. Remove from the heat.

3 Bring a large pot of salted water to a boil. Add the pasta and cook until al dente.

4 Heat the tomato sauce and add the arugula. Simmer 1 minute. Add the pasta, clams, mussels, and any liquid in the bottom of the bowl. Toss together and season with salt and pepper. Serve immediately.

Serves 6

NOTE: This can be prepared with all clams or all mussels.

"Little Ears" with Sicilian Pesto

This restorative dish comes from Erice, in the northwest corner of Sicily.

Dough

2 cups all-purpose flour
1 cup semolina flour
½ teaspoon salt
1 cup plus 3 tablespoons water

Sauce

4 cups fresh basil leaves, washed and spun dry
3 garlic cloves, minced
¼ cup pine nuts, toasted (page 277)
½ cup olive oil
¾ cup grated Parmesan cheese
Pinch of crushed red pepper
2 large tomatoes, peeled, seeded, and chopped (page 278)
Salt and freshly ground pepper
Flour for rolling and tossing

1 Combine the flours and salt on a work surface. Make a well in the center. Add the water and mix together until it forms a ball. Knead 7 to 10 minutes to form a smooth and elastic dough. Wrap in plastic wrap and let rest 30 minutes.

2 Place the basil leaves, garlic, pine nuts, and olive oil in a blender or food processor and blend at high speed until smooth. Stop and scrape down the sides. Add ½ cup cheese and the red pepper and pulse a few times to make a good thick paste. Drain the tomatoes and fold into the pesto. Season with salt and pepper.

3 Cut the dough into 4 pieces and cover with plastic wrap. With both hands, roll one of the pieces into a long snake shape, ⅜ inch in diameter. With a knife, cut it into ¼-inch pieces. Flour the work surface well. With the thumb of your right hand, press down gently in the center of each piece, rotating your thumb counterclockwise a half turn so the dough forms a round disk that is thicker on the edges and thinner in the center. The disks should be 1 inch in diameter, if they are not, let the "little ears" rest 10 minutes and rotate with your thumb again to stretch them to the right size. Toss with the flour. Repeat with the remaining dough. Store on a well-floured baking sheet covered with a kitchen towel until ready to use.

4 Bring a large pot of salted water to a boil. Add the pasta and cook until al dente, 3 to 4 minutes. Drain and toss with the pesto. Place on a platter, garnish with the remaining ¼ cup grated Parmesan cheese, and serve immediately.

Serves 6 to 8

Lemon and Herb Pansoti with Wilted Greens

This recipe is inspired by Peggy Smith and Catherine Brandel, two talented chefs I worked with for a few years at Chez Panisse Café in Berkeley, California.

1 pound Spinach Pasta Dough (recipe follows)
1 pound ricotta, drained in a cheesecloth-lined strainer for 2 hours
¼ teaspoon chopped fresh thyme
¼ teaspoon chopped fresh oregano
Pinch of chopped fresh rosemary
2 tablespoons snipped fresh chives
Zest of 2 lemons
1 egg, lightly beaten
Salt and freshly ground pepper
White rice flour to roll out the pasta
¼ cup (½ stick) butter
¼ cup extra virgin olive oil
2 small bunches of greens (turnip greens, Swiss chard, mustard greens, beet greens, escarole), washed and spun dry
Juice of ½ lemon

1 Make the pasta dough and let rest 30 minutes.

2 Combine the ricotta, herbs, lemon zest, and beaten egg. Season with ½ teaspoon salt and pepper.

3 Cut the dough into 4 pieces. Using a pasta machine, open the wheels to the widest opening. Roll the pasta dough through 4 or 5 times, folding in half each time. Dust with rice flour if the dough is sticky. Roll the dough until it is as wide as the machine. If you have started at the first opening, consider this #1. Now set the opening to #3. Roll the dough through #3 one time. Set the opening to #5 and roll the dough through #5 one time. Set the opening to #6 and roll the dough through #6 one time until you can just see the outline of your hand through it. Cut the dough into 6-inch squares. Spread a heaping tablespoon of filling in the center of each square. Spray the edges with a light mist of water. Place another square on top and seal the edges. Trim with a zigzag roller.

4 Heat the butter and olive oil in a large skillet. Add the greens and toss until wilted, 5 to 6 minutes. Season with lemon juice, salt, and pepper to taste.

5 Cook the *pansoti* in boiling salted water until al dente, 3 to 5 minutes. Place 2 on each plate and top with wilted greens and sauce.

S e r v e s   6   t o   8

Spinach Pasta Dough

The trick to getting a bright green pasta dough is to use fresh spinach that is as dry as possible.

1 bunch of spinach
2 egg yolks
1 whole egg
2½ cups all-purpose flour
½ teaspoon salt

1 Remove the stems from the spinach and wash well. Dry completely in a salad spinner.

2 Place the yolks, whole egg, and spinach in a blender. Process until completely liquefied. It should measure 1 scant cup.

3 Combine the flour and salt on a work surface. Make a well in the center and add the spinach-egg mixture. Mix with a fork or your thumb, bringing the flour in from the sides of the well. Continue until a mass is formed. Form into a ball. Knead the dough for 3 minutes.

4 Cover the dough with plastic wrap and let it rest for 30 minutes.

Makes 1 pound pasta

Potato Gnocchi with Tomatoes and Fresh Milk Mozzarella

My thanks goes to Toni Romano who taught me to make featherlight gnocchi years ago. Toni lives up to her reputation as one of the world's great gnocchi makers. Try them for yourself.

Gnocchi

1¼ pounds russet baking potatoes, peeled and quartered

Salt

4½ cups all-purpose flour

1 egg, lightly beaten

Sauce

2 tablespoons extra virgin olive oil

10 medium tomatoes, peeled, seeded, and diced (page 278), or 1½ 28-ounce cans Italian plum tomatoes, drained and chopped

½ teaspoon dried oregano

Large pinch of crushed red pepper

2 tablespoons Balsamic vinegar

1 tablespoon tomato paste

¼ cup dry red wine

1 teaspoon sugar

Salt and freshly ground pepper

1 to 2 teaspoons red wine vinegar

6 ounces fresh milk or buffalo milk mozzarella, cut into ¼-inch cubes

¾ cup grated Pecorino or Parmesan cheese

1 Place the potatoes in a saucepan and add water just to the level of the potatoes. Salt the water. Bring to a boil and cook until very soft, 25 minutes. Drain well and let sit in a colander 10 minutes.

2 Place the flour on a work surface. With a potato ricer or food mill fit with a medium disk, rice the warm potatoes evenly over the entire top of the flour. Toss together lightly with your fingers to distribute the potatoes and flour evenly.

3 Make a well in the center and add the egg. Knead together to form a ball. Knead 1 minute to gather up all of the bits of flour and potato on the work surface. Let rest on the work surface with an inverted bowl over the top 5 minutes.

4 Remove a piece of dough the size of your fist. Cover the remaining dough with the inverted bowl. Roll the piece into a long snake shape, ½ inch in diameter. Cut on a sharp diagonal into ¼-inch pieces. With the first 2 fingertips of your right hand dusted with flour and working on a floured surface, using a little pressure, roll each piece away from you ½ inch and then toward you to form a small indentation in the center, which curls back on itself like a small shell. Toss with flour. Place on a floured baking sheet. Repeat with the remaining dough.

5 Heat the olive oil in a large skillet over medium high heat. Add the tomatoes, oregano, crushed red pepper, Balsamic vinegar, tomato paste, red wine, sugar, salt, and pepper. Cook 3 to 4 minutes, until the liquid begins to evaporate and the sauce thickens slightly. Remove from the heat and puree in a blender or food processor. Season with salt, pepper, and red wine vinegar. Place in a saucepan.

6 Bring a large pot of salted water to a boil. Cook the gnocchi 15 to 20 minutes, until tender. Heat the tomato sauce. Drain the gnocchi and toss with the tomato sauce and mozzarella. Sprinkle with the grated Pecorino or Parmesan and serve immediately.

Serves 8

PASTA ALLA PUTTANESCA

Pepper Pasta with Tuna and Orange Puttanesca

Puttanesca is whore's pasta and this quick and flavorful fortifier packs a punch with almost everything "she" might have on hand. It is a true Campanian dish and appeared about fifty years ago. Every cook has her own version and this one, with its orange zest and tuna, is a welcome change.

¼ cup extra virgin olive oil
1 medium red onion, thinly sliced
4 garlic cloves, minced
6 tomatoes, peeled, seeded, and chopped (page 278), or 2½ cups canned Italian plum tomatoes, drained and chopped
4 anchovy fillets, soaked in cold water 10 minutes, patted dry, and mashed
3 tablespoons chopped capers
⅔ cup pitted and coarsely chopped black olives (page 279)
1 tablespoon tomato paste
Pinch of grated orange rind
Juice of 1 orange
Crushed red pepper to taste
Freshly ground pepper
1 6-ounce can oil-packed tuna, drained
2 tablespoons chopped fresh parsley
1 pound Black and Red Pepper Pasta Dough (recipe follows) or 1 pound dry 100% semolina linguine

1 Heat the olive oil in a skillet. Add the onions and sauté until soft, 5 minutes. Add the garlic and sauté 1 minute. Add the tomatoes, anchovies, capers, olives, tomato paste, orange rind, orange juice, red pepper, and black pepper. Simmer slowly 3 minutes.

2 Add the tuna and parsley and simmer 30 seconds.

3 Cook the pasta in a large pot of boiling salted water until al dente. Drain and immediately toss with the sauce. Serve immediately.

Serves 6

Black and Red Pepper Pasta Dough

Simply omit the black pepper and cayenne from this recipe and you will have a very good basic recipe for pasta dough.

2½ cups all-purpose flour
½ teaspoon salt
1 tablespoon medium-grind black pepper
¼ teaspoon cayenne
4 egg yolks
½ cup water
White rice flour to roll out the pasta

1 Combine the flour, salt, pepper, and cayenne and place on a work surface.

2 Make a well in the center of the flour. Combine the water and yolks and add to the well. Beat with a fork, bringing the flour in from all sides until the mixture thickens. After this, use your hands and be sure that the liquid doesn't flow out. Incorporate the rest of the liquid into the flour mixture. Form into a ball. The dough should be very dry but still able to form a ball. Knead the dough for 2 to 3 minutes. Cover the dough with plastic wrap and let it rest for 30 minutes.

3 Cut the dough into 4 pieces. Using a pasta machine, open the wheels to the widest opening. Roll the pasta dough through 4 or 5 times, folding in half each time. Use the rice flour if the dough is sticky. Roll the dough until it is as wide as the machine. If you have started at the first opening, consider this #1. Now set the opening to #3. Roll the dough through #3 one time. Set the opening to #5 and roll the dough through #5 one time. Set the opening to #6 and roll the dough through #6 one time. With the fettuccine attachment, cut the dough to make fettuccine. Cut into 12-inch lengths. Toss in the rice flour and place on a baking sheet covered with a kitchen towel.

Makes approximately 1 pound pasta

NOTE: If you make the dough one day and will not roll it out until the next, store the dough in the freezer or it will turn gray. Defrost and bring to room temperature before rolling.

Crispy Polenta Gratin with Gorgonzola and Mascarpone

The first time I tasted polenta, I couldn't under-stand what all the fuss was about. It was like the cornmeal mush I used to eat when I was a kid. The second time I had a bowl of creamy polenta with wild mushrooms, lots of sweet butter, and Parmesan cheese. It has been years and the memory still lingers with me. Today, I think of polenta as miracle food; it is basically cornmeal, ground from white or yellow corn and available at grocery stores in coarse and medium grinds. It is versatile, nutritious, comforting, and addic-tive, as the following recipe will attest.

5 cups water
Salt and freshly ground pepper
1⅓ cups coarse polenta
2 tablespoons plus 1 teaspoon butter, at
    room temperature
¼ cup mascarpone (page 276)
4 ounces Gorgonzola cheese
4 ounces mozzarella cheese, coarsely grated
½ cup grated Parmesan cheese

1 Bring the water to a boil and add 1 tea-spoon salt. Lower the heat to medium and slowly add the polenta, whisking constantly. Continue to whisk the mixture for 5 minutes. At this point, change to a wooden spoon and con-tinue to simmer, stirring periodically, until the spoon can stand in the polenta, 20 to 25 min-utes. Add 2 tablespoons butter and mix well. Season with salt and pepper.

2 In a bowl, mash the mascarpone, Gor-gonzola, mozzarella, and half of the Parmesan together with a fork. Season with pepper.

3 Preheat the oven to 425°F.

4 Using the remaining 1 teaspoon butter, butter a 2-quart baking dish. While still hot, spread half of the polenta in the gratin dish. Dab all the cheese mixture on top of the polenta evenly. Spread the remaining half of the polenta on top of the cheese. Sprinkle the top with the remaining Parmesan.

NOTE: This can be prepared 1 day ahead of time to this point and stored in the refrigerator. Bring to room temperature before baking.

5 Bake on the top shelf of the oven for 15 to 20 minutes, until hot and the edges are bub-bling and golden.

6 Remove from the oven and serve directly from the gratin dish.

Serves 6

NOTE: This can also be made in small individual 4-inch round gratin dishes. If so, the baking time should be decreased by 5 to 10 minutes.

Fried Polenta Sticks with Sweet and Hot Roasted Pepper Sauce

So you want to make a great polenta? Use a ratio of four times the amount of water to polenta and a big heavy pot (preferably copper). And to make a smooth polenta, use a whisk. Bring salted water to a boil and whisking with one hand, pour in the polenta in a "gentle shower" with the other. Once it begins to boil again, turn the heat down and stir periodically with a wooden spoon until it becomes thick (in the case of this recipe, until the spoon can stand in the center of the pot).

4 cups water

Salt and freshly ground pepper

1 cup coarse polenta

¼ cup freshly grated Parmesan cheese

2 teaspoons chopped fresh rosemary

2 tablespoons butter, cut into 6 pieces

3 red peppers, roasted (page 278)

1 cup heavy cream

¼ cup sour cream

Cayenne to taste

1 teaspoon Balsamic vinegar

2 cups all-purpose flour for dusting the polenta

1 cup olive oil for deep-frying

1 cup corn or peanut oil for deep-frying

1 Bring the water to a boil and add 1 teaspoon salt. Lower the heat to medium and slowly add the polenta, whisking constantly. Continue to whisk the mixture for 10 minutes.

At this point, change to a wooden spoon and continue to simmer, stirring periodically, until the spoon can stand in the polenta, 20 to 25 minutes. Add the Parmesan, rosemary, and butter and mix well. Season with salt and pepper.

2 While still hot, spread the polenta in a buttered 9 × 9-inch pan. Smooth the top with a rubber spatula and let it cool in the refrigerator until set, 1 hour.

3 Meanwhile, in a blender, puree the peppers until they form a smooth paste. Combine the heavy cream and sour cream in a bowl. Add the pepper puree and whisk until the cream thickens slightly but is still light. Taste and season with cayenne, vinegar, salt, and pepper.

4 Cut the polenta into 54 strips, ½-inch wide by 3 inches long. Remove from the pan and toss the polenta sticks carefully in flour to dust them lightly.

5 Heat the olive and corn or peanut oils in a large deep frying pan until the temperature reaches 375°F. Add a few of the polenta sticks and deep-fry, turning them, until they are golden brown on all sides, 2 to 3 minutes. Drain on paper towels and sprinkle them with salt. Serve immediately with the pepper sauce.

Makes 54 polenta sticks to serve 8

Gorgonzola Sauce

Gorgonzola, the famous Italian blue-veined cheese, goes wonderfully with hearty pastas. It's also a fine accompaniment to the Fried Polenta Sticks on the preceding page.

5 ounces Gorgonzola cheese, at room
    temperature
1 cup heavy cream
¼ cup sour cream
Salt and freshly ground pepper
Lemon juice to taste
Cayenne to taste

Pulse the Gorgonzola, ¼ cup heavy cream, and the sour cream in a blender or food processor just until smooth. Remove from the processor and place in a bowl. Add the rest of the heavy cream and whisk until the cream thickens slightly but is still light. Season to taste with salt, pepper, lemon juice, and cayenne.

Makes 1½ cups

Risotto with Fennel Sausage, Leeks, and Red Peppers

There is a mystique about risotto but all that it requires is arborio rice, stock, and a strong arm for stirring. Arborio rice is a short-grain rice from the Po Valley in northern Italy; it is easy to recognize by the pearly white spot on each grain. This rice was brought to Italy from the Orient by Venetian traders during the Crusades. It wasn't until the mid-sixteenth century that Italians really began to enjoy rice. Today, Italy consumes more rice per capita than any other western country. Like pasta and polenta, rice's strength is in its versatility. Witness this creative and delicious recipe for risotto with fennel sausage, leeks, and sweet red peppers.

1 pound spicy hot Italian sausage,
    preferably with fennel seeds
2 red peppers, cut into thin slices
3 cups chicken stock (page 272)
3 cups water
3 tablespoons olive oil
4 medium leeks, white and 1 inch of the
    green, cut in half lengthwise, washed,
    drained, and cut into ½-inch slices
3 garlic cloves, minced
1 ½ cups Italian arborio rice
4 tablespoons chopped fresh parsley
Salt and freshly ground pepper
¾ cup grated Pecorino or Parmesan cheese

1 Prick the sausage with a fork several times and place it in a large sauté pan with ¼ cup water. Bring to a boil and reduce the heat to medium. Cook, turning occasionally, until the fat has been rendered, the water has evaporated, and the sausage is half cooked, 8 minutes. Remove the sausage from the pan and cut into ½-inch rounds. Reserve the sausage and discard all but 1 tablespoon of the fat from the pan.

2 Return the sausage and add the peppers to the pan with the reserved fat in it and cook slowly 8 minutes. Remove the sausage and peppers with a slotted spoon and reserve.

3 Meanwhile, bring the stock and water to a gentle simmer in another saucepan on the back burner of the stove.

4 Heat the olive oil in the pan, add the leeks, and sauté 5 minutes. Add the garlic and continue to sauté 1 minute. Add the rice and continue to stir over medium heat, uncovered, 3 to 4 minutes, until the outside edge of each grain of rice is transparent and there is a tiny white dot in the interior of each grain. Add a ladle of simmering stock, ¼ to ½ cup, and stir the rice to wipe it away from the bottom and sides of the pan. When the first addition of stock has been absorbed, add another ladleful of stock and continue to stir. Keep the grains moist at all times. Stir very often to keep the rice from sticking, adding more broth, a ladleful at a time. If you run out of broth, add hot water, so that the risotto is always creamy and loose. The risotto is done in 18 to 22 minutes, when it is firm but tender, without a chalky center.

♪ Add a ladleful of broth, the sausage, peppers, parsley, salt, pepper, and half of the grated cheese. Over low heat, stir quickly to combine the ingredients. Serve immediately, garnished with the remaining cheese.

Serves 6

Risotto with Spring Vegetables

In a good risotto, the grains of rice have a very slight resistance to the tooth under their creamy exterior. The creaminess is the result of a gradual release of the arborio rice grain's starch and is achieved by first toasting the rice in olive oil or butter to harden the starch slightly. When stock is added incrementally and the rice is stirred, the released starch thickens the sauce.

2 medium artichokes, trimmed (page 278)
1 lemon
2 tablespoons olive oil
¼ pound tiny pearl onions, peeled
3 cups chicken stock (page 272)
Salt and freshly ground pepper
1½ pounds fresh fava beans, in their pods
½ pound asparagus spears, ends removed,
    cut into 1-inch lengths
1 cup green peas, fresh or frozen and
    thawed
2 cups water
1½ cups Italian arborio rice
2 tablespoons butter
1 cup grated Parmesan cheese
¼ cup chopped fresh parsley

1 Slice the artichoke hearts into thin slices. Place them in a small bowl of cold water with the juice of ½ lemon. Reserve ½ lemon.

2 Heat the olive oil in a large skillet over medium heat. Add the onions and sauté slowly, shaking the pan occasionally, for 10 minutes.

Add the sliced artichokes and sauté for about 4 minutes, turning frequently. Add ½ cup stock and a pinch of salt and cover the pot. Reduce the heat to low and cook for 10 minutes, until the onions and artichokes are soft. Uncover and cook slowly, until most of the liquid has evaporated.

3 In the meantime, peel the outer husk of the fava beans and discard. Bring a pot of water to a boil and parboil the fava beans for 30 seconds. Cool and peel. Season with salt and pepper and reserve. Blanch the asparagus in boiling salted water until tender, 5 minutes. Add the peas and continue to simmer 10 seconds. Drain and reserve the asparagus and peas with the fava beans.

4 Meanwhile, bring the remaining 2½ cups stock and the water to a simmer in another saucepan on the back burner of the stove.

5 Add the rice to the artichokes and onions and continue to stir over medium heat, uncovered, 3 to 4 minutes, until the outside edge of each grain of rice is transparent and there is a tiny white dot in the interior of each grain. Add a ladle of simmering stock, ¼ to ½ cup, and stir the rice to wipe it away from the bottom and sides of the pan. When the first addition of stock has been absorbed, add another ladleful of stock and continue to stir. Keep the grains moist at all times. Stir very often to keep the rice from sticking, adding more broth, a ladleful at a time. If you run out of broth, add warm water, so that the risotto is always creamy and loose.

The risotto is done in 18 to 22 minutes, when it is firm but tender, without a chalky center.

6 Add another ladleful of stock, the fava beans, asparagus, peas, butter, half of the grated cheese, parsley, lemon juice from the reserved ½ lemon, salt, and pepper. Over low heat, stir quickly to combine the ingredients. Serve immediately, garnished with the remaining cheese.

Serves 6

Frittata with Roasted Sweet Peppers

A frittata is a low flat cake of eggs that is cooked slowly over low heat until it is nearly firm and set inside. At the last moment, it is placed under the broiler for the final cooking. The frittata is related to the Spanish tortilla in shape and is a cousin to the French omelette, which is folded at the end of cooking to enclose the filling ingredients.

1 red bell pepper, roasted (page 278)
1 yellow bell pepper, roasted (page 278)
1 green bell pepper, roasted (page 278)
2 garlic cloves, minced
1 tablespoon extra virgin olive oil
2 teaspoons Balsamic vinegar
¼ teaspoon dried oregano
Salt and freshly ground pepper
8 eggs
3 tablespoons milk
½ cup grated Pecorino or Parmesan cheese
2 tablespoons chopped fresh parsley
2 tablespoons olive oil

1 Cut the peppers into ¼-inch strips. Toss with the garlic, extra virgin olive oil, vinegar, oregano, salt, and pepper. Let marinate 30 minutes.

2 In a bowl, whisk together the eggs, milk, cheese, and parsley until frothy. Add the peppers and their liquid and mix well. Season with salt and pepper.

3 Preheat the oven to 400°F.

4 Heat the oil in a 10-inch nonstick ovenproof skillet over medium-high heat and add the eggs and peppers. Reduce the heat to medium and cook for 7 to 8 minutes until the bottom is set and the top is still runny. Occasionally, lift the outer edges so the runny egg can run underneath. Place in the oven and continue to cook until the eggs are set and golden brown, 6 to 7 minutes.

5 Remove the frittata from the oven and loosen the bottom with a spatula. Place a serving plate over the top of the skillet and invert the frittata onto it. Cut the frittata into wedges and serve hot or at room temperature.

Serves 6

Risotto Croquettes with Smoked Ham and Mozzarella

Many years ago, when I lived in Boston, I frequented a cavernous place called Galleria Umberto on Hanover Street in the North End, the Italian area of the city. It was here that I discovered arancini, *a specialty of Sicily, and fell in love. I didn't really understand the place, though; I found it empty and cold. It wasn't until a few years ago when I spent some time in Palermo and discovered Antica Focacceria San Francesco that I understood Galleria Umberto. Antica Focacceria is a gymnasium of a place, lined completely with marble. The sound and activity reverberate as people wait in line to get inside for slices of warm* focaccia *and these delicious* arancini.

3 cups chicken stock (page 272)

1 cup water

2 tablespoons olive oil

1 small onion, minced

1½ cups Italian arborio rice

½ cup tomato sauce, homemade or canned

⅔ cup grated Parmesan cheese

1 egg yolk, beaten

Salt and freshly ground pepper

1 3-ounce slice smoked ham, cut into ⅛-inch dice

½ cup green beans or asparagus, trimmed, cut into ¼-inch lengths, and blanched

4 ounces smoked mozzarella or Scamorza cheese, cut into ¼-inch dice

Corn or peanut oil for deep frying

3 eggs, beaten

2 cups fine dry bread crumbs

1 Bring the chicken stock and water to a boil in a saucepan on the back burner of the stove. Reduce and simmer very slowly.

2 Heat the olive oil in a saucepan. Add the onion and sauté until soft, 10 minutes. Add the rice and continue to stir over medium heat, uncovered, 3 to 4 minutes, until the outside edge of each grain of rice is transparent and there is a tiny white dot in the interior of each grain. Add a ladle of stock, ¼ to ½ cup, and stir the rice to wipe it away from the bottom and sides of the pan. When the first addition of stock has been absorbed, add another ladleful of stock and continue to stir. Keep the grains moist at all times. Stir very often to keep the rice from sticking, adding more broth, a ladleful at a time. If you run out of broth, add hot water, so that the risotto is always creamy and loose.

3 The risotto is done in 18 to 22 minutes, when it is firm but tender, without a chalky center. Continue to cook, stirring, until the stock is absorbed and it is dry. Remove from the heat and add the tomato sauce and Parmesan and mix well. Cool completely. Add the egg yolk and mix well. Season with salt and pepper.

4 In a bowl, combine the ham, green beans or asparagus, and diced mozzarella.

5 There are 2 ways to form the croquettes:

(1) Pat 2 tablespoons of the rice mixture to cover the palm of one hand and place 1 tablespoon of the smoked ham mixture in the center. Gently close your hand to envelop the filling. Using both hands, shape the mass into an oval about the size and shape of a large egg. Place the croquettes on a cookie sheet and continue until you have used up all the ingredients.

(2) The alternate method is to scoop about 2 tablespoons of the rice mixture into a small ice cream scoop. Push 2 fingers into the mixture to make a small opening and put 1 tablespoon of the filling in the hole. Close the hole and finish shaping the croquette by hand.

6 Heat 3 inches of oil to 375°F.

7 Roll the croquettes in the beaten eggs, then roll them in the bread crumbs. Set on a cookie sheet or wax paper.

8 Deep-fry the croquettes in oil, a few at a time, until golden brown. Remove and drain on paper towels.

9 Serve hot, warm, or at room temperature.

Makes 24 croquettes to serve 8

Rolled Eggplant with Prosciutto and Herbs

In the Mediterranean, just about every country has a penchant for stuffing vegetables. This one is a little less time-consuming than most, and at the same time it's a very unique antipasto. This recipe for stuffed eggplant with prosciutto and herbs can be prepared completely ahead of time, even the day before, and baked when needed. My thanks goes to my friend Antonella Panarello of Caltagirone, Sicily, for sharing this recipe of her mother's.

3 medium eggplants, unpeeled
3 tablespoons coarse salt
6 tablespoons olive oil
1 medium onion, minced
1 cup fresh bread crumbs
3 tablespoons pine nuts, toasted (page 277) and coarsely chopped
3 ounces thinly sliced prosciutto, cut into very thin strips
1 teaspoon mixed chopped fresh herbs, such as thyme, rosemary, or sage
¼ cup chopped fresh parsley
1 garlic clove, minced
Pinch of crushed red pepper
6 tablespoons grated Parmesan cheese
2 ounces mozzarella cheese, coarsely grated
Salt and freshly ground pepper
Whole parsley leaves, preferably Italian

1 Cut the eggplants lengthwise into ¼-inch-thick slices. Lightly salt and drain in a colander for 30 minutes. Wash well with cold water, drain, and dry well with paper towels.

2 Preheat the oven to 350°F.

3 In a large skillet, heat 3 tablespoons oil and sauté the onions until wilted, 10 minutes. Add the bread crumbs and stir constantly until the crumbs are golden, 10 minutes. Place the mixture in a bowl with the pine nuts, prosciutto, herbs, garlic, red pepper, Parmesan, and mozzarella. Season with salt and pepper.

4 Brush both sides of the eggplant slices with the remaining 3 tablespoons oil and place on a baking sheet. Bake on the top shelf of the oven until lightly golden on each side but still malleable, 10 to 15 minutes. Pile the slices on top of one another on the baking sheet to steam and soften slightly, 5 minutes. Divide the filling evenly among the eggplant slices. Place the filling at the wide end of the eggplant slices and roll them up.

These eggplant rolls can be prepared several hours or even a day ahead of time to this point, then refrigerated until you're ready to bake them. Bring them to room temperature before baking.

5 Bake for 10 to 15 minutes, until golden. Place on a serving platter and garnish with whole parsley leaves. Serve immediately or after the rolls have cooled 10 minutes.

Makes 24 rolls to serve 6

Fennel, Prosciutto, and Parsley Salad with Shaved Parmesan

In good Italian food, there is always a juxtaposition of one kind or another: cold versus hot, sweet versus sour, spicy versus mild, raw and crunchy versus delicately soft. This lively salad is a perfect example.

3 bulbs fennel
2 tablespoons lemon juice
Salt and freshly ground pepper
¼ cup extra virgin olive oil
¼ cup olive oil
3 tablespoons orange juice
1 tablespoon Balsamic vinegar
1 garlic clove, mashed in a mortar and
　　pestle
½ cup parsley leaves, preferably Italian,
　　washed and dried
1 bunch of radishes, trimmed and thinly
　　sliced
1 3-ounce chunk Parmesan cheese
4 ounces thinly sliced prosciutto

1 Trim the fennel. Cut it in half from top to bottom. With a sharp knife, slice the fennel into paper-thin slices. Toss with 1 tablespoon lemon juice and a pinch of salt and reserve in the refrigerator.

2 In a small bowl, whisk the extra virgin olive oil, the olive oil, orange juice, vinegar, the remaining 1 tablespoon lemon juice, and garlic together. Season with salt and pepper.

3 To assemble the salad, toss the fennel, parsley, radishes, salt, and three-quarters of the vinaigrette together. Place half on a serving platter. With a cheese shaver or vegetable peeler, shave half of the Parmesan on top of the fennel. Distribute half of the prosciutto on top. Continue with the rest of the ingredients, making sure that all of the different ingredients are visible.

Serves 6 to 8

Salad of Radicchio, Arugula, Blood Oranges, Raisins, and Pine Nuts

When I read the description of this unique southern Italian salad, it intrigued me. When I tasted the salad, I was overwhelmed. The combination of ingredients and flavors is so reminiscent of North Africa, one can see the significant contribution the Arabs left here during their occupation of southern Italy.

1 medium head of radicchio, trimmed, washed, and spun dry
1 large bunch of arugula, stems removed, washed, and spun dry
1 large bulb fennel, trimmed and cut into paper-thin slices
3 blood oranges (see Note)
1 to 2 teaspoons red wine vinegar
3 tablespoons extra virgin olive oil
Salt and freshly ground pepper
¼ cup golden or sultana raisins
¼ cup pine nuts, toasted (page 277)

1 Combine the salad greens in a bowl and place in the refrigerator.

2 Grate ½ teaspoon orange zest. Section the oranges (page 279), place the sections in a bowl, and reserve.

3 Squeeze 4 tablespoons orange juice from the leftover center core into a bowl. Add the orange zest, red wine vinegar, extra virgin olive oil, ¼ teaspoon salt, and pepper and whisk together. Add the raisins and let them marinate 10 minutes.

4 Toss the salad greens with the vinaigrette. Divide among 6 individual serving plates and garnish with the orange sections, pine nuts, and raisins. Serve immediately.

Serves 6

NOTE: Any other oranges can be substituted. Blood oranges are a deliciously sweet orange with a distinctive red pulp available in the winter months.

White Bean Salad with Gremolata and Grilled Tuna

Together with tomatoes, olive oil, and garlic, dried beans or legumes are one of the strong culinary links of the Mediterranean. Lentils, chickpeas, and fava beans are thousands of years old and presumably came from the Middle East. Other legumes like cannellini or white kidney beans, navy beans, red kidney beans, and cranberry beans came from the New World, revealing that this Tuscan salad is a fairly new addition to the Italian repertoire of bean dishes.

2 cups (¾ pound) dry white, navy, or
    cannellini beans, or 2 16-ounce cans
    cannellini beans, drained and rinsed
8 cups water
2 bay leaves
Large pinch of dried thyme
½ cup extra virgin olive oil
3 to 4 lemons
Salt and freshly ground pepper
1 pound fresh tuna
2 tablespoons olive oil
3 garlic cloves, minced
¼ cup chopped fresh parsley
½ small red onion, cut in ¼-inch dice
1 medium bulb fennel, trimmed and cut
    into ¼-inch dice

1 Pick over the beans and discard any stones. Cover with water and soak overnight. The next day, drain and place the beans in a saucepan with the bay leaves, thyme, and enough water to cover by 2 inches. Simmer, uncovered, until the skins begin to crack and the beans are tender, 45 minutes to 1 hour. Drain the beans and keep warm. Combine the extra virgin olive oil, 4 tablespoons lemon juice, salt, and pepper. Add the vinaigrette to the warm beans and toss together.

2 Preheat a charcoal grill (see Note).

3 Peel 1 lemon with a vegetable peeler. Marinate the tuna with the lemon peel, pepper, and olive oil for 30 minutes.

4 Grate 1½ teaspoons lemon zest. Combine the lemon zest, garlic, and parsley. Place on a work surface and chop together until very fine. This is called gremolata. Combine with the beans, onions, and fennel and toss well.

5 Grill the tuna for 3 to 4 minutes per side, until the pink in the center just disappears and the tuna flakes. Salt and let cool 5 minutes. Break into ½- to ¾-inch pieces. Add to the white beans. Season with salt, pepper, and additional lemon juice. Serve on a platter garnished with lemon wedges.

Serves 6 to 8

NOTE: This can also be grilled on a cast-iron ridged grill or in a sauté pan. Grill or sauté 3 minutes per side, until the pink in the center just disappears and the tuna flakes.

Seafood Salad with Garden Herb Sauce

Every region in Italy bordering on the Mediter-ranean makes a seafood salad: Liguria, Tuscany, Lazio, Campania, Basilicata, Calabria, and Sic-ily. Each region has its own personal style. In the north, the seafood is tossed with good fruity olive oil, herbs, and lemon juice. In the south it is tossed with olive oil, herbs, lemon juice, pickled vegetables, olives, and capers. This version is the best of both worlds.

½ to ¾ cup fish stock (page 272), bottled
   clam juice, or water
¾ pound medium shrimp
1 pound squid, cleaned (page 279) and cut
   into ½-inch rings, tentacles reserved
2 pounds mussels, washed, beards removed
2 pounds clams, washed
Salt and freshly ground pepper
½ cup chopped fresh parsley
2 tablespoons chopped fresh chives
½ teaspoon chopped fresh thyme
¼ teaspoon chopped fresh oregano
¼ teaspoon chopped fresh rosemary
   (optional)
2 tablespoons chopped capers
2 garlic cloves, mashed in a mortar and
   pestle
4 to 5 tablespoons lemon juice
¼ cup olive oil
¼ cup extra virgin olive oil

6 slices rustic country-style bread, toasted
   or grilled
1 large garlic clove, peeled
Lemon wedges

1 Heat half of the fish stock in a skillet over medium heat. Add the shrimp, cover, and cook until almost firm, 1 to 2 minutes. Remove from the pan with a slotted spoon and cool. Remove and discard the shells. Place the shrimp in a large bowl and reserve.

2 Add the squid rings and tentacles to the pan, cover, and cook until almost firm, 30 sec-onds. Remove with a slotted spoon and add to the shrimp. Add fish stock as needed.

3 Add the mussels to the pan, cover, and cook until the mussels open, 2 to 4 minutes. Re-move the mussels from the pan with a slotted spoon as they open. Remove the mussels from the shells and discard the shells. Add the mus-sels to the seafood. Add the clams to the pan, cover, and cook until the clams open, 2 to 5 minutes. Remove the clams from the pan with a slotted spoon as they open. Remove the clams from the shells and discard the shells. Add the clams to the seafood. Reduce the cooking liq-uids until 2 tablespoons remain, 5 minutes. Toss the reduced cooking liquids with the seafood. Season with salt and pepper.

4 In a bowl, whisk together the herbs, capers, garlic, lemon juice, and both olive oils. Season with salt and pepper. Toss the seafood with the vinaigrette and let sit 30 minutes.

5 Place the seafood and vinaigrette on a platter. Rub the toasted bread lightly with the garlic and garnish the platter with the toasted bread and lemon wedges. Serve immediately.

Serves 6

NOTE: This salad is best when served within 1 hour, otherwise the herbs, in combination with the lemon juice, will turn gray.

PANZANELLA

Tuscan Bread Salad with Tomatoes and Basil

Nothing is wasted in the Mediterranean, especially bread, which at certain times in history has been worth its weight in gold. In Italy, yesterday's stale bread is made into today's fresh and flavorful salad and called panzanella. *In the Middle East, a similar salad is prepared with pita bread, cucumbers, tomatoes, scallions, and fresh garden herbs and called* fattoush, *and in Morocco their bread salad is called* shalada del khobz yabess.

½ pound coarse country-style bread, a few days old
1 cup water
6 ripe medium tomatoes, peeled, seeded, and cut into ½-inch cubes (page 278)
1 large red onion, thinly sliced
1 medium cucumber, peeled, seeded, and cut into ½-inch dice
2 garlic cloves, minced
2 tablespoons whole capers
½ cup fresh basil leaves
3 tablespoons red wine vinegar
3 tablespoons Balsamic vinegar
¾ cup extra virgin olive oil
Salt and freshly ground pepper

1 Slice the bread into 1-inch slices. Sprinkle it with water and let sit 1 minute. Carefully squeeze the bread until dry. Tear the bread into rough 1-inch shapes and let rest on paper towels for 10 minutes.

2 In a bowl, combine the tomatoes, onions, cucumbers, garlic, and capers. Tear the basil and add to the vegetables. Add the bread and toss carefully.

3 In a small bowl, combine both vinegars and the olive oil. Season with salt and pepper. Toss with the vegetables and bread and let it rest in the refrigerator 1 hour. Place on a platter and serve.

Serves 6

Yogurt and Cucumber Soup
with Mint and Dill

Lamb Broth with Summer
Vegetables and Orzo

Country White Bean and
Vegetable Soup

Avgolemono Soup with
Spiced Veal Meatballs and Rice

Baked Omelette with Zucchini,
Leeks, Feta, and Mountain Herbs

Phyllo Pizza with Three Cheeses,
Tomatoes, and Oregano

Savory Chicken, Leek, and
Feta Pie with Mountain Herbs

Lamb, Fennel, and
Orange Pie Likouressis

Fried Cheese with
Lemon and Olives

Stuffed Macaroni with
Feta, Tomatoes, and Mint

Spicy Sausages with
Tomatoes and Olives

Spicy Grilled Eggplant with
Olive Oil and Vinegar

Dilled Potato and
Leek Croquettes

Lentil and Bulgur Croquettes
with Yogurt and Mint

Stuffed Zucchini

Stuffed Tomatoes

Avgolemono Sauce

Grape Leaves Stuffed with
Rice, Currants, and Herbs

Yogurt and Cucumber Salad

Spinach Puree with Garlic

 Greece

Eggplant Salad

Salad of Oven-Roasted Beets,
Red Onions, and Olives
with Garlic Sauce

Lentil Salad with Red Peppers,
Red Onions, Feta, and Mint

Corfu Salad of Orange
Slices, Red Onions, and
Kalamata Olives

Pickled Wild Mushrooms

Pickled Squid

Squid or Octopus
Braised in Red Wine

Saffron Pilaf with
Mussels and Squid

Stewed Mussels with Feta

Swordfish Kebabs with
Red Onions, Black Olives,
and Bay Leaves

Salt Cod Roe Fritters

When twilight threatens the skies in any bustling city in Greece, the Greek has just finished his workday and heads straight for the taverna to confront the evening. Armed with a million words and a thirst to boot, you will find him perched at a waterfront table in Volos, one hand wrapped around a pearly glass of ouzo, the other picking at a plate of toothpick-skewered white feta cheese drizzled with fruity olive oil and a dash of wild oregano from the mountains. In another part of the country, maybe on the island of Zakynthos, you will find the Greek inside an old yellowing *ouzeri*, a taverna specializing in ouzo, the national drink, which is anise-flavored and packs a real punch. Shrouded in smoke, men lean on elbows as they puff on cigarettes and engage in conversation so serious they look as though they might change the world. Little bottles of ouzo dot the table accompanied by *mezethes* (me-ZE-thez), small plates of tasty morsels like olives or wedges of crimson tomatoes and crisp cucumbers dusted with sea salt.

Now head further north to the second largest city in Greece, Thessaloniki. Down by the water the new city stretches for what seems like eternity, but nestled in the congested hills is the older part of town. The whitewashed houses look as though they must be balancing on top of one another and the tiny roads are a nightmarish maze. Around every corner is a taverna, each boasting a wider array of *mezethes* or a fresher catch of fish than the one next door. It is later in the evening, say 10:00 or 11:00 P.M. Bare light bulbs are strung together around a corral of tables perched on a precipice overlooking the new city and the sea beyond. These are unpretentious surroundings. The temperature couldn't be more perfect—it is no wonder the Greeks spend most of their lives out of doors. Gentle warm breezes send a shiver of excitement. Drawn by the heady scent of olive oil and garlic, it is customary for taverna patrons to walk right into the kitchen and make their choices as they poke their heads into pots of lusty stews, give the tomatoes a proverbial squeeze, or talk to the chef who might even recommend his own favorites. The whole family is there to help, everyone talking simultaneously about the evening's seemingly endless array of offerings. Choices are made and within minutes an outside table is laden with many small plates. There is fruity white Macedonian wine and the obligatory wicker basket filled with crusty white bread and napkins rolled around forks and knives. Everyone at the table helps himself from the communal *mezethes* plates according to their own whim. It will be a long and enjoyable evening.

Mezethes, the little snacks or tempting appetizers eaten at any time of the day, are the Greek justification for two basic constituents of Greek social life—a good dose of wine or ouzo and congenial conversation. The Greeks like their drinks but they abhor drunkenness, so they wouldn't dream of drinking retsina or fiery ouzo without some sort of tasty morsel of food. Waiters do not hover over the table nor do they snatch empty plates away. Instead they promote a relaxed atmosphere and patrons are encouraged to linger and unwind after a long hot day. For example, one single small plate of *mythia me risi* (mussels pilaf) or *fassolia yigantes* (giant beans with tomatoes) can be nibbled at slowly and stretched out for an hour or more.

The *mezethes* of Greece use the freshest of seasonal ingredients. They are honest and humble, yet innovative, colorful, and pungently flavorful. They range from hot to cold and simple to complex, and vary widely in their uses from dips, salads, farinaceous dishes, dairy, and eggs to fish, game, meats, and poultry. Sometimes mezethes are eaten as a snack, a prelude to dinner, or as dinner itself.

The word *meze*, or the plural *mezethes*, means "something to whet the appetite." It is Turkish in origin, a legacy from the Ottoman Empire, which stretched into Greece. Although the Turks named *mezethes*, the custom itself dates back to Greek antiquity. Plato, the Greek philosopher who lived in the fourth century B.C., described what appeared to be a *mezethes* table as one containing small portions of olives, fresh garbanzo beans, almonds, figs, radishes, and briny cheeses.

Greece is the land of classical antiquity, mythology, romance, and fine food traditions. The oldest European cuisine, Greek food was "civilized" earlier and to a greater degree than other European cuisines. The Greeks were a bold force around the Mediterranean at the beginning of the first millennium and thought of cooking as an art. Their strong influence spread this philosophy to Italy, Turkey, and the Middle East. As the Greeks weakened, however, and the Romans thrived, Greece fell to stronger powers. The Roman Empire spread through Greece and Turkey, making its Byzantine home in Constantinople (today Istanbul) in 330 A.D. Greek cooking was so highly respected that the palaces of Constantinople employed mostly Greek cooks, setting a precedent for high gastronomic standards. By the 1450s, the Roman Empire declined and the Ottomans expanded, crossing central Asia and Asia Minor to Greece. The Ottomans occupied a majority of the countries bordering the Eastern Mediterranean for nearly 400 years and influenced the religious, historical, and culinary backbone of these countries, especially Greece. In Greece, old traditional Greek recipes were given new Turkish names like *dolmathes* for *thrion*, or rolled grape leaves, *keftethes* for croquettes, *borekakia* for savory-filled pastries, and *tzatziki*, a yogurt

and garlic sauce. Dishes and techniques specific to Turkey—like sausages called *soutzou-*
kakia, the art of pickling called *toursi, imam*
bayildi, or stuffed eggplant, the use of yogurt,
raisins, and rice for making pilaf—were transported across the Aegean to Greece. It wasn't
until 1821 that the Greeks wrestled themselves
free of Ottoman rule, but what remained was a
convivial homogeneous Greek and Turkish
cuisine oftentimes difficult to dissect.

In the following recipes, you will see
over and over again a combination of certain
key ingredients: lemons, garlic, mint, dill,
parsley, oregano, cinnamon, red wine vinegar,
and of course, ubiquitous olive oil. Greeks
have long loved the versatility, healthiness,
and variety of vegetables available, and they
make a variety of vegetable dishes using bulbous eggplants, bunches of deep red beets,
various shades of zucchini, silvery purple artichokes, large red and green peppers, salad
greens, sweet juicy tomatoes, crisp cucumbers
and fennel, and all colors, shapes, and sizes of
beans. You will also see in these recipes some
ingredients and techniques unique to Greece
like *tarama* (salted and dried mullet roe),
avgolemono sauce (an egg and lemon sauce),
skorthalia (an emulsified garlic sauce), *rigani* (a
stronger variety of oregano than the Italian
version), *elitses* olives (the tiny olives from
Crete), Kalamata olives (the large almond-
shaped purple-black olives from the southern
Peloponnese), and phyllo, or thin pastry

sheets. Rustic cheeses like feta (a salty white
sheep's milk cheese), Kefalotyri (hard yellow
goat or sheep's milk cheese like the Italian
Parmesan), and Kasseri (a firm golden sheep's
milk cheese) are a few of the favored cheeses
made in Greece.

Greece's terrain is varied—rocky hills
and valleys, snowcapped mountains, a pris-
tine cloudless sky, and a brilliant blue irides-
cent sea that surrounds the 2,500 miles of
coastline. Its perimeter is dappled with hundreds of sunbaked islands in the Aegean,
Ionian, and Mediterranean seas, yielding a tremendous amount of food for the table. Crete,
the largest Greek island, floats in the Mediterranean south of Greece, and its cuisine features elements of Greece, Asia Minor, and
Egypt. Rhodes's cuisine is closely related to
that of Turkey due to its proximity. The Venetians occupied several islands, including the
islands of Corfu, Kephalonia, and Zakynthos
off the west coast of Greece, and all of these
have adopted Venetian subtleties in their cuisine. Balkan influences in northern Greece can
be observed with the use of cabbage, hot
peppers, smoked meats, and stewed dishes.
Eastern Greece, bordering on Turkey, has
some shades of Turkish influence with the use
of sesame seeds and a love of spices. But really, does this constitute a true regional cuisine? Greek cuisine has very subtle regional
differences, unlike Italy, France, and Spain,
where these differences are more drastic. For

example, in Greece, a sauce like skorthalia is made looser in one region, thicker in another, and in some places it is thickened with potatoes while in others with various nuts. But all over Greece, *skorthalia* is made. A dish may vary, with small nuances, from kitchen to kitchen or region to region, but sometimes these differences are hardly noticeable even to the experienced cook.

Caught between the classical past and the ever-changing present, Greece has struggled to hold onto her strong culinary ties and she wears her age well. True Greek food is rustic and its flavors come through in a simple and straightforward manner as seen here with the age-old art of *mezethes*, a true testament to Greece's respect for the good things in life.

Yogurt and Cucumber Soup with Mint and Dill

This refreshing cold yogurt soup makes a perfect first course when served on a steamy hot day.

3 cups whole milk yogurt
1 large cucumber, peeled, seeded, and
    coarsely grated
2 garlic cloves, mashed in a mortar and
    pestle
3 tablespoons olive oil
1 tablespoon chopped fresh mint
2 tablespoons plus 1 teaspoon chopped
    fresh dill
2 cups cold milk
2 to 4 tablespoons white wine vinegar or
    lemon juice
Salt and freshly ground pepper
6 paper-thin slices cucumber with skin

1 Place the yogurt in a cheesecloth-lined strainer and let drip for 2 hours. Discard the water and place the yogurt in a bowl.

2 Combine the drained yogurt, grated cucumber, garlic, olive oil, mint, 2 tablespoons dill, and milk. Mix well. Add the vinegar or lemon juice, salt, and pepper to taste. Chill 1 hour until ice-cold.

3 Ladle the soup into bowls and garnish with the cucumber slices and the remaining 1 teaspoon dill.

Serves 6

Lamb Broth with Summer Vegetables and Orzo

In Greece, soups are usually served at home rather than at the taverna or restaurant, not only as a first course but also as a main course because they are so substantial. With this light yet flavorful soup, you have your choice.

¼ cup olive oil
2 medium onions, diced
2 leeks, white and 2 inches of green, quartered and diced
3 celery ribs with leaves, diced
2 carrots, peeled and diced
½ cup water
½ cup green beans, trimmed and cut into ½-inch pieces
2 small zucchini, seeded and diced
3 medium tomatoes, peeled, seeded and chopped (page 278), or 1 cup canned Italian plum tomatoes, drained and chopped
½ teaspoon chopped fresh oregano
Salt and freshly ground pepper
8 cups lamb broth (page 271)
½ cup orzo
½ cup grated Parmesan or Kefalotyri cheese
¼ cup chopped fresh parsley

1 Heat the oil in a soup pot. Add the onions, leeks, celery, and carrots. Sauté until the onions are soft, 10 minutes. Add the water, cover, and simmer slowly for 30 minutes.

2 Add the green beans, zucchini, tomatoes, oregano, salt, pepper, and lamb broth. Bring to a boil, turn down the heat, and simmer very slowly, covered, for 30 to 40 minutes. Add the orzo and continue to simmer 20 minutes.

3 Taste and season with additional salt and pepper if desired. Serve garnished with the grated cheese and parsley.

Serves 6

Country White Bean and Vegetable Soup

The pepper and olive garnish for this dish is a modern adaptation and was inspired by Paula Wolfert, but otherwise this is a classic soup made in almost every country that borders the Mediterranean. While each country adds its own nuance, the Greek cook adds a light touch of tomatoes and herbs to this healthy and hearty soup.

1 pound dried navy beans
1 red bell pepper, roasted (page 278)
1 yellow bell pepper, roasted (page 278)
1 green bell pepper, roasted (page 278)
2 tablespoons red wine vinegar
5 tablespoons extra virgin olive oil
Salt and freshly ground pepper
10 cups cold water
2 medium onions, diced
2 garlic cloves, minced
2 medium carrots, peeled and diced
1 celery rib with leaves, diced
¼ teaspoon dried thyme
¼ teaspoon dried oregano
1 tablespoon tomato paste
12 Kalamata olives, pitted and slivered
   (page 279)

1 Pick over the navy beans and discard any stones. Cover with water and soak overnight.

2 The next day, cut the roasted peppers into ¼-inch dice. Combine the peppers, vinegar,

2 tablespoons olive oil, salt, and pepper and toss to mix. Let sit at room temperature 2 hours.

3 Drain the beans and place them in a soup pot with the cold water. Simmer, uncovered, until the skins just begin to crack, 45 minutes to 1 hour.

4 In a large skillet, heat the remaining 3 tablespoons olive oil. Sauté the onions, garlic, carrots, and celery over low heat, until the onions are tender, 10 minutes. Add the vegetables, thyme, oregano, and tomato paste to the beans. Continue to simmer, uncovered, 1 hour, or until the beans and vegetables are very tender and the liquid is reduced. Taste and season with salt and pepper. Take 1½ cups soup and puree in a blender or food processor until smooth. Return to the soup pot and mix well.

5 Drain the peppers and mix with the olives. Serve the hot soup in bowls, garnished with the pepper and olive mixture.

Serves 6

NOTE: Soup can be made up to 2 days ahead. It can also be frozen. Do not garnish until ready to serve.

Avgolemono Soup with Spiced Veal Meatballs and Rice

Avgolemono, the quintessential Greek mixture of eggs (avgo) and lemon juice (lemono), dates back to antiquity and has always been referred to as the "sour sauce." Turkey is the only other country in the Mediterranean that makes this sauce but it is less popular there than in Greece.

½ pound ground veal
1 garlic clove, minced
⅓ cup grated onion
½ teaspoon grated lemon zest
2 teaspoons minced fresh mint
1 tablespoon minced fresh parsley
1 egg yolk
½ cup dry whole wheat bread crumbs
¼ cup milk
Salt and freshly ground pepper
9 cups meat stock (page 271) or chicken
    stock (page 272)
⅓ cup rice
2 eggs
Juice of 1 to 2 lemons
Chopped parsley and mint

1 Preheat the oven to 375°F.

2 In a bowl, mix together the veal, garlic, onion, lemon zest, mint, parsley, and egg yolk. Add the bread crumbs, milk, salt, and pepper and continue to mix. Form into ¾-inch meatballs. Place on an oiled baking sheet and bake the meatballs for 10 minutes. Remove from the oven and remove the meatballs from the pan with a spatula. Reserve the meatballs.

3 Bring the stock to a boil in a soup pot. Add the rice, salt, and pepper and simmer slowly, uncovered, for 10 minutes. Add the meatballs and continue to simmer 10 minutes, until the rice is cooked.

4 In the meantime, beat the eggs and the juice of 1 lemon in a bowl until light and frothy. Add 1 small ladle of boiling broth to the egg mixture and beat vigorously. Continue to add broth a ladle at a time, beating in between each addition until you have added 5 or 6 ladlefuls. Pour this mixture back into the soup pot. Taste and add additional lemon juice, salt, and pepper if desired. Serve immediately, garnished with chopped parsley and mint. Do not reheat this soup to the boiling point or it will curdle.

Serves 6

Baked Omelette with Zucchini, Leeks, Feta, and Mountain Herbs

Savory egg pies are everyday fare in the European countries that border the Mediterranean. In Spain, they make the tortilla, in France, the omelette, and in Italy, the frittata. In Greece, egg pies may not be quite as prevalent, but they are every bit as tasty. The ingredients that make this one unique are the rice, mint, and feta, so distinctively Greek, but used here in an updated context.

¼ cup long-grain white rice
¾ cup water
Salt and freshly ground pepper
3 tablespoons plus 2 teaspoons olive oil
3 leeks, white and 2 inches of green,
   chopped and washed
3 zucchini, unpeeled and coarsely grated
3 tablespoons chopped fresh mint
2 tablespoons chopped fresh dill
8 eggs, lightly beaten
5 ounces feta cheese, crumbled

1 Bring the rice, water, and a large pinch of salt to a boil. Turn down the heat and simmer, covered, 20 minutes, until the rice is cooked and the water is absorbed.

2 Preheat the oven to 325°F.

3 Heat 2 tablespoons olive oil in a large skillet over medium-low heat and sauté the leeks, covered, until soft, 10 to 15 minutes. Remove from the pan. Add 1 tablespoon olive oil to the pan and over medium heat, sauté the zucchini, uncovered, until the zucchini softens, 5 to 7 minutes. Season the zucchini with salt and pepper.

4 Combine the rice, leeks, zucchini, mint, dill, eggs, feta, salt, and pepper. Mix well.

5 Oil a 9 × 9-inch baking dish with the remaining 2 teaspoons oil. Pour the eggs and vegetables into the dish. Bake for 35 to 40 minutes, until golden and set.

6 Cut into squares and serve warm.

Serves 6

NOTE: This can be prepared several hours in advance and served at room temperature.

Phyllo Pizza with Three Cheeses, Tomatoes, and Oregano

Who uses this pastry that resembles tissue paper? How should it be handled? Where does the name come from? The word filo *is Greek for "leaf" or "page of a book" and this paper-thin dough is used by the Turks, Syrians, Lebanese, and the North Africans as well as the Greeks. Phyllo always seems to mystify the novice cook. Available either fresh or frozen in most grocery stores, it should be stored in the refrigerator until ready to use. The key to working with phyllo is keeping it covered with a slightly dampened kitchen towel. The following recipe is a modern adaptation for pizza using phyllo and is irresistible. Make it once and you'll see.*

10 sheets phyllo dough

3 tablespoons butter

3 tablespoons olive oil

½ cup (3 ounces) grated mozzarella cheese

½ cup (3 ounces) feta cheese, crumbled very
   small

½ cup grated Kefalotyri or Parmesan cheese

1 teaspoon dried oregano

Salt and freshly ground pepper

4 scallions, white and green, thinly sliced

2 large tomatoes, very thinly sliced

1 Cut the sheets of phyllo dough in half into 9 × 14-inch sheets. Place the phyllo on a work surface and cover with a slightly dampened towel. Melt the butter and olive oil together in a small saucepan. Combine the mozzarella, feta, Kefalotyri, oregano, salt, and pepper.

2 Preheat the oven to 400°F.

3 With a pastry brush, oil a sheet pan lightly with the melted butter and oil. Place 1 sheet of phyllo on the pan and brush it lightly with butter and oil. Place another layer of phyllo directly on top and brush it lightly with butter and oil. Sprinkle with a scant 2 tablespoons of the combined cheese mixture. Continue in the same manner until all the phyllo has been used.

4 Brush the top layer with butter and oil. Sprinkle with half of the remaining cheese. Sprinkle with the scallions. Place the tomatoes close together in a single layer over the scallions. Season the tomatoes with salt and pepper. Sprinkle with the remaining cheese. Trim the edges if desired.

5 Bake for 20 to 25 minutes on the top shelf of the oven, until the cheese is melted and the phyllo is golden and crisp on the edges.

Serves 6

Savory Chicken, Leek, and Feta Pie with Mountain Herbs

As I stood in front of the window, I knew I was in for a treat. I stepped inside and was immediately assaulted by the sweet smells of melted butter and golden-baked phyllo. Large round pans of pitta, or savory pie, each pan nearly as long as my arm, were balanced one on top of the other across the counter. With such a variety, how could I decide? There were the traditional pittas *of cheese and spinach but there were also some new variations like stewed chicken and artichoke or fennel, dill and wilted greens. It was tough but I finally made my selection. My slice was wrapped in wax paper imprinted with what looked like Greek hieroglyphics. Here is the recipe for the one I chose.*

Pastry

2½ cups all-purpose flour
1 teaspoon salt
¼ cup plus 1 tablespoon olive oil
½ cup water
1 egg, lightly beaten

Filling

6 leeks, white and 3 inches of green, diced
¼ cup olive oil
1 bunch of scallions, green and white, chopped
¼ cup chopped fresh parsley
⅓ cup chopped fresh dill

2 tablespoons chopped fresh mint
¾ pound raw boneless chicken meat, skin and fat removed, diced patted dry with paper towels
5 ounces feta cheese, crumbled
2 tablespoons grated Kefalotyri or Parmesan cheese
2 egg yolks, lightly beaten
Salt and freshly ground pepper

Assembly

1 tablespoon olive oil
2 tablespoons all-purpose flour
1 egg yolk, lightly beaten

1 In a bowl, combine 2¼ cups flour and salt. Add ¼ cup olive oil, water, and egg and mix well to form a ball. Flour a work surface with the remaining ¼ cup flour and knead the dough for 1 minute until smooth and elastic. Alternatively, this can be done in an electric mixer using a dough hook. Oil a large bowl with the remaining 1 tablespoon olive oil. Place the dough in the bowl and turn over to coat the top. Cover with plastic wrap and let rest at room temperature 2 hours.

2 Preheat the oven to 375°F.

3 In the meantime, wash the diced leeks in a bowl of cold water. Drain well. Heat the olive oil in a large skillet and over low heat sauté the leeks and scallions until soft, 20 minutes. Transfer to a bowl. Add the parsley, dill, mint, chicken, feta, Kefalotyri, egg yolks, salt, and pepper and mix well.

After the dough has rested 2 hours, brush a round 10 × 2-inch cake pan lightly with olive oil. (A springform pan can also be used.) Roll two-thirds of the dough into a circle ⅛ inch thick by 14 inches on a floured (using 2 table-spoons of flour) surface. Place the dough in the pan, stretching slightly so it comes up over the edges. Brush lightly with olive oil. Spread the filling evenly over the dough. Roll the other piece of dough into an 11-inch circle. Place on top of the filling so it comes up over the edges. Press the edges together and trim any excess. Roll the crust inward to form an edge. Brush the top lightly with the egg yolk. With the point of a knife, score the top, making sure that you do not cut through the crust completely.

Bake for 40 to 50 minutes, until golden brown. Remove from the oven and cool at least 15 minutes before serving. This can also be served at room temperature.

Serves 8

NOTE: This can also be made with store-bought phyllo dough, yielding a light, flaky finished product. You will need 12 sheets. Place the phyllo on a work surface and cover with a slightly dampened towel. Melt 6 tablespoons butter in a saucepan. Place 1 sheet of phyllo in the pan, letting the extra overhang the edges. Brush lightly with butter. Turn the pan one-quarter turn and place another layer of phyllo on top of the other one. Brush lightly with but-ter. Repeat with 4 more sheets of phyllo. Spread the filling evenly over the dough. Fold the ex-cess phyllo onto the filling. Place 1 sheet of phyllo on top of the filling, letting the extra overhang the edges. Brush lightly with butter. Turn the pan one-quarter turn and place an-other layer of phyllo on top of the other one. Brush lightly with butter. Repeat with 4 more sheets of phyllo. Trim the edges of phyllo so that they hang 1 inch over the edge of the pan. Tuck between the bottom layers of phyllo and the sides of the pan. With the point of a knife, score the top, making sure that you cut through only the top couple of layers of phyllo. Bake ac-cording to the directions above.

Lamb, Fennel, and Orange Pie Likouressis

Maria Likouressis and her husband, Dimitri, who live on the island of Zakynthos, are renowned for being two of the best cooks in all of Greece. I stood in her kitchen and made a sliced lemon and olive oil salad as she prepared this delicious lamb, fennel, and orange pie.

Pastry

1 tablespoon dry yeast
¾ cup warm milk
3¾ cups bread flour
½ cup plus 1 tablespoon olive oil
¼ cup water
1 teaspoon salt
1 egg, lightly beaten

Filling

1½ pounds lamb meat, cut from the leg
4 tablespoons olive oil
1 bunch of scallions, green and white, chopped
3 garlic cloves, minced
3 medium bulbs fennel, very thinly sliced
Salt and freshly ground pepper
2 large bunches of greens (spinach, arugula, collard greens, Swiss chard, turnip greens, beet greens) stems removed, washed, spun dry, and coarsely chopped
2 bay leaves, very finely crumbled
1 tablespoon orange zest

Assembly

1 tablespoon olive oil

¼ pound feta cheese, crumbled
2 tablespoons butter, melted

1 The day before you plan to serve the pie, combine the yeast and milk in a bowl and stir well to dissolve. Let sit 10 minutes until it bubbles. Add the flour, 1/2 cup olive oil, water, salt, and egg and mix until it comes together. Remove from the bowl and knead on a floured surface 6 to 7 minutes, until smooth and elastic. (Alternatively, this can be made in an electric mixer using a dough hook.) Oil a large bowl with 1 tablespoon olive oil. Place the dough in the bowl and turn it over to coat the top. Cover with plastic wrap and let sit in the refrigerator overnight.

2 The next day, trim the fat from the lamb. Cut into thin strips, ½ × 1½ inches. Heat 2 tablespoons olive oil in a large skillet. Add the lamb and sauté over medium-high heat, uncovered, 2 minutes. Remove from the pan with a slotted spoon and set aside. Reduce the heat to medium-low, add the remaining 2 tablespoons olive oil to the same pan, and sauté the scallions, garlic, fennel, salt, and pepper, uncovered, until soft, 10 minutes. Add the greens and lamb and continue to sauté, uncovered, until the greens wilt and the juices evaporate, 8 to 10 minutes. Mix well and season with salt, pepper, crumbled bay leaves, and orange zest.

3 Preheat the oven to 375°F.

4 To assemble the pie, brush a round 10 × 2-inch cake pan lightly with 1 tablespoon olive oil. Divide the dough into 2 pieces. On a floured surface, roll 1 piece of dough into a circle ⅛ inch thick by 14 inches. Place the dough in the pan, stretching slightly so it comes up over the edges. Brush lightly with olive oil. Spread the filling evenly over the dough. Crumble the feta on top of the lamb and greens. Roll the other piece of dough into an 11-inch circle. Place on top of the filling so it comes up over the edges. Press the edges together and trim any excess. Roll the crust inward to form an edge. Brush the top with melted butter. With the point of a knife, score the top, making sure that you do not cut through the crust completely.

5 Bake for 15 minutes. Reduce the heat to 325°F. and continue to bake for 45 to 60 minutes. If the top gets too dark, cover with foil and continue to bake until done. Remove from the oven and let rest 20 minutes. Remove from the pan. Cut into wedges and serve hot or at room temperature.

Serves 8

SAGANAKI

Fried Cheese with Lemon and Olives

The name of this dish derives from the thin, round, flat-bottomed aluminum pan that is traditionally used to cook this simple, yet flavorful dish of fried Kefalotyri cheese.

Olive oil for frying
1½-pound chunk Kefalotyri cheese, ½ inch thick (see Note)
2 cups water
1 cup all-purpose flour
Juice of 1 lemon
Oregano and cracked black pepper
3 lemon wedges
12 Kalamata olives

1 Heat ½ inch olive oil in a small skillet over medium-high heat. As soon as it ripples 1 minute, reduce the heat to medium-low.

2 Cut the cheese into ½-inch sticks. Place in a bowl of water. Place the flour in a bowl, remove the sticks of cheese from the water, and immediately place in the flour. Do not tap off the excess.

3 Fry the cheese sticks in a single layer until golden and crusty, turning them with a fork, about 1 to 2 minutes per side. They should be soft all the way through but not melting.

4 Serve immediately on a warm platter, drizzled with lemon juice. Sprinkle with oregano and cracked black pepper. Garnish with lemon wedges and olives.

Serves 6

NOTE: If Kefalotyri is unavailable, Italian Fontinella, Gruyère, or Romano cheese can be substituted.

Stuffed Macaroni with Feta, Tomatoes, and Mint

Htipiti is a spiced feta cheese spread that originated in Thessaloniki. It translates as "that which is beaten." This is one of my favorites and is inspired by my dear friend from Macedonia in northern Greece, Angel Stoyanof. Htipiti can be served on its own, garnished with olives and lemon wedges as a meze, *or as the filling for these irresistible filled "macaroni."*

Pasta
2 cups all-purpose flour
½ teaspoon salt
3 eggs

Filling
¾ pound feta cheese, at room temperature
6 ounces cream cheese, at room temperature
2 garlic cloves, mashed in a mortar and pestle
1 tablespoon olive oil
1 small hot pickled pepper, jalapeño or Greek torshi, minced
½ teaspoon dried oregano
¼ teaspoon dried thyme
Salt and freshly ground pepper
1 tablespoon lemon juice

Sauce
¼ cup extra virgin olive oil
5 large tomatoes, peeled, seeded, and chopped (page 278), or 2 cups canned Italian plum tomatoes, drained and chopped
2 tablespoons chopped fresh mint

1 Place the flour and salt on a work surface. Make a well in the center. In a small bowl, whisk the eggs together. Add the eggs to the well and with a fork, bring the flour in to the egg. Continue until all of the flour has been incorporated and the dough is dry to the touch but still forms a ball. Knead for 2 to 3 minutes, kneading in additional flour if it is wet. Cover with plastic wrap and let it rest 30 minutes.

2 In the meantime, place the feta, cream cheese, and garlic in a food processor. Pulse a few times to form a paste. With the motor running, add the oil in a very slow and steady stream, allowing about 1 minute from start to finish. Add the hot pepper, oregano, thyme, salt, pepper, and lemon juice. Pulse several times. Alternatively, this can be made by hand: With a fork, mash the cheeses with the garlic. With a wooden spoon, add the oil in a very slow and steady stream, mixing vigorously, about 3 minutes. Add the remaining ingredients and mix well. Reserve the mixture in the refrigerator until ready to use.

3 Lightly dust a rolling pin and work surface with flour. Divide the dough into 4 pieces. Roll the dough very thin, until you can see your hand through it. This can also be done with a pasta machine (page 134). Cut the pasta into 4-inch squares. Place 1 tablespoon cheese filling in the center of each square. Spray a mist of water around the edges or using a pastry brush, brush lightly with water. Fold over to form triangles and seal. Trim the edges. Place on a heavily floured baking sheet. Continue until all the dough has been rolled and filled.

4 Heat the olive oil in a skillet until hot. Add the tomatoes, reduce the heat to medium, and sauté, uncovered, for 2 minutes. Season with salt and pepper.

♪ Bring a large pot of salted water to a boil. Add the macaroni and simmer 4 to 5 minutes, or until done. Drain. Toss with the tomatoes. Place on a serving dish and garnish with mint. Serve immediately.

Makes 36 stuffed macaroni to serve 6

Spicy Sausages with Tomatoes and Olives

Spicy sausages are made all over the Mediterranean. Soutzoukakia, with its hint of orange and allspice, is similar to the loukanika *sausage of Greece, a holdover from the Venetian* luganega *sausage. The cumin, coriander, allspice, and garlic are Turkish influenced. It's not surprising that all of these flavors come into play, as the Venetians and Turks vied for supremacy in western Greece for years before the Ottomans finally won. The influences of this sausage are obvious when you taste the distinctive flavors of Greece, Italy, and Turkey all rolled into one.*

2 leeks, white and 3 inches of green, diced
5 tablespoons olive oil
4 scallions, finely chopped
½ cup fresh white bread crumbs
¾ cup red wine
1 tablespoon cumin seeds
1 teaspoon coriander seeds
3 allspice berries or ¼ teaspoon ground
    allspice (optional)
1¼ pounds ground lamb
4 garlic cloves, minced
1½ tablespoons grated orange zest
3 tablespoons chopped fresh parsley
½ teaspoon chopped fresh thyme
Salt and freshly ground pepper
¼ cup all-purpose flour
1 28-ounce can Italian plum tomatoes,
    ground

½ teaspoon sugar
⅓ cup pitted and coarsely chopped
    Kalamata olives (page 279)
Whole parsley leaves

1 Rinse the leeks in a bowl of cold water and drain well. Heat 2 tablespoons olive oil in a large skillet and sauté the leeks and scallions over low heat until soft, 10 minutes.

2 Soak the bread crumbs in ½ cup red wine and mix well.

3 Heat the cumin, coriander seeds, and allspice berries in a small dry skillet over medium heat until aromatic, 2 minutes. Pulverize to a fine powder in a spice grinder or a mortar and pestle.

4 Transfer the leeks, olive oil, bread, wine, and spices to a bowl. Add the lamb, garlic, orange rind, parsley, thyme, 1 teaspoon salt, and 1 teaspoon pepper. Knead together 2 to 3 minutes. Cover and refrigerate 2 hours or overnight.

5 The next day, make 1 very small patty and sauté in a small lightly oiled skillet until cooked. Taste it and correct with additional spices, salt, or pepper. Moisten your hands and form the sausages into oval shapes 2 inches long by ¾ inch and roll lightly in flour. Heat 2 tablespoons olive oil in a large skillet over medium-high heat. Sauté the sausages, uncovered, until golden on all sides, 10 minutes. Remove the sausages and drain. Discard any fat in the pan.

6 Add the remaining 1 tablespoon olive oil to the pan and heat over medium heat. Add the tomatoes, ¼ cup red wine, sugar, salt, and pepper and simmer, uncovered, 10 minutes. Add the sausages and continue to simmer very slowly, covered, 30 minutes. Taste the sauce and season with salt and pepper.

7 Serve warm, garnished with olives and parsley leaves.

Makes 24 sausages to serve 6 to 8

NOTE: These sausages can be made 1 day in advance and reheated before serving.

MELITZANES TIGANITES

Spicy Grilled Eggplant with Olive Oil and Vinegar

A specialty of one of my favorite ouzeris in Greece. The technique and ingredients for this simple and delicious dish are so typically Mediterranean, it could easily make its way onto just about any table around the sea.

> 9 long thin Japanese eggplants or 2 small
>   eggplants
> Salt and freshly ground pepper
> ½ cup plus 2 tablespoons olive oil
> 3 garlic cloves, mashed in a mortar and
>   pestle
> 2 teaspoons red wine vinegar
> ¼ teaspoon crushed red pepper
> 2 tablespoons chopped fresh parsley

1 Start a charcoal grill (see Note).

2 Slice the eggplant into ¼-inch slices crosswise. If you are using Japanese eggplant, there is no need to salt them. With the larger eggplants, set the slices in a colander and salt them lightly. Let sit 30 minutes. Rinse with water and pat dry with paper towels.

3 Place the eggplant slices in a bowl and drizzle with ½ cup olive oil, black pepper, and a large pinch of salt. (Use salt only if you are using Japanese eggplants, otherwise omit the salt here.) Grill the eggplant slices over a hot fire, turning occasionally, until they are golden and tender, about 10 to 12 minutes.

4 Combine the garlic with the remaining 2 tablespoons olive oil and vinegar. Place the eggplant on a serving platter and brush the olive oil, vinegar, and garlic evenly over the top. Sprinkle with the crushed red pepper, salt, and parsley.

Serves 6

NOTE: These can also be baked in the oven: Oil a sheet pan and spread the eggplant slices in a single layer on the sheet pan. Bake on the top shelf of a 400°F. oven for 15 minutes, turning occasionally, until golden on both sides.

Dilled Potato and Leek Croquettes

I tasted potato croquettes in Greece, Italy, and Turkey. Each country served its own version, but essentially it was the same delicious croquette with a slight twist of flavors. These croquettes are made with potatoes, leeks, dill, cheese, and a splash of vinegar, but the choice of other aromatics is up to you.

1½ pounds brown russet baking potatoes, scrubbed well
3 leeks, white and 2 inches of green, coarsely chopped and washed
2 egg yolks
3 scallions, white and green, finely chopped
¼ cup chopped fresh dill
⅔ cup grated Kefalotyri or Parmesan cheese
½ teaspoon white wine vinegar
Salt and freshly ground pepper
Olive oil for frying
¾ cup all-purpose flour
2 eggs, lightly beaten
2 ½ cups fine dry bread crumbs
Dill sprigs

1 Boil the potatoes and leeks in a large pot of boiling salted water for 25 to 30 minutes, until the potatoes are tender. Drain and let cool. Peel the potatoes. Pass the potatoes and leeks through the fine disk of a food mill or pulse a few times in a food processor until the mixture is smooth. Do not mix so long that the mixture gets gluey.

2 Add the egg yolks, scallions, dill, cheese, vinegar, 1 teaspoon salt, and pepper. Mix well. Cover and refrigerate 3 hours.

3 Heat ½ inch olive oil in a large skillet to 375°F.

4 With floured hands, shape the mixture into croquettes 1½ inches long by ¾ inch wide.

5 Place the flour, beaten eggs, and bread crumbs each in their own individual bowls. Season all 3 with salt and pepper. Dust the croquettes in the flour first, then in the eggs, and then in the bread crumbs. After each is breaded, place on a baking sheet until all are made. Store in the refrigerator until ready to use.

This recipe can be prepared to this point up to 6 hours in advance.

6 Fry the croquettes a few at a time, turning occasionally, until golden on all sides, 3 to 4 minutes. Serve them hot on a platter, garnished with dill sprigs.

Makes 20 croquettes to serve 6 to 8

NOTE: After the croquettes have been cooked, they can be kept warm in a 350°F. oven until ready to serve.

Lentil and Bulgur Croquettes with Yogurt and Mint

Jews have lived in Macedonia for nearly 2,000 years. Thessaloniki, the largest city in Macedonia, was known as the "Queen of Israel" for 400 years until the Jews there fell victim to the Holocaust. The rich culinary heritage of the Jews continues to be seen today, and these savory, spiced lentil and bulgur croquettes are a perfect example.

½ cup lentils
⅓ cup medium-fine bulgur or cracked
   wheat
4 tablespoons olive oil
1 small onion, finely chopped
1 ½ teaspoons ground cumin
4 tablespoons chopped fresh mint
2 tablespoons chopped fresh parsley
1 tablespoon plus 1 teaspoon lemon juice
2 eggs, lightly beaten
3 tablespoons all-purpose flour
Salt and freshly ground pepper
1 cup plain whole milk yogurt
Mint leaves

1 Pick over the lentils and discard any stones. Wash the lentils and place in a large saucepan with 2 cups water. Bring to a boil, turn down the heat, and simmer, uncovered, 30 minutes, until tender. At the end of the cooking time, add enough additional water to just cover the lentils. Remove from the heat. Stir in the bulgur, cover, and set aside 1½ hours.

2 Heat 2 tablespoons olive oil in a large skillet. Add the onions and sauté until soft, 7 minutes. Add the cumin and stir well. After the lentils and bulgur have sat for 1½ hours, add the onions, 3 tablespoons mint, the parsley, 1 tablespoon lemon juice, the eggs, flour, 1 teaspoon salt, and pepper to taste. Mix well. If the mixture is still wet, add an additional tablespoon of flour.

3 Combine the yogurt with the remaining 1 tablespoon mint and 1 teaspoon lemon juice, salt, and pepper. Reserve.

4 Heat the remaining 2 tablespoons olive oil in a large skillet. Drop batter by the tablespoonful to form 2-inch cakes. Sauté the cakes, uncovered, until golden brown, 2 minutes per side. Drain on paper towels. Garnish with the minted yogurt and mint leaves.

Makes 18 croquettes

NOTE: The sauce can be varied. If desired, omit the mint and add the same amount of dill and/ or ¼ cup grated cucumbers and/or 1 small garlic clove, mashed in a mortar and pestle.

KOLOKITHAKIA YEMISTA

Stuffed Zucchini

4 to 6 medium zucchini, 1¼ inch diameter, washed, ends trimmed

½ medium onion, coarsely grated

2 tomatoes, peeled, seeded, and chopped (page 278), or 1 cup canned Italian plum tomatoes, drained and chopped

¼ cup long-grain white rice

1 ½ tablespoons chopped fresh dill

2 ½ tablespoons chopped fresh parsley

Salt and freshly ground pepper

3 tablespoons olive oil

½ cup water

Avgolemono Sauce (page 173)

1 Preheat the oven to 350°F.

2 Cut the zucchini in 1½-inch lengths. With a melon baller, scoop out the seeds and pulp from the center, leaving the bottom of each "stump" intact. Reserve. Chop the seeds and pulp and reserve.

3 Combine the reserved zucchini, onions, tomatoes, rice, dill, parsley, ½ teaspoon salt, and pepper. Stuff the hollowed-out zucchini very loosely with filling just below the level of the top. Do not pack the filling as the rice will expand. Place zucchini, filling side up, in a baking dish large enough to hold the squash tightly. Pour the olive oil and water into the bottom of the baking dish. Cover tightly with foil and bake 50 minutes, or until the rice is tender. Remove from the oven, uncover, and pour the juices from the pan into a measuring cup to make the Avgolemono Sauce. Reserve the zucchini.

4 Place the zucchini on a serving platter and drizzle the Avgolemono Sauce over the top or pass separately.

Serves 6

DOMATES YEMISTES

Stuffed Tomatoes

6 firm medium tomatoes, washed

5 tablespoons olive oil

½ medium onion, coarsely grated

⅓ pound ground veal

¼ cup long-grain white rice

1 ½ tablespoons chopped fresh parsley

1½ tablespoons chopped fresh dill

Salt and freshly ground pepper

¼ cup water

Avgolemono Sauce (recipe follows)

1 Preheat the oven to 350°F.

2 With a small knife, cut around the top of the tomato but leave ½ inch attached to form a flap. With a spoon, scrape out the pulp and reserve. Reserve the tomatoes.

3 Heat 2 tablespoons olive oil in a skillet. Sauté the onions and veal until the veal turns gray. Strain the tomato pulp and reserve the juices. Chop the pulp, add to the veal, and continue to sauté, uncovered, until the juices evaporate, 2 to 3 minutes. Add the rice, parsley, dill, ½ teaspoon salt, and pepper. Turn off the heat.

4 Stuff the hollowed-out tomatoes very loosely with the filling just below the level of the top. Do not pack the filling as the rice will expand. Place the flap back on top. Place the stuffed tomatoes tops up in a baking dish large enough to hold the tomatoes tightly. Combine the reserved tomato juice, the remaining 3 tablespoons olive oil, and water and pour into the bottom of the baking dish. Cover tightly with foil and bake 40 minutes, or until the rice is tender. Remove from the oven, uncover, and pour the juices from the pan into a measuring cup to make the Avgolemono Sauce. Reserve the tomatoes.

5 Place the tomatoes on a serving platter and drizzle the Avgolemono Sauce over the top or pass separately.

Serves 6

NOTE: The stuffed zucchini or tomatoes can be served hot or at room temperature. They can be prepared up to 1 day in advance and baked the day they will be served. The sauce should never be made in advance but should be prepared just before the dish is served.

Avgolemono Sauce

What makes the stuffed vegetables of Greece unique is the avgolemono sauce. This sauce is meant to accompany the Stuffed Zucchini, the Stuffed Tomatoes, or any stuffed vegetable.

Stock reserved from cooking vegetables
1 cup chicken stock (page 272)
2 eggs
Juice of 2 lemons

1 Add enough chicken stock to the reserved juices from either the zucchini or tomatoes to make 1½ cups. Reduce by ½ cup, about 10 minutes, and keep warm.

2 In a bowl, beat the eggs until light and very foamy, about 3 minutes. Beating continuously, gradually add the lemon juice, a few drops at a time. Beating continuously, gradually add the hot stock to the egg-lemon juice, a few tablespoons at a time. When all of the stock has been added, pour the contents into a saucepan and heat very gently until it coats the back of a spoon and thickens slightly, 2 to 4 minutes. Do not let the mixture boil or get too hot or it will curdle.

3 Remove from the heat and keep warm in a double boiler set over warm water.

Makes 1 ¹/₂ cups

Grape Leaves Stuffed with Rice, Currants, and Herbs

Dolmathes *came to Greece by way of the Ottoman Empire, which was in its heyday in the sixteenth century. Originally this dish was palace food but today* dolmathes *are commonplace for everyone from the field worker to the prosperous city dweller in Greece, Turkey, Cyprus, and the Middle East.* Dolma *is a Turkish word that means "stuffed." Many different kinds of leaves can be stuffed—lettuce, cabbage, spinach, and the most preferred, grape leaves.*

1 jar (16 ounces) preserved vine leaves or 7 dozen fresh young vine leaves

¾ cup extra virgin olive oil

2 medium onions, finely minced

⅓ cup pine nuts

1 cup chopped scallions, white and green

1 cup long-grain white rice

¼ cup chopped fresh parsley

3 tablespoons chopped fresh mint

3 tablespoons chopped fresh dill

3 tablespoons chopped fresh fennel greens or leaves

⅓ cup currants

Pinch of cinnamon

Salt and freshly ground pepper

2 cups water

2 fennel stalks (optional)

2 dill sprigs

Juice of 2 lemons

Lemon wedges

1 cup plain whole milk yogurt or 1 cup Yogurt and Cucumber Salad (recipe follows) (optional)

1 Rinse the vine leaves and blanch a few at a time, in boiling water for 1 minute. Cool in a bowl of cold water and then drain. Cut off the tough stems.

2 Heat ½ cup olive oil in a large skillet and sauté the onions until soft. Add the pine nuts, scallions, and rice and stir over heat for 3 minutes. Stir in the herbs, currants, cinnamon, ½ teaspoon salt, pepper to taste, and 1 cup water. Cover and cook over low heat for 15 minutes, until the rice is cooked and the water is absorbed.

3 To shape the rolled grape leaves, place a leaf, smooth side down, on a work surface and put a heaping teaspoon of the filling near the base of the leaf at the stem end. Fold the stem end and sides over the filling and roll up toward the point of the leaf, making a little bundle. After you have used up all the filling, you should have some leaves left over.

4 Line a heavy 4-quart saucepan with a few leaves and place the fennel stalks and dill sprigs on the bottom. Sprinkle with a pinch of salt. Pack the rolls in close together, seam side down. Sprinkle each layer with the remaining ¼ cup olive oil and lemon juice. Add the remaining 1 cup water and cover the top of the rolls with leaves. Invert a small heatproof plate on top to keep the rolls in shape. Cover the saucepan tightly and bring to a boil. Turn the heat down and simmer slowly for 1½ hours.

♪ Remove from the heat and leave for 2 hours, until the liquid is absorbed. Let cool to room temperature. Serve warm or at room temperature, garnished with lemon wedges and/or plain yogurt or tzatziki.

Makes 5 dozen

NOTE: These can be made 1 week before they are to be served and stored in the refrigerator. Bring to room temperature before serving.

TZATZIKI

Yogurt and Cucumber Salad

Yogurt plays an important role in the eastern and southern Mediterranean and tzatziki, *the heady yogurt, garlic, and cucumber spread or salad, appears throughout Greece and the Middle East. Variations of this dish appear in the Middle East, Egypt, and even in some parts of North Africa. In Greece,* tzatziki *is made with the highest fat content yogurt available, preferably from the sheep. In the United States, draining the yogurt for 2 hours provides an adequate alternative.*

2 cups whole milk yogurt
Salt
½ medium cucumber, peeled and seeded
3 to 4 garlic cloves, mashed in a mortar and
    pestle
1 tablespoon chopped fresh dill
2 teaspoons chopped fresh mint
1 tablespoon extra virgin olive oil
1 tablespoon lemon juice

1 Combine the yogurt and ¼ teaspoon salt in a cheesecloth-lined strainer over a bowl and let it drain for 4 hours.

2 In the meantime, grate the cucumber with a coarse grater to make 1 cup total. Place the grated cucumber in another cheesecloth-lined strainer. Salt lightly and let drain 30 minutes.

3 Combine the yogurt, cucumber, garlic, herbs, and olive oil. Mix well. Add the lemon juice to taste and season to taste with salt. Let sit 1 hour before using.

Makes 2¹/₄ cups

Spinach Puree with Garlic

On every meze *table in Greece, there are always a mass of tiny bowls filled with dips, spreads, and purees of all varieties—pungent yogurt with garlic and cucumbers; smoky eggplant spread; creamy white potato, garlic, and olive oil sauce; pale rose* taramasalata; *a puree of chick-peas with lemon and cumin. The presence of these dishes on the* meze *table is a holdover from the Turkish domination of Greece, whose influence extends even further east to the countries of Syria, Lebanon, Iraq, and Egypt. The following recipe, which resembles the classic* skorthalia, *is delightfully simple and packed with robust flavor.*

1 cup coarsely chopped spinach, washed
   and dried
½ cup fresh bread crumbs
¼ cup cold water
¾ cup plus 2 tablespoons walnuts
½ cup olive oil
3 garlic cloves, minced
1 teaspoon lemon juice or white wine
   vinegar
Salt and freshly ground pepper
Lemon wedges
Crusty bread

1 Preheat the oven to 350°F.

2 Bring a pot of salted water to a boil. Add the spinach to the boiling water and drain immediately.

3 Soak the bread crumbs in the cold water and squeeze well to remove any excess moisture. Discard the water.

4 Place the walnuts on a baking sheet and bake 5 to 7 minutes, until they are golden and hot to the touch. Chop 2 tablespoons and reserve for a garnish.

5 Place the spinach, bread crumbs, ¾ cup walnuts, oil, garlic, and lemon juice in a blender or food processor. Blend to obtain a smooth paste. Taste and season with salt and pepper.

6 Spread the puree on a plate. Sprinkle with the reserved walnuts and garnish with lemon wedges. Serve with crusty bread.

Makes 1 ¹/₂ cups

Eggplant Salad

Daphne Zepos may be a Greek goddess. She got so excited about my book project that she spent several weeks in Greece translating for me. Her love of her native country is boundless, and her friendship is truly an honor. When we got back to San Francisco, she tested this recipe for me and we tasted the results together. Her eyes sparkled and I think for a few moments she was back in Greece.

1 large eggplant, smoked (page 277)
½ small red bell pepper, roasted (page 278)
2 garlic cloves, minced
½ medium onion, grated
¼ teaspoon dried oregano
¼ teaspoon ground cumin
2 tablespoons lemon juice
2 tablespoons extra virgin olive oil
Salt and freshly ground pepper
Chopped fresh parsley
3 lemon wedges
Crusty bread

1 Preheat the oven to 350° F.

2 Place the smoked eggplant on a baking sheet and bake 20 minutes, or until the pulp is soft and a skewer goes into the flesh easily. Cool in a bag with the pepper. Remove the skin from the eggplant and squeeze the flesh gently between paper towels to remove any excess moisture. Remove the skin, stem, and core from the pepper and finely dice. Reserve.

3 In a food processor or blender, pulse the eggplant flesh a few times. Add the garlic, onion, oregano, cumin, and lemon juice. Gradually add the olive oil with the motor running. Season with salt and pepper and pulse a few more times. Place in a bowl and fold in the peppers. Let sit at room temperature for 1 hour.

4 To serve, mound the salad on a serving plate and garnish with the chopped parsley and lemon wedges. Serve with crusty bread.

Serves 6

Salad of Oven-Roasted Beets, Red Onions, and Olives with Garlic Sauce

Irene Fotiadis is a well-respected caterer who performs miracles for her clients in Thessaloniki. I was lucky enough to work with her one day as she gracefully transformed Greek classics into modern dishes. Skorthalia, which dates back to antiquity, is Greece's unique garlic sauce; it is linked to France's aioli and rouille and Spain's romesco *and* allioli *by a common thread of abundant mashed garlic. Unlike the sauces of the western Mediterranean,* skorthalia *has a strong starchy base, either nuts and soaked bread (as in this recipe) or mashed potatoes. Here, Irene's version of* skorthalia *is used as the dressing for a flavorful salad of roasted beets, red onions, and black olives.*

2 bunches of beets (8 to 9 beets)
¼ cup extra virgin olive oil
½ teaspoon dried oregano
Salt and freshly ground pepper
1 bulb garlic, whole, unpeeled, and cut in half crosswise
1 8-ounce loaf country-style coarse white bread, crusts removed
4 cups water
½ cup ground walnuts
¼ cup vegetable oil
¼ cup olive oil
3 to 4 tablespoons white wine vinegar
2 tablespoons Mayonnaise (page 273)

3 large garlic cloves, mashed with a mortar and pestle
1 small red onion, peeled and cut into thin rings
24 Kalamata olives
Chopped fresh parsley

1 Preheat the oven to 350°F.

2 Wash the beets and place in a baking dish. Drizzle with the extra virgin olive oil. Sprinkle with the oregano, salt, and pepper. Break the garlic bulb into cloves and scatter over the beets. Cover with foil and bake for 1 hour, or until the beets can be easily skewered. Remove from the oven and cool the beets. Peel the beets, cut into thin slices, and drizzle with the strained oil from the baking dish.

3 Place the bread in a bowl and pour the water over the bread to soak. Remove the bread from the water immediately and drain for 1 hour. Squeeze the bread to remove any excess moisture. Discard the water.

4 Grind the walnuts in a food processor or blender. Add the bread, salt, vegetable oil, olive oil, 2 tablespoons vinegar, mayonnaise, and garlic in a blender or food processor and puree to obtain a smooth paste. Taste and season with salt, pepper, and additional vinegar if desired.

5 Place the beets, red onions, and olives on

a serving plate. Place a spoonful of garlic sauce on the side of the plate or pass in a separate bowl. Garnish with the parsley.

Serves 6

NOTE: The beets can be cooked up to 24 hours in advance. The garlic sauce should be made the same day. Assemble just before serving.

FAKES SALATA

Lentil Salad with Red Peppers, Red Onions, Feta, and Mint

Lentils are very much enjoyed in Greece, the most popular dish being the famous soupa fakes, *or lentil soup flavored with stewed tomatoes and garlic. The following recipe is not a salad you would be served in a Greek home or restaurant. Although all of the ingredients are indigenous to Greece, here they are assembled in a new and updated way.*

1 cup dry lentils

3 bay leaves

4 whole garlic cloves, peeled and bruised

¼ teaspoon dried oregano

6 tablespoons extra virgin olive oil

6 tablespoons red wine vinegar

2 garlic cloves, minced

½ teaspoon ground cumin

Salt and freshly ground pepper

1 small red onion, diced

1 medium red bell pepper, seeded and finely diced

3 tablespoons chopped fresh mint

6 ounces feta cheese, crumbled

18 Kalamata olives

1 Pick over the lentils and discard any stones. Wash the lentils and place in a large saucepan with the bay leaves, bruised garlic, and oregano. Cover with water by 2 inches. Bring to a boil, turn down the heat, and simmer, uncovered, 30 minutes, until tender. Drain and cool.

2 To make the vinaigrette, whisk together the olive oil, vinegar, garlic, cumin, salt, and pepper in a small bowl.

3 Toss the vinaigrette with the lentils, onions, red pepper, ½ teaspoon salt, and pepper. Let sit 20 minutes. Taste and season as needed with additional salt, pepper, and vinegar.

This salad can be prepared 6 hours in advance up to this point.

4 To serve, toss the lentil salad with the mint and place on a platter. Garnish with the crumbled feta and the olives.

Serves 6

Corfu Salad of Orange Slices, Red Onions, and Kalamata Olives

Traditionally, this salad is made with olives, sweet juicy oranges, onions, and paprika on the island of Corfu, located off the northwest coast of Greece near Albania. This modern version combines oranges, olives, red onions, and mint, instead of the paprika, and the whole salad is linked together by fruity extra virgin olive oil, a splash of red wine vinegar and a touch of garlic. The result is a masterpiece of colors and full flavors.

6 seedless oranges

3 tablespoons orange juice

½ teaspoon orange zest

1½ teaspoons red wine vinegar

1 garlic clove, mashed in a mortar and
    pestle

¼ cup extra virgin olive oil

Salt and freshly ground pepper

½ small red onion, thinly sliced into rings

18 Kalamata olives

12 mint leaves

1 With a knife, cut the top and bottom off of the oranges. Cut off the skin, leaving no white pith remaining. Cut the oranges into ¼-inch slices.

2 In a small bowl, whisk together the orange juice, orange zest, red wine vinegar, garlic, olive oil, ¼ teaspoon salt, and pepper.

3 To serve, arrange the orange slices, onions, and olives on a platter. Drizzle with the dressing. Pile the mint leaves on top of one another and roll up. Cut into thin ribbons. Sprinkle on the salad and serve immediately.

Serves 6

Pickled Wild Mushrooms

Pickling as a way of preserving is a very common practice all over the Mediterranean, especially in Greece where almost every vegetable is pickled, or toursi. *In many international kitchens, the infamous vegetables "a la Grecque" are served, but in Greece they are simply referred to as "marinated vegetables." This full-flavored dish of marinated wild mushrooms is a welcome sight on any* meze *table from coast to coast in Greece.*

1½ pounds small button mushrooms

½ pound wild mushrooms (porcini, morels, field, or chanterelles)

1 cup dry white wine

1 cup white wine vinegar

½ cup extra virgin olive oil

4 garlic cloves, thinly sliced

4 bay leaves

2 teaspoons coarse salt

20 whole black peppercorns, cracked with a mortar and pestle

15 coriander seeds, cracked with a mortar and pestle

6 sprigs fresh parsley

2 sprigs fresh oregano or ¼ teaspoon dried

2 sprigs fresh thyme or ¼ teaspoon dried

2 sprigs fresh fennel or ¼ teaspoon fennel seeds

1 tablespoon chopped fresh parsley

1 To clean the mushrooms, use a soft towel or mushroom brush and brush gently. Trim any bruised spots and discard. If the wild mushrooms are large, cut to the same size as the button mushrooms.

2 Place the wine, vinegar, olive oil, garlic, bay leaves, salt, peppercorns, coriander seeds, parsley sprigs, and half of the oregano, thyme, and fennel in a saucepan. Bring to a boil, cover, and simmer very slowly, 45 minutes. Strain with a fine-mesh strainer, using the back of a wooden spoon to extract all the liquid from the solids. Place the liquid back in a saucepan. Discard the solids.

3 To the liquid in the saucepan, add the mushrooms, the other half of the herbs, and enough water to almost cover the mushrooms. Bring to a boil, turn the heat down, and simmer, uncovered, 3 minutes, stirring occasionally. With a slotted spoon, remove the mushrooms and herbs and place in a bowl. Reduce the liquid until 1 cup remains, 10 minutes. Pour the hot liquid over the mushrooms and mix well. Let cool. Cover and refrigerate overnight.

4 Serve at room temperature, garnished with the chopped parsley.

Serves 6

KALAMARAKIA TOURSI
Pickled Squid

On the idyllic island of Zakynthos, ferries arrived every few hours unloading tons of holiday guests who had made their way to this tiny remote island to enjoy the notorious Easter weekend. Clad in skimpy clothes and carrying fluorescent-striped beach bags, the island was ripe for what was to come—forty-eight hours of eating, drinking, celebrating, and merrymaking. Bukios, the popular outdoor taverna just off the main street, knew what to expect. In advance, they had prepared jars of their famous pickled squid. All weekend, the taverna was jam-packed with island natives and knowing tourists who ate and enjoyed this pungent meze.

1½ pounds medium squid, cleaned
   (page 279)
½ cup bottled clam juice
3 tablespoons olive oil
⅓ cup white wine vinegar
½ cup dry white wine
4 garlic cloves, thinly sliced
½ to ¾ teaspoon pickling spices
½ teaspoon dried oregano
Salt and freshly ground pepper
¼ red bell pepper, finely diced
¼ green bell pepper, finely diced
1 small pickled green pepper, peperoncini
   or Greek *toursi*, finely diced (see Note)
2 thin lemon slices
3 lemon wedges
Whole parsley leaves, preferably Italian

¼ cup black olives (Greek Elitses, Kalamata, Niçoise)

1 Slice the squid bodies into rings and leave the tentacles whole.

2 Bring the clam juice to a boil in a saucepan and reduce by half, 2 minutes. Add the olive oil, vinegar, wine, garlic, pickling spices, oregano, salt, and pepper and simmer over low heat, uncovered, for 10 minutes. Add the squid and simmer 30 to 40 seconds, stirring occasionally. Pour the contents of the pan into a bowl. Add the red, green, and pickled peppers and the lemon slices and mix well. Cover and refrigerate overnight.

3 The next day, bring the squid to room temperature. Place the squid and juices on a platter and garnish with the lemon wedges, parsley leaves, and black olives.

Serves 6 to 8

NOTE: Greek *toursi* are available in specialty Greek and Middle Eastern grocery stores. Peperoncini, readily available in most grocery stores, can be substituted.

Squid or Octopus Braised in Red Wine

Squid and octopus are a common offering on the menu of any Greek restaurant within a stone's throw from the sea. Squid should be cooked for either a very short time on high heat or a long time at a slow simmer to produce a deliciously tender product. Octopus needs to be tenderized in the effective but time-consuming manner of smashing the beast against a rock for a laborious hour. It is then strung on a clothesline to dry in the Mediterranean breezes. The following dish can be prepared with either squid or octopus and is pleasing either way.

2 pounds medium squid, cleaned (page 279), or octopus (see Note)
2 tablespoons olive oil
2 medium onions, thinly sliced
4 garlic cloves, minced
2 cups dry red wine
4 tomatoes, peeled, seeded, and chopped (page 278), or 2 cups canned Italian plum tomatoes with juice, chopped
4 tablespoons chopped fresh parsley
½ small cinnamon stick
2 whole cloves
1 bay leaf
Pinch of fresh or dried thyme
Pinch of sugar (optional)
Salt and freshly ground pepper
2 tablespoons lemon juice

1 If you are using octopus, see the Note at the end of the recipe. For squid, slice the squid into rings and leave the tentacles whole. Wash well and dry.

2 Heat the olive oil in large skillet and sauté the onions until soft, 10 minutes. Turn the heat up to medium and add the squid and garlic. Saute for 8 to 10 minutes, stirring occasionally. Add the wine, tomatoes, 3 tablespoons parsley, cinnamon stick, cloves, bay leaf, thyme, sugar, salt, and freshly ground pepper. Reduce the heat and simmer very slowly over low heat, uncovered, until the squid is tender and the liquid has thickened, 1 hour.

3 Remove the cinnamon stick, cloves, and bay leaf. Add the lemon juice and stir well.

4 Place on a plate and serve warm or at room temperature, garnished with the remaining 1 tablespoon parsley.

Serves 6

NOTE: If you are using octopus, be sure that it has been cleaned and tenderized when you buy it. Then wash the octopus, place it in a pot with 1 cup water, and simmer over medium heat, covered, for 30 minutes, until the octopus is bright pink. Drain and cool. Cut into large bite-size pieces. Follow the above recipe, but after you simmer it, covered, for 1 hour with the wine, tomatoes, and spices, uncover it and simmer very slowly an additional hour, adding more wine if the mixture dries out.

Saffron Pilaf with Mussels and Squid

Saffron is the threadlike stigma of a violet-colored crocus, contributing both flavor and a distinctive yellow-orange color to various dishes. The combination of rice and saffron are certainly no strangers to Mediterranean cooking. Spanish paella, Milan's famous risotto Milanese, and this Greek specialty of saffron pilaf with mussels and squid are three familiar dishes.

¾ cup dry white wine

2 tablespoons chopped fresh parsley

2 bay leaves

2 pounds mussels, washed,
   beards removed

1 pound squid, cuttlefish, or calamari

¼ cup extra virgin olive oil

1 medium onion, minced

3 garlic cloves, minced

1 carrot, peeled and diced

1 bunch of chopped scallions, white and
   green

3 tomatoes, peeled, seeded, and chopped
   (page 278), or 1 cup canned Italian plum
   tomatoes, peeled and chopped

1 red bell pepper, roasted (page 278) and
   diced

1 large pinch of saffron, revived (page 279)

1½ cups water

1 cup clam juice or fish stock (page 272)

1 cup long-grain white rice

Salt and freshly ground pepper

2 tablespoons lemon juice

1 tablespoon coarsely chopped fresh parsley

6 lemon wedges

1 Heat the white wine, parsley, and bay leaves in a skillet. Add the mussels, cover, and cook until the mussels open. Remove the mussels as soon as they open and reserve mussel juices. Remove the mussels from all but 12 opened shells and reserve for a garnish. Discard the empty shells.

2 Wash the squid. Separate the body from the head by tugging gently. Pull any remaining insides and the transparent quill bone from the body and discard. Remove the tentacles by cutting just below the eyes of the head. Remove the beak by turning the head inside out and pressing the center. Discard the small round beak. Remove the skin from the body by scraping with a knife. Slice the squid into thin rings and cut the tentacles into bite-size pieces. Wash well. Heat the mussel juices over medium-high heat and cook the squid for 30 seconds, uncovered, stirring constantly. Remove the squid and reserve. Reserve the mussel juices.

3 Heat the olive oil in a large skillet. Add the onions, garlic, carrots, and scallions and sauté slowly, uncovered, until the vegetables are soft, 10 minutes. Add the tomatoes, red pepper, and saffron and simmer 20 minutes. Add the water, fish stock, rice, and mussel juices and cook until the rice is tender and the liquid is gone, 20 to 25 minutes.

4 When the rice is done, add the mussels, squid, and lemon juice and toss together. Let sit 2 minutes.

5 To serve, mound the rice, mussels, and squid in the center of a platter. Garnish with the reserved mussels in their shells, parsley, and lemon wedges.

Serves 6

MITHIA SAHANAKI
Stewed Mussels with Feta

Feta is the most widely used cheese in Greece. Also known as farmhouse cheese, this salty white moist cheese is made with either sheep's or goat's milk. Feta, meaning "slice," gets its name from the way it is cut into blocks. This unique and unlikely combination of shellfish and feta can be made with mussels or shrimp. I admit, I never thought I would enjoy this tangy classic dish as much as I do.

¼ cup olive oil
½ medium onion, finely chopped
4 large tomatoes, peeled, seeded, and
    coarsely chopped (page 278) or 2 cups
    canned Italian plum tomatoes, drained
    and coarsely chopped
1 cup dry white wine (Sauvignon Blanc)
¼ teaspoon dried oregano
Pinch of crushed red pepper
1 teaspoon red wine vinegar
2 pounds mussels, washed, beards removed
6 ounces feta cheese, crumbled
Salt and freshly ground pepper
1 tablespoon coarsely chopped fresh parsley

1 Heat the olive oil in a large skillet over low heat and sauté the onions until soft, 10 minutes. Increase the heat to high. Add the tomatoes, wine, oregano, red pepper, and vinegar and stir well. Reduce the heat and simmer, uncovered, until thick, 20 to 30 minutes.

2 Add the mussels and cover the pan. As the mussels open, 8 to 10 minutes, remove them from the pan and keep them warm on a platter. Cook until all the mussels have opened. Remove the mussels from their shells and discard the shells.

3 Return the mussels to the pan. Add the feta and stir well. Simmer slowly 30 seconds. Season with salt and pepper.

4 Pour the mussels and sauce onto a platter and garnish with parsley. Serve immediately.

Serves 6

Swordfish Kebabs with Red Onions, Black Olives, and Bay Leaves

Souvlaki, or skewered meat or fish, trade is brisk in Greece. Vendors set up shop in large delivery trucks equipped with small charcoal grills and makeshift chimney pipes attached to the side for ventilation. A small pit of coals glows with a warm light. Suddenly a tiny flame bursts as the juices drip onto the embers. Waiting just a few more moments for my swordfish souvlaki to cook, I impatiently shift from one foot to another. The ferry blows its horn signaling a few minutes to departure. I exchange a few drachma for my souvlaki and run for the ferry. I jump aboard. As the ferry pulls slowly from the dock, I take my first bite. With herbaceous oils dripping down my chin, I smile. I'm in heaven.

1 lemon

1 1¼-pound swordfish steak, ¾ inch thick

¾ cup olive oil

½ teaspoon dried oregano

Salt and freshly ground pepper

1 small red onion

12 Kalamata olives

12 small firm cherry tomatoes

24 bay leaves

12 small wooden skewers, soaked in water
    30 minutes

½ teaspoon chopped fresh oregano

6 lemon wedges

1 With a vegetable peeler, remove the peel from 1 lemon. Juice the lemon. Cut the swordfish into ¾-inch cubes. Place the swordfish in a bowl with the lemon peel, ¼ cup olive oil, oregano, and pepper and let marinate 2 hours.

2 Cut the onion into quarters and separate into individual pieces. Place the onions, olives, cherry tomatoes, and bay leaves in the same bowl with the swordfish. Toss to coat the vegetables with oil.

3 Start a charcoal grill.

4 Skewer a swordfish cube, bay leaf, cherry tomato, onion piece, olive, bay leaf, swordfish cube, and onion piece in that order on each of the 12 skewers, pushing all ingredients close together. Set the kebabs on a platter until ready to grill. Reserve the marinade.

5 Whisk together 3 tablespoons lemon juice, the remaining ½ cup olive oil, ¼ teaspoon salt, pepper, and fresh oregano. Taste and season with additional lemon juice, salt, and pepper and reserve.

This recipe can be done 6 hours ahead to this point.

6 Grill the swordfish kebabs over a medium-hot fire for 5 to 8 minutes. Turn every few minutes and brush with the marinade occasionally. Remove from the fire and place on a platter.

Whisk the vinaigrette and drizzle on the kebabs. Garnish with the lemon wedges and serve immediately.

Serves 6

NOTE: These skewers can also be cooked under the broiler for 5 to 8 minutes. Turn every few minutes and brush with the marinade occasionally.

TARAMOKEFTETHES

Salt Cod Roe Fritters

The lovely seaside town of Volos is renowned for its fishing fleet. Small fishing boats bob between the calm shallow inlet harboring Volos and the Aegean Sea. In Volos, I met Stavroula Spyrou, a spry little woman who specializes in cooking a bounty of seafood while talking a blue streak. This simple family favorite is one she graciously shared with me.

⅓ cup (3½ ounces) *tarama* or salted cod roe (see Note)
2 tablespoons hot water
Juice of ½ lemon
1 cup fresh bread crumbs
1 cup cold water
2 medium onions, grated
5 scallions, finely chopped
½ cup chopped fresh dill
¼ cup chopped fresh parsley
Freshly ground pepper
Oil for deep-frying
¾ cup all-purpose flour
1 teaspoon baking powder
¼ teaspoon salt
6 lemon wedges
Dill and parsley sprigs

1 Mash together the *tarama*, hot water, and lemon juice. Soak the bread crumbs in the cold water and squeeze well to remove any excess moisture. Discard the water. In a bowl, mix the tarama, bread crumbs, onions, scallions, dill, parsley, and pepper.

2 Pour the oil to the depth of 1½ inches into a deep saucepan. Heat to 375° F.

3 Form the mixture into 1-inch balls. Combine the flour, baking powder, and salt. Dredge the balls in the flour mixture. Deep-fry a few at a time, until golden on all sides, 3 to 4 minutes. Do not overcrowd the pan. Remove from the pan with a slotted spoon and drain on paper towels. Serve immediately, garnished with the lemon wedges and dill and parsley sprigs.

Serves 6

NOTE: Lidia Kitrilakis of Peloponnese, the Oakland, California, wholesaler of upscale Greek food products, informed me that an average-quality *tarama* is available in most supermarkets in major United States cities. Peloponnese is in the process of importing excellent *tarama*, which will be available at grocery and specialty food stores. If *tarama* is unavailable, Lidia substitutes domestic whitefish caviar.

Lentil Soup with Swiss Chard
and Lemon

Carrot, Butternut Squash,
and Coriander Soup

Pilaf Pie with Chicken, Sultanas,
and Sweet Spices

Onion Yogurt

Turkish Lamb and Tomato Pizza

Flaky Cheese-Filled Pastry
with Herbs

Turkish Ravioli with
Lamb, Mint, and Yogurt

Spiced Chick-pea Croquettes with
Tahini Sauce and Herb Salad

Tahini and Cumin Sauce

Warm Chick-peas with Spinach

Zucchini Pancakes wtih
Scallions and Herbs

Slowly Simmered Brown Beans
with Egyptian Aromatics

Syrian Stuffed Bulgur Croquettes
with Pine Nuts and Spices

Yogurt and Mint Sauce

Bulgar and Lamb Tartar
Rolled in Lettuce Leaves

Chicken and Lemon Kebabs with
Three Savory Sauces

Yogurt and Lemon Sauce

Green Herb Sauce

Circassian Chicken

Pickled Turnips

Okra Stewed with Tomatoes,
Pearl Onions, and Cilantro

Artichoke Hearts Stewed with
Fava Beans and Lemon

Sweet Stuffed Red Onions

Turkish White Bean Salad with
Colored Peppers and Herbs

Cucumber and Feta Salad with
Dill and Mint

The Levant
Turkey and the Middle East
Syria, Lebanon, Israel, and Egypt

Syrian-Lebanese Bulgur, Mint,
and Parsley Salad

Syrian Toasted Bread and
Summer Vegetable Salad

Tel Avivian Citrus, Avocado,
and Watercress Salad

Hot Spiced Cheese Puree
"Goreme"

Red-Hot Smoked Tomato Relish

Turkish Spicy Hot Chick-Pea
and Garlic Puree

Smoked Eggplant Cream

Baked Stuffed Eggplant
to Make a Priest Faint

Eggplant Puree with Tahini

Eggplant Sandwiches

Saffron and Rice Stuffed Squid

Turkish Batter-Fried Mussels
with Garlic and Pine Nut Sauce

In the land of carpets and prayer rugs, every street hawker in Istanbul has a brother or uncle more than willing to offer a special price for just about anything you might or might not want. As you stand wavering between doubt and mistrust, he invites you to share his *meze,* or appetizer table, which is never too small and the offerings never too meager for a new friend to partake. If you were to take him up on his offer, you would find that even in the shabbiest environs grandmother's relics are taken from the closet, dusted, and polished for the occasion. The air is heady with the lofty scent of mint, cumin, and coriander, and a low linen-clad table is beautifully set. Kilim-upholstered cushions are gathered around the perimeters. You find yourself sitting cross-legged on a Persian carpet with pile so deep you seem to get lost in the who, where, and why of this magical land. An endless parade of colorful small plates crowds the center of the communal table. This avalanche of appetizers is accompanied by plenty of warm disklike flat bread used as a scoop to gather bites of food. Seasoned with pungent spices, garlic, and wild herbs; moistened with yellow-gold olive oil, sesame seed paste, and butter; and rolled in all kinds of leaves and pastry, the *meze* experience is almost dizzying.

The people of the Eastern Mediterranean—Turkey, Syria, Lebanon, Israel, and Egypt—are incredibly hospitable and their *meze* table is true confirmation. The origin of *meze* can be traced to ancient Persia, where raw-tasting wines were tempered by bites of various foods. Today *meze* appears in every home, café and restaurant before the main course. This is a time of relaxation—a time to take a deep breath and catch up with oneself in a relaxed and aesthetically pleasing environment. It might be on a balcony in Cappadocia amid the stark loveliness of the moonlike formations, at one of the famous fish restaurants moored to the quay under the Galata Bridge in Istanbul, or at a terrace restaurant in the herb-laden hills above Beirut where the cedar trees act as an umbrella against the penetrating sun. This is not a time to sit on the edge of one's chair but instead to sit back and forget one's troubles and the stresses of daily life. *Meze* is meant to revitalize the spirit and soul and satisfy the stomach and heart. *Meze* is true evidence of the Middle Easterner's passion for leisure.

The most important element of *meze* is its versatility, limited only by the availability of ingredients. Give the Syrian or the Lebanese cook a group of raw materials and he can concoct variation upon variation of appetizing and sumptuous dishes with the same ingredients. For example, there are over 100 different preparations for eggplant. *Mezes* can be exact or diminished replicas of main courses. They range from overly simple to refined, sophisticated, and technically complicated. What could be better than the simplicity of perfectly roasted and salted hazelnuts, pistachios, and chick-peas or a wedge of vine-sweetened melon with a thick slice of creamy white cheese? On the other hand, the skillful and dedicated cook will spend the whole day making delicate paper-thin pastry called *yufka* to make borek or savory pies. It is hard to say which is better when there is such a variety and range of starters—salads, various purees, stuffed vegetables and leaves, assorted olives, roasted nuts, egg pies, tiny spiced kebabs, pastries, soups, stewed legumes, deep-fried croquettes, and different vegetable dishes. And just when you think that you have eaten your last bite, another tray of small *meze* plates emerges from the depths of the kitchen, this time with a completely new selection, making this ceremony last for hours.

To accompany *meze*, the drink of choice is a cool glass of *raki* or *arak* (or *zabib* in Egypt), the Middle Eastern version of Greek ouzo or French pernod. Although Islam—still the backbone of Turkey, Syria, Lebanon, and Egypt—forbids drinking alcohol, somehow, for some people, *raki* escapes scrutiny here. A suitable companion to *meze*, *raki* is an anise-flavored colorless distillation of grape mash also known as "lion's milk" because it turns a cloudy white when water is added and it roars with strength. *Raki*

is matured in oak for one to three months, then filtered and bottled in narrow cylindrical bottles. It registers at a high 87 proof. The *meze* table and *raki* table are interchangeable terms for the appetite-whetting prelude, which often surpasses in quality, quantity, and flavor the main course that follows.

The countries of Turkey, Syria, Lebanon, Israel, and Egypt, often referred to as the Levant, are a gentle blend of the Middle East, Greece, the Balkans, Asia, Byzantium, and North Africa. Christians, Moslems, and Jews have intermingled here for centuries, though not always under the most congenial of circumstances. These lands are the intersection of many civilizations fertilized by centuries of continuous interaction.

Turkey, actually straddling Asia and Europe, is the home of the Ottoman Turks who in 1453 changed the name of the Byzantine capital from Constantinople to Istanbul and its religion from Christianity to Islam. Originating in Asia, the Turks swept across the Middle East, Asia Minor, and Greece and dominated these countries for nearly 400 years. The palace sultan's penchant for extravagance and variety was largely responsible for the level of sophistication in the Middle Eastern kitchen. At its ceremonial zenith, 1,400 cooks, mostly from other countries, were employed at Topkapi Palace in Istanbul. The Ottoman rulers were dubbed the "Frenchmen of the East" because of their dexterity in the kitchen.

Turkey is the crossroads between Europe and Asia, where East meets West, and the influences of both of these rich and varied cuisines can be seen as an inspiration to one another in the Middle East. Constantinople (or Istanbul today) is a cosmopolitan city made up of Arabs, Serbs, Jews, Venetians, Circassians, Bulgarians, Genoese, Armenians, Greeks, and Turks who continue to leave an indelible mark on the cuisine. *Tarator*, a sauce of olive oil, garlic, and nuts much like the Greek *skorthalia*, is made here. Shish kebab, meat or fish on skewers, and *doner* kebab, layered slices of marinated lamb roasted on a gigantic spit, are Turkish in origin. Lamb is the livestock of choice in Turkey and the rest of the countries that border the eastern Mediterranean because lamb adapts well to the barren and arid terrain. Pilav, in various forms, is popular, as well as paprika-steeped oil as a favored garnish. Some of the most delicious yogurt in the world is made in Turkey.

The cuisines of Syria and Lebanon are closely linked. A melting pot of Arabic cultures, the food is some of the most diverse and exotic of the Mediterranean. These two countries, bordering the eastern Mediterranean, have always been on the trade route for spices and rice between the East and the West. The food here is redolent of spices and herbs, and the aromas of mint, parsley, allspice, and cinnamon fill the air. Turkey has ruled and overpowered Syria and Lebanon over the years,

and thus the food continues to be Turkish influenced. As in Turkey, briny black olives are eaten at every meal and of course a basket of warm disk-shaped flat bread or pita bread forms the centerpiece. Lemon and garlic are very pronounced. Rice, dried beans, and bulgur, an earthy cracked wheat that is hulled and parboiled, are some of the most important ingredients in the Syrian-Lebanese larder. Bulgur is the main ingredient in making kibbeh and *tabouleh* salad. Yogurt and *labneh*, a yogurt cheese, are also used often, along with tahini or sesame seed paste, and stuffed grape and cabbage leaves. Olive oil is used for flavoring and cooking in nearly every dish.

Israel, the land of historical turmoil, is indeed a Jewish state but it retains an Arabic presence that is visible in its cooking. Falafel, spiced chick-pea croquettes, are a favorite first course and are sold on every corner as street food. There are a variety of refreshing salads with fruits and vegetables like citrus and avocados. Judaism's strong dietary restrictions have influenced the food prepared in Israel where pork or shellfish are rare, as are meals that combine meat and dairy products. Matzo, or unleavened crackers, makes its way into many dishes, especially during Passover.

When the civilization of ancient Greece was still in its infancy, Egypt was already 2,000 years old and the most sophisticated in the West. The Nile River, the longest river in the world, has always been the country's defining feature, providing Egypt with transportation, irrigation for farming, a strong fishing industry, and innumerable droughts and floods. It also divides Egypt from Israel. Although Egypt is part of North Africa geographically, its food relates more closely to the Middle East and Turkey. Peasants constitute three-fifths of the population and they subsist mostly on cereal grains, legumes, seasonal vegetables, and round loaves of bread baked in beehive-shaped clay ovens. *Ful medames,* an ancient staple of both the wealthy and the poor Egyptian table, is made with soaked and slow-cooked brown beans, mashed with salt and garlic, and accompanied by an assortment of highly aromatic condiments, virgin olive oil, hard-boiled eggs, lemon wedges, chopped parsley, and chopped onions. These ingredients transcend their humble beginnings to create a flavorful and satisfying dish. *Ta'amiya,*

the cousin to Israeli falafel and the national dish of Egypt, is made with fava beans instead of chick-peas, coriander, garlic, onions, and red pepper and is said to be the best around the Mediterranean. One can readily find *ta'amiya* served as a first course sandwiched between bread or sold by street vendors. Cumin, coriander, mint, dill, and tahini are favored aromatics.

Cooking techniques are simpler in the Levant than in the western Mediterranean countries of France, Spain, or Italy, but strong and distinctive flavors are not compromised. Over thousands of years, a multifaceted cuisine has developed and flourished. The ingredients of these five countries are not exotic and rare or the cooking techniques difficult to follow. Instead, flavors are combined to produce an unusual and distinctive array of dishes, as sampled here in these *meze* recipes.

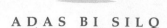

Lentil Soup with Swiss Chard and Lemon

I have had a long love affair with Middle Eastern food. My first day of art school, I was standing in line waiting to register for a painting class and met Pamela Altieri, a Lebanese classmate. A week later, she invited me to her family's home to have dinner. When I walked through the door, I was struck by the Lebanese music that filled the background and the heady scent of garlic, lemons, and roasted lamb. This is how my fixation with Middle Eastern food began twenty-four years ago. To this day I can still remember the flavors of this soup her grandmother served.

1 cup brown lentils
4 cups water
4 cups chicken stock (page 272)
1 large bunch of Swiss chard, stems
   removed, washed
¼ cup olive oil
1 large onion, finely chopped
4 garlic cloves, minced
½ cup chopped fresh cilantro or coriander
   leaves
Salt and freshly ground pepper
⅓ cup lemon juice
Lemon wedges

1 Wash the lentils and place them in a large pan with the water and chicken stock. Bring to a boil, cover, and simmer until tender, 1 hour.

2 Remove the stems from the Swiss chard. Wash well and chop coarsely.

3 Heat the oil in a skillet. Add the onions and sauté until soft, 10 minutes. Add the garlic and continue to sauté, 2 minutes. Add the Swiss chard, cover, and cook for 1 minute. Uncover and continue to cook, uncovered, until the Swiss chard wilts, stirring often, 3 to 4 minutes.

4 Add the onions, garlic, Swiss chard, cilantro, salt, and pepper to the lentils. Stir well and add the lemon juice. Cover and simmer slowly 15 minutes. Taste and season with salt, pepper, and more lemon juice if needed.

5 To serve, heat the soup and ladle into bowls. Garnish with the lemon wedges.

Serves 6

NOTE: This can be prepared 1 day in advance. Adjust the seasonings before serving and serve hot.

Carrot, Butternut Squash, and Coriander Soup

This exotic Syrian soup bursts with a complex blend of sweet and hot flavors. Fresh coriander and a few tablespoons of seasoned yogurt swirled into the soup make a striking garnish.

1½ to 2 pounds butternut squash
3 tablespoons olive oil
1 large onion, chopped
1 teaspoon paprika
1½ teaspoons cumin
¾ teaspoon turmeric
1 teaspoon ground coriander
Salt and freshly ground pepper
4 carrots, trimmed, peeled, and coarsely
    chopped
1 teaspoon sugar
3 cups chicken stock (page 272)
3 cups water
½ cup plain yogurt
2 tablespoons chopped fresh cilantro or
    coriander leaves

1 Preheat the oven to 375°F.

2 Cut the squash in half horizontally. Place on a lightly oiled baking sheet and bake for 45 to 60 minutes, until the squash is soft and can be easily skewered. With a spoon, remove the seeds and discard. Scrape the pulp from the skin. Reserve the pulp and discard the skin.

3 Heat the olive oil in a soup pot. Add the onions and sauté until soft, 10 minutes. Add the paprika, cumin, turmeric, coriander, salt, and pepper and sauté 2 minutes, stirring occasionally. Add the squash, carrots, and sugar and sauté 10 minutes. Add the chicken stock and water. Bring to a boil, reduce, and simmer, uncovered, 30 minutes, until the carrots are soft. Cool for 15 minutes.

4 Puree in a blender in several batches for 3 minutes each time until the soup is very smooth and light. If desired, the soup can be thinned with water or stock. Taste and season with salt and pepper.

5 Season the yogurt with salt and pepper and stir well.

6 To serve, heat the soup. Pour into bowls and garnish with the coriander and yogurt.

Serves 6

NOTE: This can be prepared 2 days ahead of time and heated before serving. Garnish when serving.

Pilaf Pie with Chicken, Sultanas, and Sweet Spices

Asia introduced rice to Persia in the sixth century and later its use spread to the rest of the Middle East and Greece. The Arabs carted the rice to Spain in the eighth century and planted it in Andalusia, making way for the multitude of paella and rice dishes. It was transported to Italy and used there for risotto. Today rice is a staple of the Middle Eastern table for stuffings, dolmas, and pilav. In this recipe, it is made into a phyllo pie of chicken, golden raisins, allspice, cinnamon, and cloves.

1 3- to 3½-pound chicken
2 onions, peeled and quartered
1 carrot, peeled and coarsely chopped
2 bay leaves
4 parsley sprigs
12 black peppercorns
¾ cup long-grain white rice
Salt and freshly ground pepper
½ cup pine nuts, toasted (page 277)
½ cup sultana or golden raisins
10 tablespoons butter, melted
½ pound phyllo dough
2 eggs, lightly beaten
½ teaspoon allspice
Large pinch of cinnamon
Large pinch of ground cloves

1 Place the chicken, onions, carrots, bay leaves, parsley sprigs, peppercorns, and 8 cups water in a large saucepan. Bring to a boil, turn the heat down, and simmer, uncovered, 1 hour. Turn off the heat and allow the chicken to cool in the water. Remove the chicken from the pan and reserve the stock. Remove the skin and discard. Remove the meat from the bones. Cut the chicken meat into bite-size pieces, moisten with ¼ cup chicken stock, and reserve. Place the bones in a saucepan with the stock and reduce by half, 20 to 30 minutes. Strain, skim off the fat, and reserve.

2 Place the rice in a bowl with 1½ teaspoons salt and pour 3½ cups boiling water over the rice. Let stand until the water cools to lukewarm. Drain and wash the rice under cold water. Drain.

3 Place 2½ cups chicken broth, a pinch of salt, the pine nuts, and raisins in a saucepan. Bring to a boil. Add the rice, reduce the heat to low, and cook, covered, until the rice absorbs all the water and is cooked, 15 minutes. Remove from the heat and let stand 10 minutes.

4 Preheat the oven to 350°F.

5 Brush a 9-inch springform pan lightly with butter. Line the pan with 1 sheet of phyllo that will hang over the outside of the pan and brush it lightly with melted butter. Arrange 6 more sheets of phyllo, brushing each layer lightly with butter, turning the pan slightly so that the overhanging phyllo is even on all sides. Toss together the chicken, rice, eggs, and spices. Taste and season with 1 teaspoon salt and pepper. Place the filling in the pan and pat down slightly. Cut 8 circles of phyllo the same size as the circumference of the pan. Place 1 circle on top of the filling, brushing lightly with butter. Place 3 more circles on top, brushing lightly with butter between each layer. Fold in the first layer of phyllo to cover and seal the top. Brush with butter. Repeat to fold in all layers. Place the remaining 4 circles on top, brushing lightly with butter between each layer. Brush the top with butter. Bake for 35 to 40 minutes, until golden. Remove from the oven and let rest 10 minutes.

6 Cut into wedges and serve hot or warm.

Serves 6 to 8

YOGURT SALCASI

Onion Yogurt

Middle Easterners love onions in any guise, cooked, raw, or marinated. Onions are used in soups, kebabs, stews, salads, and as a garnish. In this versatile recipe, the onions' acidity is tempered by marinating them in salt and vinegar. Later they are combined with yogurt for a healthy and irresistible sauce or condiment.

3 cups whole milk yogurt
Salt
2 medium onions, peeled
1 tablespoon plus 1 to 2 teaspoons white
    wine vinegar

1 Combine the yogurt and ½ teaspoon salt. Place the yogurt in a cheesecloth-lined strainer over a bowl and let it drain 4 hours.

2 Cut the onions first in half and then into very thin slices. Sprinkle with 1 teaspoon salt and 1 tablespoon vinegar and let sit 30 minutes, occasionally rubbing the onions and salt together.

3 Wash the onions and pat them dry. Combine the yogurt and onions together and mix well. Season with salt and 1 to 2 teaspoons vinegar.

Makes 2 cups

Turkish Lamb and Tomato Pizza

Lahmaçun means "dough with meat" and is an Arab version of Italian pizza. The crust of the lahmaçun *is very thin and when taken from the oven, the crust should still be soft and pliable. To eat this excellent* meze, *simply roll it up and eat it while still warm.*

Dough

1 package active dry yeast
1 cup lukewarm water (110°F.)
2 tablespoons butter, melted
2 tablespoons olive oil
1 teaspoon salt
3 cups all-purpose flour

Filling

2 tablespoons olive oil
1 large onion, finely chopped
1 pound ground lamb
2 large tomatoes, peeled, seeded, chopped, and drained (page 278), or 1 cup canned Italian plum tomatoes, drained and chopped
2 tablespoons tomato paste
⅓ cup chopped fresh parsley
¼ cup pine nuts, toasted (page 277)
Large pinch of ground cinnamon
Large pinch of ground allspice
Large pinch of ground cloves
¼ teaspoon crushed red pepper
Salt and freshly ground pepper
1 tablespoon lemon juice
4 tablespoons butter, melted

1 Combine the yeast and ¼ cup lukewarm water in a bowl and mix well. Let stand 10 minutes until the yeast is dissolved. Add the remaining lukewarm water, the butter, olive oil, salt, and flour. Mix well. Knead 7 to 10 minutes, until smooth and elastic. Place in an oiled bowl and turn the dough over to coat the top with oil. Cover with plastic wrap and let rise in a warm place (75°F.), until doubled in volume, 1 hour.

2 Heat 2 tablespoons olive oil in a large skillet and sauté the onions until soft, 10 minutes. Add the lamb, tomatoes, tomato paste, parsley, pine nuts, spices, red pepper, ½ teaspoon salt, and ½ teaspoon black pepper and cook slowly, uncovered, 10 minutes. Add the lemon juice and mix well.

3 Preheat the oven to 450°F.

4 Divide the dough into 15 egg-size pieces on a floured board. Flatten with your hands or roll each piece of dough into a circle 5 to 6 inches in diameter by ⅛ inch thick. Place close together on an oiled baking sheet and let rest 10 minutes.

5 Spread 1 heaping tablespoon filling on top of each circle of dough going right up to the edges. Brush the pizzas lightly with melted butter.

6 Bake the pizzas 8 to 10 minutes, until very lightly golden around the edges but still soft enough to roll.

Makes 15 small pizzas to serve 6 to 8

Flaky Cheese-Filled Pastry with Herbs

Börek, boregi, briouats, briks, *empanadas,* pittas, *and* pastillas *are the various names for the small turnovers from the countries surrounding the Mediterranean Sea.* Borek *is a generic term for a whole range of Turkish pastries that come in various shapes, such as triangles, squares, semicircles, and cigar rolls. They are made with puff pastry, leavened dough, short crust, or* yufka, *the Turkish version of phyllo dough, and stuffed with anything from greens and leeks to cheese and herbs.* Börek *are delicious on their own, but they are also an excellent accompaniment to a bowl of hot soup.*

12 ounces feta cheese
4 tablespoons grated Kefalotyri or
    Parmesan cheese
1 egg, lightly beaten
Pinch of nutmeg
2 tablespoons chopped fresh chives
2 tablespoons chopped fresh dill
2 tablespoons chopped fresh mint
2 tablespoons chopped fresh parsley
4 tablespoons pine nuts, toasted (page 277)
Salt and freshly ground pepper
8 ounces phyllo dough
6 tablespoons butter, melted

1 To make the filling, mash together the feta, Kefalotyri, egg, nutmeg, chives, dill, mint, parsley, pine nuts, salt, and pepper. Reserve.

2 With a scissors, cut the phyllo into 3-inch-wide by 18-inch-long strips. Place the strips on top of one another and cover with a slightly dampened towel. Melt the butter in a small saucepan.

3 Preheat the oven to 375°F.

4 Take 1 strip and place it on a work surface. Brush it lightly with butter. Take another strip, place it on top of the first one, and brush it lightly with butter. To make triangular-shaped pastries, place a heaping teaspoon of filling at one end about 1 inch in from the edge. Fold 1 corner over the filling to meet the other side, forming a triangle. Now lift the triangle and continue to fold as you would a flag, until the whole strip is folded into a small triangular parcel, making sure that there are no holes.

5 Brush the top with butter and place on a buttered baking sheet. Repeat with the rest of the phyllo.

6 Bake for 15 to 20 minutes, until golden brown and crisp.

7 Serve hot from the oven, warm, or at room temperature.

Makes 25 to 30 pastries to serve 6

NOTE: These can be prepared 2 weeks in advance and stored in the freezer until they are ready to use. Defrost before baking.

MANTI

Turkish Ravioli with Lamb, Mint, and Yogurt

I told Mieke that I had never tasted manti. *In less than twenty-four hours, the energetic Mieke Schweren organized the women of Goreme, in central Turkey, to prepare a lavish* meze *table at Mieke's authentically restored fifteenth-century restaurant, Konak Turk Evi, nestled in the hills above the small town. The sun shone through the windows and onto a low, round table fit for a sultan, packed with village specialties, including this rustic dish of fabulous* manti.

Dough
1¾ cups all-purpose flour
½ cup whole wheat flour
½ teaspoon salt
1 egg
1 egg yolk
½ cup water

Sauce
1 cup chicken stock (page 272)
4 cups yogurt drained in a cheesecloth-lined
 strainer for 2 hours
4 garlic cloves, mashed in a mortar and
 pestle
3 tablespoons extra virgin olive oil
Salt and freshly ground pepper

Filling
½ pound lean ground lamb

½ small onion, grated
3 tablespoons minced fresh parsley
Salt and freshly ground pepper
1 cup white rice flour
12 fresh mint leaves

1 For the dough, place the flours and salt on a work surface. Make a well in the center. Mix together the egg, egg yolk, and water and pour into the well. With a fork, gradually bring the flour into the well to mix together. When it is almost combined, gather the mixture into a ball and knead for 2 to 3 minutes. It will be a rough dough. Cover with plastic wrap and let rest 30 minutes.

2 Place the chicken stock in a saucepan and reduce by half, 5 minutes.

3 Beat together half the reduced chicken stock, the yogurt, garlic, olive oil, salt, and pepper until light and creamy. Set aside at room temperature.

4 For the filling, combine the lamb, onion, parsley, salt, and pepper. Knead together for 2 minutes and set aside.

5 Divide the dough into 4 pieces. Cover with an inverted bowl so they do not dry out. Lightly flour a surface with the rice flour and with a floured rolling pin, roll the dough until you can almost see the outline of your hand through it. Alternately you can use a pasta machine, rolling the dough to the full width of the machine, 5 inches (see page 134).

6 Cut the dough into 2½-inch squares. Place a scant ½ teaspoon filling in the center of each square. Lightly mist the squares with a spray bottle filled with water. Fold each square in half to form a triangle. Press together to seal the edges. Place the ravioli on a floured baking sheet in a single layer. Repeat with the other 3 pieces of dough.

7 Bring a large pot of salted water to a boil. Drop the ravioli into the water and simmer for 3 to 5 minutes, stirring occasionally, until the dough is cooked. Strain and toss with the remaining reduced chicken stock.

8 Pile the mint leaves on top of one another. Roll up and cut into thin ribbons. Toss the ravioli with the yogurt sauce. Place on a platter and garnish with the mint.

Serves 8

NOTE: This dough can be made up to a week ahead of time and frozen. If you are not rolling the dough for 24 hours, store in the freezer and defrost when needed. If the filled ravioli are not being used for 24 hours, store the ravioli in the freezer and remove when ready to cook. Boil the ravioli while still frozen.

FALAFEL OR TA'AMIYA
Spiced Chick-pea Croquettes with Tahini Sauce and Herb Salad

In the past, dishes based on legumes and cereal grains have been looked upon as foods for the poor. Today they are eaten both in the home of the peasant farmer and the city dweller. Highly seasoned with aromatics like garlic, spices, onions, and herbs, legumes and cereal grains can be taken to new heights. Falafel, the national dish of Israel, and ta'amiya, *its Egyptian equivalent, are perfect examples. I have taken an old classic recipe and modernized it by serving it with an herb salad and onion yogurt or, if you prefer, the more traditional tahini sauce.*

2 cups (¾ pound) dry chick-peas (see Note)
2 tablespoons medium-fine bulgur or
    cracked wheat
¼ cup boiling water
1 medium onion, finely chopped
⅓ cup chopped fresh parsley
½ bunch chopped fresh cilantro or
    coriander leaves
10 garlic cloves, minced
4 teaspoons ground cumin
1 tablespoon ground coriander
1 teaspoon turmeric
¼ to ½ teaspoon cayenne
1 teaspoon baking soda
Salt and freshly ground pepper
Vegetable oil for deep-frying

4 large sprigs mint, washed and dried
½ small bunch of fresh cilantro or coriander
    leaves, washed and spun dry
½ small bunch of fresh parsley leaves,
    washed and spun dry
2 handfuls of salad greens, washed and
    spun dry
2 tablespoons extra virgin olive oil
1 tablespoon lemon juice
2 cups Tahini and Cumin Sauce
    (recipe follows) or Onion Yogurt
    (page 197)

1 Pick over the chick-peas and discard any stones. Cover with water and soak 12 to 15 hours. Drain.

2 Place the bulgur in a bowl and add the boiling water. Stir well and let stand 30 minutes.

3 Place the chick-peas and onions in a food processor or blender and process until they form a thick pasty consistency. Add the bulgur and its liquid, the parsley, cilantro, garlic, spices, baking soda, 1½ teaspoons salt, and ½ teaspoon pepper and pulse a few times to mix well. Remove from the processor or blender and knead for 1 minute. Let rest 30 minutes.

4 Take walnut-size lumps of the paste and roll into balls. Make into slightly flattened balls

1½ inches by ½ inch. Place on a baking sheet and let rest 30 minutes.

These can be prepared up to this point 24 hours in advance.

5 Heat 1 inch of oil to 375°F. Deep-fry the falafel, a few at a time, until they are golden on both sides, 2 to 3 minutes. The falafel can be kept warm in a 350°F. oven until ready to serve.

6 Toss the mint, ground coriander, parsley, greens, olive oil, and lemon juice together. Sea-son with salt and pepper and place on a platter. Place the falafel on the greens and garnish with the Tahini and Cumin Sauce or Onion Yogurt.

Makes 20 to 30 croquettes to serve 6

NOTE: In Israel, these croquettes are made with chick-peas, but in Egypt, where they originated, they are made with dried peeled fava beans. Fava beans can be substituted for the chick-peas. Simply soak them before processing them in the food processor and proceed as above.

SALATA TAHINI
Tahini and Cumin Sauce

Tahini and cumin complement one another well. This simple sauce is versatile and an excellent ac-companiment to grilled skewers of chicken, fish, pork, or beef or just simply served with warm pita bread.

2 garlic cloves, mashed with a mortar and
  pestle
Juice of 1 lemon
⅓ cup tahini
½ teaspoon ground cumin
2 tablespoons chopped fresh parsley
Salt

Place the garlic in a bowl and slowly whisk in half of the lemon juice. Gradually whisk in the tahini and 4 to 5 tablespoons water. Add the cumin and parsley and mix well. Season with salt and additional lemon juice if needed.

Makes 1 cup

Warm Chick-peas with Spinach

Chick-peas and spinach are a favorite around the Mediterranean, having emigrated from Persia to the Middle East and across North Africa to Spain, where they were introduced by the Moors during their 700-year occupation of Spain. I happen to be partial to this tasty Middle Eastern version.

1⅓ cups (½ pound) dry chick-peas
1½ pounds spinach
¼ cup olive oil
1 large onion, minced
1 tomato, peeled, seeded, and chopped
    (page 278), or ½ cup Italian plum
    tomatoes, drained and chopped
3 tablespoons tomato paste
Salt and freshly ground pepper
2 garlic cloves, minced
1 tablespoon minced fresh mint
Crusty bread

1 Pick over the chick-peas and discard any stones. Cover with water and soak overnight. The next day, place in a saucepan with enough water to cover by 2 inches. Simmer, uncovered, until the skins begin to crack and the beans are tender, 1 to 1¼ hours. Drain.

2 Trim the stems from the spinach. Wash the spinach and coarsely chop. Reserve.

3 Heat the oil in a large skillet. Add the onions and sauté, uncovered, until very soft, 15 minutes. Add the tomatoes and tomato paste. Cook slowly 10 minutes. Add the spinach and chick-peas and cook together, uncovered, until the spinach is wilted, 6 to 8 minutes. Add the salt, pepper, garlic, and mint and toss together.

4 To serve, mound the chick-peas and spinach on a platter and serve with crusty bread.

Serves 6

Note: This can be prepared 1 day in advance. To serve, bring to room temperature or heat gently.

Zucchini Pancakes with Scallions and Herbs

We simply didn't want to leave. The Kalkan Han, an exquisitely restored inn located in the little fishing village of Kalkan on the Turkish Mediterranean, had been our base for a few days longer than we had expected. It was our last morning and I had just woken from a dreamy sleep. I threw open the shutters to see the clear sky and azure sea and just as I did, a donkey let out a bray that brought me back to reality: We had to pack and go. We went up to the roof balcony to enjoy one last breakfast and when we said our good-byes, our host Ersin gave me this recipe of his mother's as a memento.

1½ pounds zucchini, coarsely grated
Salt and freshly ground pepper
1 bunch scallions, white and green, minced
6 ounces feta cheese, crumbled
½ cup chopped fresh dill
½ cup chopped fresh mint
¼ cup chopped fresh parsley
2 eggs, lightly beaten
½ cup all-purpose flour
Olive oil for frying

1 Place the zucchini in a colander and sprinkle with ½ teaspoon salt. Let sit 1 hour to drain. Pat dry between paper towels.

2 Place the zucchini in a bowl and add the scallions, feta, dill, mint, parsley, and eggs. Mix well. Sift the flour over the top and stir to mix. Season with salt and pepper.

3 Heat a large skillet containing a thin film of oil. Drop tablespoons of the batter into the hot oil, spreading them to make thin 2-inch pancakes. Cook until golden brown, 2 minutes on each side.

4 Serve hot or at room temperature.

Serves 6

Slowly Simmered Brown Beans with Egyptian Aromatics

This simple Egyptian peasant dish of ful medames *originated in the Middle Ages. After the* hammam, *or public baths, were closed and the heat was turned off for the night, poor food stall–keepers took advantage of the leftover embers to slowly stew their beans in huge pots until dawn. In the morning, the soft and delicate beans were ready. Today, these beans can be simmered on the stove, a bit less romantic, but just as flavorful.*

1½ cups small brown beans (see Note)
¼ cup red or orange lentils
Salt and freshly ground pepper
3 garlic cloves, minced
¼ cup extra virgin olive oil
¼ cup chopped fresh parsley
3 hard-boiled eggs, coarsely chopped
½ bunch of scallions, green and white, chopped
2 tomatoes, cut in ½-inch dice
Crushed red pepper
6 lemon wedges
2 tablespoons ground cumin
2 tablespoons paprika
1 cup Tahini and Cumin Sauce (page 203)
1 loaf rustic country-style bread

1 Pick over the beans and discard any stones. Cover with water and soak overnight. The next day, place the drained beans and the lentils in a saucepan with enough water to cover by 1 inch. Simmer the beans and lentils very slowly, covered, until the beans are very soft but not mushy, 1½ to 2 hours. As they cook, check the beans from time to time to see if they have enough water. Add more boiling water if necessary.

2 In the meantime, mash 1 teaspoon salt and the garlic together with a mortar and pestle or mix together in a small bowl. Reserve.

3 Place each garnish in an individual bowl: olive oil, parsley, hard-boiled eggs, scallions, tomatoes, crushed red pepper, lemon wedges, cumin, paprika, and Tahini and Cumin Sauce.

4 When the beans are done and very little water remains, gently stir in the garlic, salt, and pepper and place in a large serving bowl. Taste for additional seasoning. Place the beans on the table accompanied by the garnishes. Serve with the bread.

Serves 6

NOTE: Egyptian brown beans, or *ful medames*, are a small brown bean grown in Southeast Asia and Egypt, where they are a staple of the diet. They can often be found in Greek and Middle Eastern specialty food stores. If unavailable, substitute any small bean that has a delicate flavor like pinto, navy, or fava beans.

Syrian Stuffed Bulgur Croquettes with Pine Nuts and Spices

Kibbeh making is a labor of love. Made the traditional way, with a mortar and pestle, it takes over an hour to pound the kibbeh mixture to the correct texture and thus the task has always been reserved for the devout cook. The familiar pounding sound of the heavy pestle against the sides of the mortar can still be heard in the villages of Syria and Lebanon throughout the day. With the invention of the food processor, kibbeh making requires much less time and muscle power.

Kibbeh

1½ cups medium-fine bulgur or cracked
    wheat
½ pound lean tender lamb cubes
1 medium onion, minced
Salt and freshly ground pepper

Filling

2 tablespoons olive oil
1 small onion, minced
3 tablespoons pine nuts
Large pinch of ground allspice
Large pinch of ground cinnamon
Small pinch of ground cloves
Small pinch of ground ginger
Small pinch of ground nutmeg
¼ pound lean ground lamb
Corn or peanut oil for deep-frying
1 recipe Yogurt and Mint Sauce (recipe
    follows)

1 For the kibbeh, soak the bulgur in cold water to cover for 20 minutes and drain. Place the bulgur on paper towels for 5 minutes.

2 Place meat, onions, salt, and pepper in a food processor and blend together 1 minute. Add the bulgur in 3 batches and continue to mix until the mixture is like a soft dough, 3 minutes.

3 For the filling, heat the oil in a skillet and sauté the onions until soft, 10 minutes. Add the pine nuts and spices and continue to sauté, uncovered until the pine nuts are golden, 2 minutes. Add the ground lamb and sauté until it is cooked, 4 minutes. Season with salt and pepper.

4 Pour 2 inches of oil into a deep saucepan and heat to 375°F.

5 With wet hands, take an egg-size piece of kibbeh and shape into a ball. With 2 fingers, make a small indentation and fill with filling. Place a small amount of kibbeh on the opening to close. Shape the kibbeh into a small football shape.

6 Deep-fry a few kibbeh at a time until golden brown, about 2 to 3 minutes. Drain on paper towels.

7 Place warm stuffed kibbeh on a platter and serve with Yogurt and Mint Sauce.

Makes 18 kibbeh to serve 6

CACIK

Yogurt and Mint Sauce

Cacik *is made all over the Eastern Mediterranean. In Greece and Turkey, it is made with cucumbers, garlic, dill, and/or mint. The Persians omit the mint and substitute dill and golden or sultana raisins. In Iraq, fresh coriander is the herb of choice. In this Lebanese version of* cacik, *cucumber is omitted altogether and a healthy amount of mint is added at the end.*

2 cups yogurt
Salt
3 garlic cloves, mashed with a mortar and
   pestle
2 tablespoons olive oil
¼ cup chopped fresh mint

1 Combine the yogurt and ¼ teaspoon salt. Place the yogurt in a cheesecloth-lined strainer over a bowl and let it drain 4 hours.

2 Place the drained yogurt in a bowl and discard the water that has drained. Add the garlic, olive oil, and mint and mix well. Let sit 1 hour before using.

Makes 1 ½ cups

CIGKOFTE

Bulgur and Lamb Tartar Rolled in Lettuce Leaves

If you like tartar, Siribom is for you. Siribom, an outstanding restaurant on the Asian side of Istanbul, specializes in meat and features a charcoal brazier or grill, a common cooking apparatus in the Middle East. The idea is to pull a chair up to the counter along side the grill and watch the chef turn the kebabs over the glowing embers as they cook to golden perfection. But don't forget to

order this piquant and irresistible appetizer to enjoy while you wait for your kebab.

⅓ cup (2 ounces) medium-fine bulgur or
   cracked wheat
1 cup very hot water
¼ pound lean tender lamb, preferably from
   a rack
1 small onion

1 very small tomato, peeled, seeded and
   chopped (page 278)
3 garlic cloves, mashed in a mortar and
   pestle
2 tablespoons tomato paste
2 teaspoons paprika
¼ to ½ teaspoon cayenne
½ teaspoon ground cumin
Salt and freshly ground pepper
2 scallions, white and green, minced
¼ teaspoon grated lemon rind
1 tablespoon chopped fresh parsley
1 small head of butter, Bibb or leaf lettuce
½ bunch fresh parsley leaves
½ bunch of fresh cilantro or coriander
   leaves
6 radishes, cut into thin slices
6 lemon wedges

1 Place the bulgur in a bowl. Pour 1 cup
very hot water over it and drain immediately.
Discard the water and let the bulgur stand 10
minutes.

2 Finely chop the meat by hand, with
the fine blade of a meat grinder, or in a food
processor.

3 Knead the meat and bulgur by hand for
10 minutes or in an electric mixer set on slow
speed for 5 to 7 minutes.

4 Grate the onion. Add the onion, tomatoes, garlic, tomato paste, paprika, cayenne,
cumin, salt, and pepper to the meat-bulgur mixture. Knead again for 5 minutes (or 3 minutes
with a mixer). Let stand in the refrigerator for 1
hour.

5 Add the scallions, lemon rind, and parsley and mix well. Taste and season with salt
and pepper. Bring to room temperature. Take
walnut-size pieces of the lamb-bulgur mixture.
With your first 3 fingers and your thumb, press
the mixture to make free-form shapes with finger indentations.

6 Tear the lettuce leaves into very large
pieces. Wash and spin dry the parsley leaves,
cilantro, and lettuce. Place on a platter. Place the
pieces of tartar on top of the herbs and lettuce.
Serve slightly chilled, garnished with radish
slices and lemon wedges. To eat, roll the tartar
in lettuce leaves and drizzle with lemon juice.

Serves 6

NOTE: This can be prepared up to 6 hours in advance and stored in the refrigerator until ready
to serve.

This is also excellent served with Red-Hot
Smoked Tomato Relish (page 223).

Chicken and Lemon Kebabs with Three Savory Sauces

The word kebab, or skewered meat, is one thousand years old. Nomadic tribes used their swords to skewer cuts of meat and cook them over an open flame. Today the technique has changed slightly and bamboo and steel skewers are used instead of swords, but the tradition continues throughout the Middle East, North Africa, and Greece. For this kebab recipe, soak bamboo skewers in lemon juice to give the chicken an extra lemony tang.

4 large chicken breasts, skin and bones
    removed
3 lemons
18 bay leaves
1 teaspoon dried oregano
6 garlic cloves, sliced
¼ cup extra virgin olive oil
Salt and freshly ground pepper
12 8-inch bamboo skewers
1 large onion, peeled, cut into 8 wedges,
    and separated
6 lemon wedges
1 cup each Yogurt and Lemon Sauce, Green
    Herb Sauce (recipes follow), and/or
    Tahini and Cumin Sauce (page 203)

1 Cut the chicken breasts into ¾- to 1-inch cubes. Peel the lemons with a vegetable peeler and reserve the peels. Juice the lemons.

2 Place the chicken in a bowl with the lemon peel, ¼ cup lemon juice, bay leaves, oregano, garlic, olive oil, a pinch of salt, and freshly ground pepper. Toss well to coat and let marinate 1 to 6 hours, the longer the better.

3 Soak the skewers in ½ cup water and the remaining lemon juice for 1 hour.

4 Heat a charcoal grill, ridged grill, or broiler.

5 Using the skewers, alternate the chicken with the lemon peel, bay leaves, and onion pieces.

6 Cook the skewers on a hot grill, ridged grill, or under the broiler for 4 to 6 minutes, turning until golden and cooked through. Sprinkle with salt. Remove from the grill and place on a platter garnished with lemon wedges. Serve with 1, 2, or 3 sauces.

Serves 6

TITBEELET LABAN
Yogurt and Lemon Sauce

The making of yogurt is as old as the Bible. No-madic tribes stored milk in leather pouches. The hot summer sun and desert heat would curdle the milk, making a product even more versatile and healthy. The word yogurt *is Turkish and it means "to thicken." The Turks introduced yogurt to the Islamic Middle East and Europe. Today, yogurt is made with cow's, goat's, or sheep's milk and is an excellent source of protein, potassium, calcium, phosphorus, and vitamin B. Yogurt is used to tenderize meat, to enrich stews, to dress salads, and to make sauces.*

1 garlic clove, mashed in a mortar and
   pestle
1 tablespoon extra virgin olive oil
1 tablespoon olive oil
½ cup yogurt
3 tablespoons lemon juice
Salt and freshly ground pepper

Place all the ingredients in a blender and process until well mixed. Taste and add additional lemon juice, salt, and pepper if needed.

Makes 1 cup

SALKHA
Green Herb Sauce

This is the Middle Eastern version of Italian salsa verde. It is a great accompaniment to grilled chicken kebabs but goes equally well with fish.

½ cup olive oil
¼ cup extra virgin olive oil
Pinch of cayenne
Large pinch of ground allspice
Large pinch of ground cumin
Small pinch of cinnamon
1 tablespoon chopped fresh chives
3 tablespoons chopped fresh cilantro or
   coriander leaves

½ teaspoon chopped fresh oregano
1 scallion, white and green, minced
2 tablespoons chopped fresh parsley
2 garlic cloves, minced
4 tablespoons lemon juice
Salt and freshly ground pepper

Place all the ingredients in a blender and process until well mixed. Taste and add additional lemon juice, salt, and pepper if needed.

Makes 1 cup

Circassian Chicken

Ataturk, the twentieth-century Turkish reformer and modernist whose bronze bust and concrete statue can be seen all over Turkey, loved this chicken and walnut dish. It originated in the area of Circassia in the northern Caucasus. The beautiful Circassian girls introduced this recipe when they were imported to Turkey as part of the sultan's harem. It not only became a favorite of the sultans and Ataturk, it is also well loved by the countries of Lebanon and Syria.

1 3- to 3½-pound chicken
2 onions, peeled and quartered
1 carrot, peeled and coarsely chopped
2 celery ribs, coarsely chopped
2 bay leaves
4 parsley sprigs
12 black peppercorns
6 cups water
2 tablespoons good-quality paprika
¼ teaspoon cayenne
1 tablespoon walnut oil
2 cups walnuts, toasted (page 277)
2 slices coarse white bread, crusts removed
5 garlic cloves, mashed in a mortar and
    pestle
Salt and freshly ground pepper
Walnut halves toasted (page 277)

1 Place the chicken, onions, carrots, celery, bay leaves, parsley sprigs, peppercorns, and water in a large saucepan. Bring to a boil, turn the heat down, and simmer, uncovered, 1 hour.

Turn off the heat and allow the chicken to cool in the water. Remove the chicken from the pan and reserve the stock. Remove the skin and discard. Remove the chicken meat from the bones, tear into long strips, and moisten with ¼ cup chicken stock. Reserve. Place the bones in the saucepan with the stock and reduce by half, 8 to 10 minutes. Strain, skim off the fat, and reserve.

2 Heat 1 tablespoon paprika and a pinch of cayenne in a dry skillet until aromatic, 30 seconds. Add the walnut oil and turn off the heat. Let stand 30 minutes.

3 Place the walnuts in a food processor or blender container and process to obtain a rough paste. Soak the bread in ½ cup chicken stock and add the bread and stock to the food processor. Pulse a few times. Add the remaining 1 tablespoon paprika, the remaining cayenne, garlic, 1 teaspoon salt, and pepper. Process until smooth. Add ¾ to 1 cup chicken stock gradually until a thick creamy consistency is obtained. It should be pourable. Season to taste with salt and pepper.

4 Toss the chicken pieces with half of the walnut sauce. Place on a platter and top with the remaining walnut sauce. Drizzle with the paprika-walnut oil and garnish with the walnut halves. Serve at room temperature.

Serves 6

NOTE: This can be made 1 day in advance. To serve, bring to room temperature.

Pickled Turnips

The Turks, like the Greeks and Italians, adore pickled vegetables. Apicius, the first-millennium Roman cookbook writer, even wrote about the famed pickled cucumbers of Cappudocia in central Turkey. Other pickled vegetables are carrots, squash, peppers, eggplants, artichokes, onions, okra, cauliflower, and turnips. Flavored with garlic and pickling spices, these brilliantly colored magenta pickled turnips are striking and flavorful when served with pickled peppers.

2 pounds small white turnips
2 medium beets, peeled and cut into thin
   slices
6 garlic cloves, thinly sliced
2 tablespoons chopped celery leaves
2 ¼ cups water
1 ½ cups white wine vinegar

2 tablespoons salt
1 teaspoon pickling spices
Small pinch of crushed red pepper

1 Peel the turnips and cut into quarters. Pack the turnips, beets, garlic, and celery leaves into sterilized jars, alternating raw beets between the layers at regular intervals.

2 Bring the water and vinegar to a boil. Add the salt, pickling spices, and crushed red pepper and stir to dissolve the salt. Pour over the vegetables, making sure that the vegetables are completely covered with liquid. If not, add a little extra vinegar. Seal the jars. Leave in a warm place (at least 75°F.) for 7 to 10 days.

Makes 2 quarts

Okra Stewed with Tomatoes, Pearl Onions, and Cilantro

Zeytinyaglilar is the word used in the Middle East to describe a whole array of vegetable dishes that are cooked in olive oil, do not contain meat, and are served at room temperature. In this dish, okra, a tropical plant native to Africa, is the primary ingredient.

2 pounds fresh okra
¾ pound pearl onions
6 tablespoons olive oil
6 garlic cloves, minced
3 tomatoes, peeled, seeded, and chopped (page 278), or 1¼ cups Italian plum tomatoes, drained and chopped
Salt and freshly ground pepper
1 cup water
1 tablespoon coriander seeds, ground in a mortar and pestle
Juice of 1 to 2 lemons
¼ cup chopped fresh cilantro or coriander leaves

1 Wash and dry the okra. Cut off the stems.

2 Bring a pot of water to a boil. Add the onions and simmer 1 minute. Remove the onions and peel.

3 Heat the olive oil in a large skillet over medium heat. Add the onions and sauté, uncovered, until they are golden, 15 minutes, shaking the pan periodically. Reduce the heat, add the okra, and sauté, uncovered, 5 minutes. Add the garlic and sauté 1 minute. Add the tomatoes, salt, pepper, and water. Cover and simmer slowly, 20 minutes. Add the ground coriander seeds and the juice of 1 lemon and simmer 5 to 7 minutes, uncovered, until the liquid reduces by half.

4 Remove from the heat and stir in the chopped cilantro. Taste and season with salt, pepper, and more lemon juice.

5 Serve warm or at room temperature.

Serves 6

NOTE: This can be prepared 24 hours in advance. Bring to room temperature and add the fresh cilantro just before serving.

Artichoke Hearts Stewed with Fava Beans and Lemon

This is a favorite dish of the Copts, a native Christian religious sect from Egypt. This vegetable stew has been served for many years during lent when abstinence from animal products is required. At this time of year, the diet is made exclusively of wheat and vegetables and it takes some culinary ingenuity to produce such a delicious dish as this popular one.

6 large artichokes, trimmed (page 278)
Juice of 3 lemons
3 pounds fava beans (or 1 10-ounce package frozen fava beans)
¼ cup olive oil
3 garlic cloves, minced
3 cups water or vegetable stock (chicken stock optional, page 272)
3 carrots, peeled and cut in ½-inch slices
1½ teaspoons chopped fresh marjoram or oregano
Salt and freshly ground pepper

1 Cut the artichoke hearts into quarters. Place the hearts in a bowl of cold water with the juice of 1 lemon. If using fresh fava beans, remove from pod. Boil the fava beans 30 seconds in boiling water. Remove the skins and discard. If using frozen beans, omit this step.

2 Place the artichoke hearts in a saucepan with the juice of 1 lemon, olive oil, garlic, and water. Bring to a boil and reduce the heat to a simmer. Simmer very slowly, uncovered, 10 minutes. Add the carrots, marjoram, salt, and pepper and continue to simmer, covered, 20 to 30 minutes, until the artichokes are tender. Add the fava beans and simmer slowly, covered, 5 minutes. Remove from the heat and cool in a bowl. Taste and season with salt, pepper, and lemon juice.

3 Place the vegetables and cooking juices on a platter. Serve warm or at room temperature.

Serves 6

NOTE: This can be prepared 1 day in advance. Bring to room temperature or gently warm before serving.

Sweet Stuffed Red Onions

I wonder why the beautiful Lycian Coast of Turkey has not been exploited like the Amalfi Coast of southern Italy. We scoured this part of the Mediterranean for just about every Roman ruin there was to be found. Talking to some Turkish friends, we realized there was one more ruin we couldn't miss, though it was two hours away by hired boat. The weather was perfect and the water was calm so we took a ride. After viewing the spectacular ruins, we motored a few more minutes to the island of Kekova, where we enjoyed a rustic outdoor lunch featuring these sweet stuffed onions.

6 medium red onions, peeled
Salt and freshly ground pepper
1 teaspoon sugar
⅓ pound ground lamb
3 tablespoons pine nuts, toasted (page 277)
⅓ cup long-grain white rice, rinsed
3 tablespoons golden raisins
1 tomato, peeled, seeded, and chopped (page 278), or ½ cup canned Italian plum tomatoes, chopped and drained
1 tablespoon tomato paste
¼ cup chopped fresh parsley
2 tablespoons chopped fresh mint
¼ teaspoon ground allspice
¼ teaspoon ground cinnamon
2 tablespoons olive oil
¾ to 1 cup chicken stock (page 278)
Juice of ½ lemon
Whole parsley leaves, preferably Italian

1 Preheat the oven to 375°F.

2 Cook the onions in boiling salted water for 15 minutes. Remove and cool. Trim ½ inch off the top of the onions. Trim just enough off the bottom of the onion so it will stand upright but will not fall apart. With a small knife, cut the centers out of the onions, leaving a ½-inch-thick shell. Discard the centers. Season the inside with salt, pepper, and sugar.

3 Combine the lamb, pine nuts, rice, raisins, tomatoes, tomato paste, parsley, mint, allspice, cinnamon, oil, ¾ teaspoon salt, and pepper. Mix well. Stuff the onions three-quarters full with this mixture, to allow for the expansion of the rice. Place the onions close together in a baking dish. Put the chicken stock, with a pinch each of allspice and cinnamon, in a saucepan, bring to a boil, and pour ¾ cup stock between the onions. Squeeze the lemon juice on top. Cover with foil and bake until the onions are tender and the filling is cooked, 45 to 50 minutes. Periodically check to see if the pan needs additional stock.

4 Remove from the pan carefully and pour the juices from the pan over the filling. Let cool slightly. Serve warm, garnished with parsley leaves.

Serves 6

NOTE: These can be done 1 day in advance. To serve, warm gently.

Turkish White Bean Salad with Colored Peppers and Herbs

Legumes are a popular and inexpensive source of protein around the Mediterranean. In this recipe, white beans are made into a colorful and substantial salad that is a welcome addition to any meze *table.*

2 cups (¾ pound) dry white, navy, pea,
    Great Northern, or kidney beans
Salt and freshly ground pepper
Juice of 2 lemons
⅓ cup olive oil
⅓ cup extra virgin olive oil
3 garlic cloves, minced
⅓ cup chopped fresh parsley
1 tablespoon chopped fresh mint
1 tablespoon chopped fresh dill
1 teaspoon chopped fresh oregano
1 large red onion, finely chopped
½ red bell pepper, finely diced
½ green bell pepper, finely diced
3 hard-boiled eggs, quartered
⅓ cup Kalamata or Niçoise olives

1 Pick over the white beans and discard any stones. Cover with water and soak overnight. The next day, place the beans in a saucepan with enough water to cover by 2 inches. Simmer, uncovered, until the skins begin to crack and the beans are tender, 40 to 60 minutes. Drain. Place in a bowl, season with salt and pepper, and drizzle with half of the lemon juice. Toss well. Let stand 20 minutes.

2 In a small bowl, whisk together the remaining lemon juice, both olive oils, the garlic, parsley, mint, dill, oregano, salt, and pepper. Toss the beans with the vinaigrette. Add the onions and peppers and toss again. Taste and season with salt, pepper, and additional lemon juice if desired.

3 Place the beans on a platter and garnish with the hard-boiled eggs and olives.

Serves 6 to 8

Cucumber and Feta Salad with Dill and Mint

My Egyptian friend Nabih made this salad for me in a matter of minutes. When it was done and I tasted it, I couldn't believe how flavorful it was for the amount of work. Of course, I asked for the recipe. He was delighted to share it, letting me know that it was one of his family favorites. It happens to be one of my favorites also.

8 ounces feta cheese
¼ cup extra virgin olive oil
2 to 3 tablespoons fresh lemon juice
1 tablespoon water
Salt and freshly ground pepper
1 large cucumber, peeled, seeded, and cut in ½-inch dice
1 small red onion, cut in ¼-inch dice
1 tablespoon chopped fresh mint
1 tablespoon chopped fresh parsley
1 tablespoon chopped fresh dill
Dill and mint sprigs
3 lemon wedges
Pita bread

1 Crumble the feta into a bowl and mash together with the olive oil, lemon juice, water, salt, and pepper. Add the cucumbers, onions, mint, parsley, and dill.

2 Place on a serving plate and garnish with sprigs of dill and mint and lemon wedges. Serve with warm pita bread.

Serves 6

NOTE: This can be prepared 1 day ahead of time. Bring to room temperature before serving.

Syrian-Lebanese Bulgur, Mint, and Parsley Salad

Bulgur is usually thought to be the backbone of Middle Eastern winter food and yet tabouleh *celebrates the arrival of summer.* Tabouleh, *the national dish of Syria and Lebanon, is made with soaked bulgur, which imparts an earthy quality, an equal amount of parsley, lots of refreshing herbs, sweet ripe tomatoes, and crunchy cucumbers. The outcome is a healthy and substantial summer salad.* Tabouleh *is served with crisp romaine lettuce leaves or triangles of pita bread used as a scoop instead of the usual fork.*

1 cup medium-fine bulgur or cracked wheat
⅔ cup extra virgin olive oil
4 to 5 garlic cloves, minced
¾ to 1 cup lemon juice
1 large bunch of scallions, white and green,
    cut in ¼-inch dice
2 large bunches of parsley chopped
¼ cup chopped fresh mint
5 large tomatoes, cut in ¼-inch dice
2 medium cucumbers, peeled, seeded, and
    cut in ¼-inch dice
Salt and freshly ground pepper
Romaine lettuce leaves or pita bread

1 Place the bulgur in the bottom of a large salad bowl. Mix together the olive oil, garlic, and lemon juice and drizzle over the bulgur. Layer the next 5 ingredients in the order listed. Season the top layer of cucumbers well with salt and pepper and cover with plastic wrap. Refrigerate at least 24 hours and up to 48 hours.

2 Bring to room temperature. Season with 1 teaspoon salt. Toss together and serve with romaine lettuce leaves or warm pita bread.

Serves 6 to 8

Syrian Toasted Bread and Summer Vegetable Salad

*F*attoush, *the cousin of Italian* panzanella, *is a Syrian peasant bread salad made with leftover pita and fresh summer vegetables like cucumbers, tomatoes, scallions, and fragrant herbs.*

2 small cucumbers, peeled, seeded, and cut
    in large dice
Salt and freshly ground pepper
Juice of 2 lemons
2 large garlic cloves, mashed in a mortar
    and pestle
½ cup olive oil
3 medium tomatoes, coarsely chopped
½ bunch scallions, green and white, thinly
    sliced
⅓ cup chopped fresh parsley
¼ cup chopped fresh mint
1 tablespoon chopped fresh cilantro or
    coriander leaves
Pinch of chopped fresh thyme (optional)
2 large or 4 small loaves pita bread, toasted
    or stale, torn into rough 1-inch pieces

Black olives (optional)

1 Salt the cucumbers and let drain 30 minutes. Rinse under cold water and dry well.

2 Whisk together half of the lemon juice, the garlic, and olive oil. Season with ½ teaspoon salt and pepper. Combine the vinaigrette with the cucumbers, tomatoes, scallions, parsley, mint, cilantro and thyme. Season with salt and pepper and mix well.

3 Place toasted or dry bread in a salad bowl. Sprinkle with the remaining half of the lemon juice and let sit 5 minutes. Add the vegetables and vinaigrette to the bread and mix well. Taste and season as needed with salt, pepper, and lemon juice. Garnish with black olives and serve immediately.

Serves 6

Tel Avivian Citrus, Avocado, and Watercress Salad

Make sure that the citrus fruits you choose are juicy and sweet. This cool and refreshing Israeli salad is best when served on a hot summer day.

2 large avocados
3 tablespoons lemon juice
1 tablespoon white wine vinegar
6 tablespoons extra virgin olive oil
¼ teaspoon lemon zest
Salt and freshly ground pepper
3 oranges
1 small grapefruit
1 very small young bunch of watercress or
    arugula, washed and spun dry
10 large mint leaves

1 Cut the avocados in half. With 2 hands, twist to divide into 2 pieces. Remove the pit and discard. With a large spoon, scoop out the flesh from both halves. Cut into thin slices. Repeat with the other avocado.

2 Make a vinaigrette by whisking together the lemon juice, vinegar, olive oil, lemon zest, salt, and pepper. Drizzle the avocado slices with one-third of the vinaigrette.

3 With a knife, cut the top and bottom off of the oranges and grapefruit. Do not peel. Cut off the skin with a knife, leaving no white pith remaining. Cut the oranges into ¼-inch slices. Cut the grapefruit into quarters and then into ¼-inch slices.

4 Remove any tough stems from the watercress or arugula. Place in a bowl and season lightly with salt and pepper. Toss with 1 tablespoon vinaigrette.

5 Randomly place the avocados, orange slices and grapefruit slices on a platter, alternating the colors. Drizzle the vinaigrette over the top. Garnish with watercress or arugula. Pile the mint leaves on top of one another, roll up, and cut into very thin ribbons. Sprinkle on the salad and serve.

Serves 6

Hot Spiced Cheese Puree "Goreme"

Cappudocia, in central Turkey, is a fairy-tale landscape formed by the wind, which over thousands of years has carved away at the soft rock to create supernatural amorphous formations. The softness of the rock has also enabled man to carve his own cave dwellings from its soft stone mass. This is where I met Aris, who hospitably invited me inside her humble cave dwelling to show me a true Cappudocian kitchen and way of life. She showed me how she grinds wheat, stores beans and apples for the winter, and makes thick creamy yellow yogurt. She offered me a bite of her special spicy cheese puree and when my eyes rolled back in my head, she gave me her recipe.

1¼ cups yogurt
Salt and freshly ground pepper
10 ounces feta cheese
2 garlic cloves, mashed in a mortar and
    pestle
½ to 1 teaspoon cayenne
1 teaspoon paprika
1 tablespoon plus 1 teaspoon extra virgin
    olive oil
Black olives
Pita bread

1 Combine the yogurt and ¼ teaspoon salt and mix well. Place the yogurt in a cheesecloth-lined strainer over a bowl and let drain 2 hours.

2 Place the yogurt and feta in a bowl. With a fork, mash them together to obtain a smooth paste. Add the garlic, cayenne, paprika, 1 tablespoon olive oil, and black pepper and mix well. Alternatively, this can be pureed in a food processor or blender.

3 Spread the puree on a serving plate. Drizzle with the remaining 1 teaspoon olive oil and garnish with the olives. Serve with warm pita bread.

Serves 6

NOTE: This can be prepared 24 hours in advance and refrigerated. Bring to room temperature before serving.

Red-Hot Smoked Tomato Relish

This tomato condiment can be found on many meze tables in Turkey. The first time I tasted it, I loved it. Luckily, I began to see it again and again and finally managed to get the recipe. This refreshing yet spicy tomato relish is best when served with warm crusty bread, pita, grilled skewers of lamb or chicken, or just by the spoonful.

1 pound ripe tomatoes
1 long green sweet pepper or ½ green bell
   pepper
½ cucumber (2-inch piece), peeled and
   seeded
½ medium onion, grated and drained
2 garlic cloves, mashed with a mortar and
   pestle
½ teaspoon chopped fresh mint (optional)
Large pinch of chopped fresh thyme
   (optional)
½ teaspoon paprika
¼ teaspoon cayenne
Large pinch of crushed red pepper
1 tablespoon olive oil
2 teaspoons red wine vinegar
Salt and freshly ground pepper
Whole parsley leaves

1 Place the tomatoes and green pepper in a hot dry black iron skillet for 10 minutes over medium-high heat, turning occasionally, until lightly blackened and blistered. (Alternatively, the tomatoes and peppers can be cooked on a charcoal grill. Cut the tomatoes in half and with the cut sides up, grill the tomatoes 20 minutes and grill the pepper until black on all sides, 10 minutes.) Place the pepper in a plastic bag and steam 10 minutes. Peel, seed, and chop the tomatoes. Place them in a sieve and let drain 30 minutes. Seed and chop the pepper. Combine the tomatoes and the pepper.

2 Coarsely grate the cucumber and place in a sieve. Salt lightly and let sit 10 minutes. Combine the tomatoes, pepper, cucumbers, onions, garlic, mint, thyme, paprika, cayenne, crushed red pepper, olive oil, vinegar, salt, and pepper. Place on a work surface and chop until you get a fine paste. Alternatively, this can be done in a food processor by pulsing to get the desired texture. Taste and season with salt, pepper, and vinegar.

3 Place on a plate and garnish with parsley leaves.

Makes 1 ¹/₂ cups to serve 6

NOTE: This can be prepared 1 day in advance. Bring to room temperature before serving.

Turkish Spicy Hot Chick-pea and Garlic Puree

Toasted ground sesame seeds mixed with oil is called tahini, one of the most important ingredients of the Lebanese and Syrian kitchen. Tahini is always used to make the very popular hummus, *a chick-pea and garlic puree. In the following recipe, cayenne and paprika are added to give the dish a real kick. Cayenne and paprika are optional and if you eliminate them, you will have the classic Middle Eastern* hummus.

1⅓ cup dry chick-peas (8 ounces) or
    1 14-ounce can cooked chick-peas
Juice of 3 lemons
½ cup tahini or sesame seed paste
2 tablespoons water
4 tablespoons olive oil
6 garlic cloves, mashed in a mortar and
    pestle
Salt
¾ teaspoon cayenne
1½ teaspoons sweet paprika
¼ teaspoon cumin
1 teaspoon chopped fresh parsley
6 lemon wedges
5 Kalamata or Niçoise olives
Pita bread

1 Pick over the chick-peas and discard any stones. Cover with water and soak overnight. The next day, drain and place in a saucepan with enough water to cover by 2 inches. Simmer, uncovered, until the skins begin to crack and the chick-peas are very tender, 1 to 1¼ hours. Drain the chick-peas and reserve a few whole ones for a garnish. Reserve the cooking liquid.

2 In a food processor or blender, puree the chick-peas, the juice of 2 lemons, tahini, water, 3 tablespoons olive oil, garlic, ¾ teaspoon salt, cayenne, 1½ teaspoons paprika, and cumin until a soft creamy paste is obtained. Taste and season with additional salt and lemon juice if needed.

3 Place on a plate and drizzle with the remaining 1 tablespoon olive oil. Sprinkle with parsley and a pinch of paprika. Garnish with the lemon wedges, black olives, and reserved whole chick-peas. Serve with warm pita bread.

Serves 6

NOTE: The cayenne is optional. If you do not want the *hummus* to be spicy hot, omit the cayenne. This can be made 2 days ahead. Bring to room temperature before serving.

IZGARA PATLICAN

Smoked Eggplant Cream

Eggplant is one of the most common Mediterranean vegetables, and eggplant dips are equally ubiquitous in the region. This smoked version has also been nicknamed "poor man's caviar." In Middle Eastern villages, it is obvious when someone is making a batch of this fragrant eggplant cream because there is a familiar smoky smell of eggplant roasting on an open fire.

2 large eggplants
4 tablespoons lemon juice
Salt and freshly ground pepper
4 garlic cloves, mashed in a mortar and
    pestle
Large pinch of cumin
½ teaspoon paprika
Pinch of crushed red pepper
¼ cup extra virgin olive oil
Kalamata or Niçoise olives
Lemon wedges
1 teaspoon chopped fresh parsley
Pita or crusty bread

1 There are 3 different methods for cooking the eggplants, depending upon the amount of smokiness desired. If strong smokiness is desired, heat a charcoal grill. Roast the eggplants over a very slow and steady fire, turning occasionally, until cooked on all sides, the skin is black, and the eggplants are soft, about 30 to 40 minutes. If medium smokiness is desired, place the eggplants directly on the high flame of a gas jet, turning constantly, until the skin is black

and wrinkled, 5 to 10 minutes. Place the eggplants on a baking sheet and bake in a 375°F. oven for 15 to 20 minutes, until very soft. If no smokiness is desired, bake the eggplants on a baking sheet in a 375°F. oven for 30 to 40 minutes, until very soft.

2 Cool the eggplants slightly. Cut them in half, scoop out the pulp, chop coarsely. Discard the skin. Drizzle the eggplant with 3 tablespoons lemon juice and sprinkle with salt. Let drain in a colander 30 minutes.

3 In a large bowl, mix together the garlic, cumin, paprika, red pepper, and black pepper. With the back of a spoon, press the eggplant gently to extract any additional liquid. Add the eggplant to the spices and mash all the ingredients together until it becomes a puree.

4 Heat the olive oil in a large skillet. Add the eggplant puree and sauté over low heat for 10 minutes, stirring occasionally. Cool to room temperature. Taste and season with salt, pepper, and the remaining 1 tablespoon lemon juice.

5 Place on a plate and garnish with the black olives, lemon wedges, and chopped parsley. Serve with pita or crusty bread.

Serves 6

NOTE: This can be served either warm or at room temperature. It can be made up to 48 hours ahead and stored in the refrigerator until ready to use. Bring to room temperature before serving.

Baked Stuffed Eggplant to Make a Priest Faint

The title of this recipe is an intriguing one with two possible derivations. In Turkey, there was a priest who was reputed to be both a real glutton and a true gourmet. One theory has it that the priest's cook was distraught about trying to impress his employer. With market-fresh jet-black eggplant, he did his best. The priest loved it and ate until he "swooned away," or fainted. The second theory is that due to the priest's tight-fistedness, he was shocked at how much olive oil was used and he fainted at the expense of the finished product.

6 small thin Japanese eggplants
Salt and freshly ground pepper
6 cups water
7 tablespoons extra virgin olive oil
3 medium onions, thinly sliced
4 garlic cloves, minced
3 tomatoes, peeled, seeded, and chopped
     with juice (page 278) or 1 ¼ cups canned
     Italian plum tomatoes, chopped with
     juice
⅓ cup chopped fresh parsley
½ teaspoon dried oregano
¼ cup currants
¼ teaspoon ground allspice
¼ teaspoon cinnamon
1 teaspoon honey
2 tablespoons lemon juice
1 tomato, thinly sliced

1 Remove the stems from the eggplants and cut the eggplants in half lengthwise. Make 4 evenly spaced incisions lengthwise in each eggplant. Dissolve 4 tablespoons salt in 6 cups water and soak the eggplant for 30 minutes.

2 Heat 2 tablespoons olive oil in a large skillet and sauté the onions over low heat, uncovered, until very soft, 20 minutes, stirring occasionally. Add the garlic and continue to cook 5 minutes. Add the tomatoes, ¼ cup parsley, and oregano and simmer until almost dry, 5 to 10 minutes. Add the currants, allspice, cinnamon, salt, and pepper. Set aside.

3 Preheat the oven to 350°F.

4 Rinse the eggplant well. Squeeze gently and dry well with paper towels. Heat 3 tablespoons oil in a skillet over medium-low heat, uncovered, and sauté the eggplant on all sides, until the cut side is golden brown and the eggplant is cooked through, 8 to 12 minutes. With a spoon, scoop the pulp from the inside of the shell, leaving the skin and ¼ inch of the lining intact. Finely chop the pulp and add to the tomatoes and onions. Mix well. Taste and season with salt and pepper.

5 Place the eggplant shells in a baking dish just large enough to accommodate them. Fill with the tomato and onion stuffing. Pour ¼ cup water into the bottom of the dish. Combine the honey, lemon juice, the remaining 2 tablespoons olive oil, salt, and pepper and drizzle evenly over each eggplant. Top each stuffed eggplant with a tomato slice. Cover and bake the eggplant for 15 minutes. Uncover and bake an additional 10 minutes, adding water as necessary. Cool to room temperature. Reserve the pan juices.

6 To serve, place the eggplant on a platter, drizzle with the pan juices, and garnish with the remaining parsley.

S e r v e s 6

NOTE: This can be done completely 24 hours ahead of time. Store in the refrigerator and bring to room temperature before serving.

BABA GHANNOUJ

Eggplant Puree with Tahini

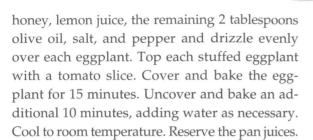

This rich creamy puree is a combination of smoky eggplant and tahini spiked with fresh squeezed lemon juice and plenty of crushed garlic. In Turkey, this delicious dish is called mutabbul, *but more commonly throughout the world it is called* baba ghannouj, *its Lebanese name.*

2 large eggplants, smoked 10 to 15 minutes (page 277)
4 to 5 garlic cloves, mashed in a mortar and pestle
Salt
Juice of 3 lemons
½ cup tahini or sesame seed paste
Large pinch of cumin
2 tablespoons extra virgin olive oil
1 tablespoon chopped fresh parsley
¼ cup Kalamata or Niçoise
Pita or crusty bread

1 Preheat the oven to 375°F.

2 Place the eggplants on a baking sheet and bake in the oven 15 to 20 minutes, until very soft. The eggplants can also be roasted in the oven for the entire time until very soft, 35 to 45 minutes. Cool slightly, peel the skin, and discard it.

3 Place the pulp in a bowl and mash to make a paste. This can also be done in a food processor by pulsing until the desired consistency is obtained. Add the garlic and salt and mix well. Add the lemon juice, tahini, and cumin and mix well. Taste and season with salt, lemon juice, or tahini if desired.

4 Place the puree on a plate. Drizzle the olive oil on top, and sprinkle with the parsley. Place the olives around the sides. Serve at room temperature with warm pita or bread.

S e r v e s 6

NOTE: This can be prepared 2 days in advance and stored in the refrigerator. Bring to room temperature before serving.

Eggplant Sandwiches

The Turks boast more than 150 different preparations of eggplant. This one is truly unique. Traditionally, the eggplant is usually fried in a skillet in olive oil. I find that with this technique, the eggplant absorbs too much oil. Instead I have opted for brushing the eggplant slices with olive oil and baking them in the oven. Whether the eggplant is fried or baked, I am certain you will enjoy the flavors.

3 medium eggplants (3 pounds total)
Salt and freshly ground pepper
3 tablespoons olive oil
4 ounces cream cheese
4 ounces fresh milk mozzarella, grated
2 tablespoons chopped fresh dill
2 tablespoons chopped fresh parsley
3 tablespoons chopped fresh chives
3 eggs, lightly beaten
2 cups fine dry bread crumbs
Vegetable or peanut oil for deep-frying
6 lemon wedges
2 tablespoons chopped fresh parsley

1 Preheat the oven to 375° F.

2 Cut the stems off the eggplants. With a vegetable peeler or sharp knife, peel the skin in ½-inch-wide strips vertically so you get striped eggplants. Discard the peel. Slice the eggplants horizontally into ½-inch slices. Place in a colander and salt each slice. Let stand 30 minutes. Rinse well and pat dry with paper towels.

3 Brush a baking sheet liberally with olive oil. Place the eggplant slices in a single layer on the baking sheet. Brush the tops of the eggplant with olive oil and bake for 20 to 30 minutes, turning occasionally, until light golden on both sides. Cool.

4 Mash together the cream cheese, mozzarella, dill, parsley, chives, 1 tablespoon of the beaten eggs, salt, and pepper. Spread the cheese mixture on half of the eggplant slices. Find another eggplant slice about the same size and sandwich them together.

5 Heat ¼ inch oil to 375°F. in a large skillet.

6 Season the bread crumbs with salt and pepper. Dip the eggplant sandwiches in the remaining beaten eggs and then lightly in the bread crumbs.

These can be prepared 1 day ahead to this point.

7 Fry the sandwiches for 2 to 3 minutes, until golden. Drain on paper towels. Serve immediately, garnished with the lemon wedges and parsley.

Makes 18 to 20 sandwiches to serve 6

NOTE: As you make these, they can be kept warm in a 375° F. oven until ready to serve. Do not hold them for more than 15 minutes.

Saffron and Rice Stuffed Squid

There is a whole string of fish restaurants under the Galata Bridge in Istanbul where hawkers try to lure you in with promises of freshness and abundance. However, they mention nothing of price. Luckily I was warned about the prices of the various fish dishes—some can be astronomical. At one restaurant I tasted this stuffed squid dish. It was not only very tasty but curiously one of the more reasonable choices.

1½ pounds squid, cleaned (page 279)
½ cup olive oil
1 large onion, finely chopped
¼ cup short-grain white rice
¼ cup pine nuts, toasted (page 277)
3 tablespoons chopped fresh parsley
Salt and freshly ground pepper
2 pinches of saffron threads, revived
   (page 279)
3 medium onions, thinly sliced
2 tablespoons boiling water
1 cup fish stock (page 272) or bottled clam
   juice
2 to 3 tablespoons lemon juice
6 lemon wedges
Whole parsley leaves, preferably Italian

1 Leave the squid bodies whole. Chop the tentacles and reserve them separately.

2 Heat ¼ cup olive oil in a skillet and sauté the onion, uncovered, until soft, 10 minutes. Add the tentacles, rice, pine nuts, parsley, salt, pepper, and a pinch of saffron. Stuff the bodies one-half to two-thirds full and close the opening by weaving a toothpick through it, making sure that you have left some space for the rice to expand.

3 Heat the remaining ¼ cup olive oil in a large skillet. Sauté the squid, uncovered, for 5 minutes, stirring occasionally. Remove the squid from the pan and reserve.

4 Add the onions to the pan and sauté, uncovered, 10 minutes. As the onions begin to soften, cover and continue to sauté slowly, until the onions are golden and very soft, 15 to 20 minutes.

5 When the onions are golden, add the remaining saffron and its liquid and a pinch of salt and pepper. Place the squid on top of the onions and add 1 cup fish stock. Bring to a boil, reduce the heat to a simmer, cover, and simmer 20 minutes. Uncover and reduce the juices by one-third, 2 to 3 minutes. Remove from the heat and add the lemon juice to the onions. Remove the toothpicks from the squid. Place the onions on a platter and top with the squid. Garnish with the lemon wedges and parsley.

Serves 6

NOTE: This can be made 1 day in advance. Bring to room temperature or warm gently before serving.

Turkish Batter-Fried Mussels with Garlic and Pine Nut Sauce

Mitko lumbered across the street with his hand outstretched, a hand that is bigger than life. We shook hands for the first time and were instantly friends. As we trudged through the chaotic markets and streets of the European side of Istanbul, I began to see the city through his eyes, the eyes of a native. Mitko loves this city like no other. Walking across the Bosporus, the strait of water that divides the old and new Istanbul, Europe, and Asia, he told me his story. Mitko Stoyanof is a third-generation baker and has the largest bakery on the Asian side of Istanbul. We walked and talked all the while, stopping for bites to eat along the way—roasted chestnuts and sweet plump dried apricots. As we got closer to his bakery, we happened upon a stall surrounded by people. What was the attraction? "Haven't you had any deep-fried mussels yet?" he said. We made it to the front of the line in no time. In front of me was a sizzling pool of golden-fried mussels. He forked over a few lira for a couple of skewers and when I took a bite, I immediately understood the fuss.

1½ cups all-purpose flour
Salt and freshly ground pepper
1 egg, separated
2 tablespoons olive oil
¾ cup beer
1 slice coarse white bread, crusts removed
½ cup pine nuts, toasted (page 277)
2 garlic cloves, mashed with a mortar and
  pestle
¼ cup extra virgin olive oil
2 to 4 tablespoons lemon juice
40 mussels
Vegetable oil for deep-frying
Lemon wedges
Parsley sprigs

1 Sift 1 cup flour and ½ teaspoon salt together. Make a well in the center and add the beaten egg yolk, olive oil, and beer. With a whisk, mix well but not enough to make it stringy. Let the batter rest for 1 hour at room temperature.

2 Soak the bread in ¼ cup water for 1 minute. Squeeze dry and discard the water. Place the pine nuts in a blender or food processor and pulverize until finely ground. Add the bread and garlic and pulse a few times to make a paste. In a small bowl, combine the olive oil, 2 tablespoons lemon juice, and ¼ teaspoon salt. With the machine running, add this mixture in a steady stream. Taste and season with salt, pepper, and additional lemon juice, if desired. Thin with water until it is thick and pourable. Let the sauce sit 30 minutes before serving. It will thicken as it sits, so thin with water if needed.

3 Scrub the mussels well. Place in a bowl of hot water and as the mussels just begin to open, use a knife to open them completely. Remove the mussels from their shells and discard the beards. Reserve the mussels in the refrigerator.

4 Heat the vegetable oil in a deep saucepan to 375°F.

5 Beat the egg white stiffly and fold into the batter. Toss the mussels in the remaining ½ cup flour to coat and tap off any excess. Dip the mussels in the batter. Deep-fry a few at a time until golden, 1 to 2 minutes, turning them to brown evenly. Remove with a slotted spoon and drain on paper towels.

6 Place the mussels on a serving platter. Garnish with the lemon wedges and parsley sprigs and serve immediately with the garlic and pine nut sauce.

Serves 6

NOTE: The sauce should be served at room temperature. It will keep in the refrigerator for 1 week.

Lamb Soup with Lentils, Harissa,
and Cilantro

Couscous Soup with
Chicken, Tomatoes, and Mint

Harissa, a Spicy Hot Condiment

Chick-Pea Soup with
Squash and Cilantro

Moroccan Minestrone

Moroccan Baked Phyllo Rolls
with Shrimp and Scallops

Tunisian Sweet and
Hot Pepper Tomato Relish

Baked Phyllo Triangles with
Lamb and Moroccan Spices

Tunisian Potato, Scallion, and
Fried Egg Turnovers

Flaky Moroccan Chicken Pie

Preserved Lemons

Moroccan Pizza Bread
with Herb Salad

Ras El Hanout

Couscous with Chick-peas
and Caramelized Onions

Harissa Sauce

Tunisian Omelette with Hot
Sausage, Peppers, and Eggplant

Maghreb Lamb Sausage

Lamb Kefta Stewed with
Hot Tomatoes

Warm Spiced Lentils

Fava Bean Puree

Algerian Eggplant Jam

North Africa
Morocco, Algeria, and Tunisia

Warm Olives with
Preserved Lemons

Beet, Orange, and Walnut Salad

Couscous Salad with Tomatoes
and Hot Green Peppers

Tomato, Onion, and
Preserved Lemon Salad

Fennel Salad with
Preserved Lemons and Garlic

Moroccan Carrot, Radish,
and Orange Salad

Orange, Black Olive, and
Cilantro Salad

Mussels Steamed with
Cumin and Tomatoes

Braised Clams with Preserved
Lemons and Cilantro

Grilled Tuna Skewers
with Moroccan Spices

idden in the old *medina*, or center of town, are the residential homes of Marrakesh. The Moroccans are notoriously hospitable and a dinner invitation is coveted. A mysterious man wearing a djellabah, a long robe, and carrying a gas lantern guides you down the long dark alley leading to the home of your host tucked within the labyrinth of the *medina*. The door opens, exotic music fills your ear, and warm light pours onto the alley. Your host welcomes you, and as you step inside, the glow of candles is everywhere. The central courtyard opens to the clear night sky and gentle night breezes stir the palms that grow toward the moon and stars. As the music breaks, a fountain, the crowning centerpiece of the courtyard, serenades you with flowing water. Bouquets of roses and musky incense act as a fragrant backdrop. The walls, floors, and ceilings are ablaze with colored mosaic tiles of every imaginable color and pastel-painted ironwork frames the windows. Arches open onto adjoining rooms filled with bolsters, ottomans, cushions, and hassocks of brightly woven tapestries that frame the round highly burnished brass trays placed on low carved wooden tripods. It is here that you will gather for the next couple of hours to eat small plates of first courses, several at a time, followed by several

more. Some will be fragrant, some spicy, some creamy and smooth, some crunchy and tart. And it is here that you will witness the true glories of Moroccan hospitality.

Just a few miles across the Strait of Gibraltar from Spain and less than 100 miles across the Mediterranean from Sicily lie the magical and exotic countries of Morocco, Algeria, and Tunisia, virtually a world of their own tucked into the northwestern corner of Africa. Scrub-covered red-ocher and sandgray ridges rise out of the Mediterranean, sculpted by generations of goats, lambs, and wind erosion. This land is bathed in sunlight, from the coast to the mountains and the Sahara desert beyond. Morocco, Algeria, and Tunisia, often referred to as the Maghreb, share many regional dishes, common ingredients, and a shared history of invaders who imparted their culinary heritage to this mystical desert oasis.

The Maghreb has seen wave after wave of invasion for a few thousand years. Phoenician traders, en route to Spain in 800 B.C., set up trading posts on the coast of Tunisia, at the mouth of the upper basin of the Mediterranean. One of these posts was the city of Carthage, which the Phoenicians lifted to new heights of culture, elegance, and riches. Phoenician cooking methods, recipes, and the propagation of ingredients like the olive, grape, and fig, still figure in the cuisine of this region. The Carthaginians dominated parts of

North Africa, Sicily, Spain, Sardinia, and Corsica until 200 B.C., when the city fell to the Romans. In 146 B.C., Rome, recognizing that Carthage was its potential rival in the Mediterranean, destroyed, plowed, and salted Carthage, so nothing would grow again. The Maghreb remained under Roman rule for several hundred years and the reverberations of this domination can be seen in the Maghrebi *diffa*, similar to the old Roman banquet, where a great succession of dishes extends for hours. The Roman influence can also be seen with the cultivation of the olive and the use of olive oil as a cooking medium.

After the fall of the Roman Empire, the Berbers, indigenous North Africans from the mountains and deserts, became increasingly powerful in the Maghreb. Their most important culinary contribution is *harira* soup. About the same time, Moslem crusaders began their movement westward out of southwest Asia (or Arabia) and across North Africa. In 670, they conquered Tunisia, and later Algeria and Morocco. They delivered the word of Mohammed, the Islamic religion, a new Arabic language, and foods from the eastern Mediterranean: *smen*, or preserved butter, spices, dates, citrus, almonds, rice, and sugarcane. The Islamic religion and dietary restrictions spread quickly.

In 711 A.D., the Berbers and Moslems created a Moorish force that went across the Strait of Gibraltar to conquer Spain, and for centuries, a cultural and culinary exchange existed between Morocco and Spain. For example, gazpacho was first introduced to Spain by the Moors as a soup of garlic, bread, water, and almonds. When the tomato and pepper were brought to Spain from the New World, they were added to the soup and a new version was transported back to Morocco.

The Moslems remained a powerful religious and political force in the Maghreb for many centuries, with intermittent rule by the Ottoman Turks. Later the Maghrebi states were declared independent states, until the beginning of the nineteenth century when France invaded Algeria, Tunisia, and Morocco. The French brought political order, modernization of facilities, a strong Western influence, and the grapevine. In 1956, Morocco and Tunisia were finally pronounced free states and in 1962, Algeria achieved her independence from France.

Today, a vast majority of North Africans are Arab speaking and Moslem. The laws of Islam govern the people. Moslems observe one month of fasting from sunrise to sunset, the ninth month of the Moslem calendar. This observance is called Ramadan—a period of atonement and forgiveness. Like the Jews, Moslems abstain from eating pork.

The souk, or marketplace, is the hub of life in North Africa and it is distinguished by the extraordinary vitality of its sights, sounds, and smells. The buzz of daily activity resonates through the labyrinth of market passageways that are lined with shops, vendors, beggars, and donkeys. Shop owners have meticulously built pyramids of melons, pears, lemons, oranges, peaches, figs, prickly pears, onions, peppers, garlic, squash, and rosy tomatoes. Gigantic basins are piled high with all colors of olives, some preserved with lemons, others with spicy hot pepper, cumin, and garlic. Like an open-air department store, the spice shop can be found next to the carpet shop, which is next door to the fishmonger, next to the jewelry and fabric shop. Haggling and bargaining are expected and provoked. In the main square, the water seller, in his brightly woven red garb, brushes elbows with the snake charmer, the letter writer, and the newspaper reader. Makeshift restaurants serve skewers of lamb and chicken roasted on braziers or clay grills. Cauldrons of *harira*, a minestronelike soup, simmer for hours and then are served to patrons, who enjoy a bowl as they sit and chat with friends.

Respect for food and the enjoyment of eating is foremost in Morocco, Algeria, and Tunisia. Food is eaten with a crust of bread or with the thumb and the first two fingers of the right hand, thus hand washing is a ritual: The hands are held over a bowl while warm, rose-perfumed water is poured over them from a large copper kettle. Then, the hands are dried with a starched white linen towel. Meals are taken communally, each person serving him-

self directly from the plates in the center of the round table. Stories are exchanged in a relaxed atmosphere as the diners go from the table to repose, leaning on their elbows and oversized embroidered pillows for support. The consumption of alcohol is forbidden in the Koran, the bible of the Islamic religion, and this prohibition is more closely observed in the Maghreb than in the Levant. The focus of the table in most cases is on food rather than on alcoholic beverages but this doesn't mean that an occasional glass of wine or fig liqueur doesn't appear from time to time.

To begin the meal, baked pastries, soups, tiny meat on skewers, and small plates of condiments and salads, called *mukabalatt* in Arabic, fill the center of the table. Salads, or *sheladatt*, are the most common first course; rarely fewer than four and sometimes as many as twenty different salads are served, depending upon the number of guests and how the abundance of the harvest has inspired the cook. These colorfully contrasted small plates are served both hot and cold, and the intense flavors vary: spiced, salted, sweetened, and soured. The textures vary as well, from raw and crunchy to soft and jamlike. The range is tremendous: grated carrots with orange wedges, orange flower water, and cinnamon; minced lamb with cumin, paprika, onions, and garlic; chopped tomatoes with cilantro, preserved lemons, and sweet red onions; and an eggplant puree stewed in olive oil and garlic until it resembles jam. These first courses inspire the appetite and refresh the palate. Sometimes the first course plates are cleared away before the main course arrives, but at other times they are left throughout the meal.

One of the greatest and most popular dishes of the Maghreb is couscous. These golden granules are made from hard durum wheat, moistened with water, rolled in finely ground flour, and formed into pellets the size of a pinhead. Couscous is the name of the granules as well as the preparation that features them. To make couscous traditionally, four steps are used—washing the couscous, steaming, resting, and steaming the couscous again. What results is a mound of fluffy golden grains. Other dishes common to Morocco, Algeria, and Tunisia are stews, kebabs, *merguez* sausage, and the fiery condiment made of red-hot red peppers, garlic, and olive oil called *harissa*. Baked and fried pastries are made with a phyllolike dough called *warka*. Although phyllo can be substituted, the result will not be completely authentic. *Warka* dough is made by dabbing a ball of dough onto a hot metal drum, whereas Greek and Middle Eastern phyllo is a rolled pastry. Cooking implements in the Maghreb include the clay brazier, the mortar and pestle, and skewers for roasting kebabs.

Morocco is fairly isolated in the northwest corner of Africa, bordering the Mediterranean Sea and the Atlantic Ocean. Sheltered from invasion by both the mountains and the sea, it is the least Europeanized part of the Mediterranean. *Bisteeya* is the pride of the Moroccan kitchen; it is a poultry stew, usually pigeon, encrusted in featherlight *warka*, and dusted with cinnamon and sugar. Spices and lemons preserved in salt are indispensable in many recipes and provide a uniquely floral fragrance. *Harira* is a peppery and lemony soup thickened with meat, beans, and vegetables. *Ras el hanout*, or "top of the shop," is a highly aromatic spice mixture integral to many dishes as a marinade or flavor enhancer.

Algeria is sandwiched between Morocco and Tunisia, though its food is more similar to that of Morocco. However, Algeria has been more strongly influenced by the French because of their recent 130-year occupation (in comparison to only 40 years in Morocco). The French influence is seen in the production of wine and the baking of baguettes in Algeria, instead of the round thin disks of rustic country bread common in Morocco. Stuffed vegetables, an Ottoman invention, are very much enjoyed here. Besides these more obvious differences, many of the dishes in Morocco and Algeria overlap.

Tunisia faces Italy and addresses the eastern basin of the Mediterranean Sea. Its food, some of it similar to Morocco and Algeria, has a few peculiarities: *brik*, a thin, deep-fried envelope of crisp pastry enclosing a raw egg; *chakchouka*, an intensely hot, deep-red soup;

and the liberal use of *harissa*, the fiery hot condiment paste added in abundance to many dishes. Women are not seen in the Tunisian kitchen as often as they are in Morocco, where the cooking, whether in a restaurant or home, is always done by a woman.

But ultimately, the kitchens of the Maghreb share a great deal. Spices are used liberally to enhance the brilliance of the food. The cuisine is technically very simple, prepared without the use of stocks or rich sauces. Instead, a complexity is developed with the juxtaposition of flavors and textures, delighting all five senses. These first courses of North Africa should transport you to this enchanting land.

Lamb Soup with Lentils, Harissa, and Cilantro

In an area of the world that has gone through its share of hardship, soups have provided needed sustenance over the years. When the poor farmer had a bin of dried legumes, garden vegetables, and a lamb bone, spices were used to heighten the flavors of the finished product. This soup is heavily spiced with cumin, paprika, bay leaves, lemon peel, harissa, *and at the end, a big bunch of chopped cilantro, Maghreb's favorite herb, is thrown in. The result is nutritious, economical, substantial, and very flavorful.*

¾ pound lamb cubes, cut into small pieces
1 tablespoon butter
1 tablespoon olive oil
½ teaspoon cumin
½ teaspoon paprika
2 bay leaves
1 2-inch piece of lemon peel
¼ to ½ teaspoon *harissa* (or ¼ teaspoon cayenne) (page 241)
8 cups water (or 4 cups water and 4 cups beef stock, page 271)
¾ cup lentils (see Note)
1 medium onion, cut in ½-inch dice
1 carrot, cut in ½-inch dice
¾ cup chopped fresh cilantro or coriander leaves
Salt and freshly ground pepper

1 In a soup pot, combine the lamb, butter, olive oil, cumin, paprika, bay leaves, lemon peel, *harissa*, and 2 cups water. Simmer slowly, covered, until the lamb is tender, 1½ to 2 hours.

2 Add the remaining 6 cups water, lentils, onions, and carrots. Simmer 20 to 30 minutes, until the lentils are just tender. Discard the bay leaves and lemon peel. Add the cilantro, salt, and pepper.

3 Serve immediately.

Serves 6

NOTE: This soup can be made 1 to 2 days in advance.

NOTE: Any dry beans can be substituted. If using dry beans, soak them overnight and simmer the next day with the onions and carrots until tender.

Couscous Soup with Chicken, Tomatoes, and Mint

In North Africa, couscous is usually cooked by steaming but in this soup, the couscous is boiled. When you add the couscous, simmer the broth briskly and stir vigorously so the couscous doesn't lump together.

1 small (3 pounds) chicken, cut into 4
    pieces, skin removed
1 tablespoon olive oil
1 tablespoon butter
1 tablespoon tomato paste
2 tomatoes, peeled, seeded, and chopped
    (page 278), or ¾ cup canned Italian plum
    tomatoes, drained and chopped
1 onion, coarsely grated
½ teaspoon cumin
½ teaspoon paprika
¼ teaspoon turmeric
¼ teaspoon *harissa* (recipe follows)
1 cinnamon stick
Salt and freshly ground pepper
8 cups water
½ cup couscous
3 tablespoons chopped fresh mint
2 tablespoons chopped fresh parsley
2 tablespoons chopped fresh cilantro or
    coriander leaves
1 to 2 teaspoons lemon juice

1 In a soup pot, place the chicken pieces, olive oil, butter, tomato paste, tomatoes, onion, cumin, paprika, turmeric, *harissa*, cinnamon stick, ½ teaspoon salt, ½ teaspoon pepper, and 2 cups water. Simmer gently, covered, until the chicken is cooked, 45 minutes. Remove the chicken from the broth and let cool. Remove all the bones and tear the chicken into 1-inch pieces. Add the chicken back into the soup.

2 Add the remaining 6 cups water and bring the soup to a simmer. Using a spoon, stir the broth constantly as you add the couscous slowly. Add the mint, parsley, and cilantro and simmer, uncovered, stirring occasionally, 10 minutes.

3 Season with salt, pepper, and lemon juice and serve immediately.

Serves 6

Harissa,
a Spicy Hot Condiment

Harissa is a fiery hot condiment used as a flavor enhancer in many dishes in Morocco, Algeria, and especially Tunisia, where they prefer their food extra hot. Harissa may also be purchased by the tube or in a small can in specialty food stores and some grocery stores.

½ ounce dried hot red chili peppers
1 garlic clove, coarsely chopped
Large pinch of salt
¼ cup olive oil

1 Place the peppers in a saucepan, cover with water, and simmer 2 minutes. Turn off the heat and let soak for 1 hour. Drain and cut them into small pieces. Place them in a mortar with the garlic and salt and pound them, or use a blender, to make a fine puree. Spoon into a jar and cover with the olive oil. Cover tightly and refrigerate.

2 *Harissa* can be kept in the refrigerator for up to a year as long as the top surface is covered with olive oil.

Makes ¹/₂ cup

Chick-pea Soup with Squash and Cilantro

I have made this soup several times and each time I make it I like it more and more. The final flavor is a little bit sweet, but nothing that a good handful of cilantro, a squeeze of fresh lemon juice, and even some freshly grated Parmesan can't balance.

1 pound chick-peas

Stock
 2 to 2½ pounds lamb or beef bones
 8 cups water
 2 bay leaves
 1 onion, coarsely chopped
 1 carrot, coarsely chopped

Soup
 2 tablespoons olive oil
 2 medium onions, cut in ½-inch dice
 2 carrots, cut in ½-inch dice
 6 garlic cloves, minced
 1 small (1 pound) butternut squash, peeled, and cut in ½-inch dice
 2 large pinches of saffron threads, revived (page 279)
 ¾ cup chopped fresh cilantro or coriander leaves
Salt and freshly ground pepper
1 to 2 teaspoons lemon juice

1 Pick over the chick-peas and discard any stones. Cover with water and soak overnight. The next day, drain and place in a saucepan with enough water to cover by 2 inches. Simmer, uncovered, until the skins begin to crack and the beans are tender, 50 to 60 minutes.

2 Place the lamb, water, bay leaves, onion, and carrot in a soup pot. Bring to a boil. Turn the heat down and simmer slowly until the stock has a good flavor, 2 to 3 hours. Replenish the water to the original level as needed. Strain, discard the bones and vegetables, and reserve the stock.

3 Heat the olive oil in a soup pot and add the onions and carrots. Saute slowly until the onions are soft, 12 minutes. Add the garlic and continue to sauté 2 minutes. Add the stock, chick-peas, and butternut squash and simmer slowly 20 minutes. Add the saffron and cilantro and simmer 3 minutes. Season with salt, pepper, and lemon juice.

4 Ladle the soup into bowls and serve immediately.

Serves 6

Moroccan Minestrone

Ramadan is the ninth month of the holy Muslim year and is marked by fasting during the daylight hours. When the bells chime to announce sundown, the Moroccan family gathers for a substantial bowl of harira. Harira *is a peppery, lemony soup, made robust with legumes, meat, vegetables, and spices, thickened at the last moment with flour and a beaten egg, and accompanied by wedges of lemon and fresh dates.*

½ cup chick-peas
3 tablespoons olive oil
1½ pounds beef or lamb, trimmed and cut
   in small cubes
2 medium onions, chopped
¼ cup chopped celery
1 28-ounce can whole tomatoes, with juice
1 tablespoon tomato paste
¼ teaspoon ground ginger
¼ teaspoon turmeric
¼ teaspoon cinnamon
½ teaspoon saffron threads, revived (page
   279)
Salt and freshly ground pepper
9 cups water
1 cup dried lentils
1 egg, lightly beaten
½ cup spaghetti, broken into small pieces
3 tablespoons all-purpose flour
¼ cup chopped fresh cilantro or coriander
   leaves
¼ cup chopped fresh parsley
Juice of 1 lemon
1 lemon, cut into wedges

1 Pick over the chick-peas and discard any stones. Cover with water and soak overnight.

2 In a soup pot, heat the oil. In batches, add the meat and sauté until well browned on all sides, 8 to 10 minutes. Remove and set aside. Add the onions and celery and sauté until the onions are soft, 7 minutes.

3 Puree the tomatoes, tomato paste, ginger, turmeric, cinnamon, saffron, and 1 teaspoon pepper until smooth. Add the tomatoes and meat to the onions. Add 6 cups water, the lentils, and chick-peas and bring to a boil. Turn the heat down and simmer 2 hours, until the meat and chick-peas are very tender.

4 Thirty minutes before serving, add the beaten egg and stir briskly until it makes strands. Add 2 cups water and the pasta and cook until tender, 10 minutes. Season with salt and pepper.

5 Bring the soup to a boil. Blend the flour with the remaining 1 cup water and add to the soup pot, mixing vigorously. Simmer slowly 5 minutes. Add the cilantro, parsley, lemon juice, salt, and pepper to taste.

6 Serve garnished with lemon wedges.

Serves 6 to 8

NOTE: This soup can be prepared 1 day in advance. To serve, bring it to a low boil, taste, and season with salt, pepper, and lemon juice.

Moroccan Baked Phyllo Rolls with Shrimp and Scallops

Fried and baked triangular and cigarette-shaped stuffed pastries are made in many countries that border the eastern and southern Mediterranean. In Morocco they are called briouats, *in Tunisia,* briks, *in Turkey,* bourek *and* böregi, *and in Greece,* bourekakia. *They are made with featherlight pastry resembling phyllo and they melt in your mouth. These* briouats *are filled with fresh scallops and shrimp, tomatoes, and Moroccan aromatics. This is only one filling idea—the possibilities are limitless.*

2 tablespoons olive oil
¼ pound scallops
¼ pound medium shrimp, peeled
2 garlic cloves, minced
Salt and freshly ground pepper
¼ cup onion, finely chopped
1 large tomato, peeled, seeded, and
    chopped (page 278)
3 tablespoons chopped fresh parsley
3 tablespoons chopped fresh cilantro or
    coriander leaves
¾ teaspoon cumin
½ teaspoon paprika
Pinch of cayenne
Pinch of saffron threads, revived (page 279)
¼ cup fresh bread crumbs
½ pound phyllo dough
½ cup butter, melted
Lemon wedges

1 Heat 1 tablespoon oil in a skillet and sauté the scallops, shrimp, and half the garlic over low heat for 2 minutes. Season with salt and pepper. Remove the seafood from the pan, chop coarsely, and reserve in a bowl. In the same pan, add 1 tablespoon oil, the onions, and tomatoes and simmer 10 minutes. Add the remaining garlic, parsley, cilantro, cumin, paprika, cayenne, saffron, salt, and pepper. Continue to simmer slowly until the moisture is evaporated, 10 minutes. Add the seafood and bread crumbs and mix well. Season with salt and pepper.

2 Preheat the oven to 375°F.

3 Cut the phyllo into 4 equal strips, 4 inches wide. Cover with a damp towel until ready to use. Brush 1 strip lightly with melted butter and place another one on top. Brush it lightly with butter. Place a heaping teaspoon of filling along the short end. Fold the sides in and roll, forming a cigar shape. Brush lightly with butter. Repeat with the remaining phyllo and filling. Place on a greased baking sheet and bake until golden, 15 minutes.

4 Serve immediately, garnished with lemon wedges.

Makes 30 pastries to serve 6

NOTE: These can also be made into triangles. Cut 3-inch-wide strips of phyllo. Brush 1 strip lightly with melted butter and place another one on top. Brush lightly with butter. Place a heaping teaspoon of filling at one end and fold the corner in to make a triangle. Fold along the line as you would in folding a flag. Brush lightly with butter and proceed as above to bake.

MESHWIYA

Tunisian Sweet and Hot Pepper Tomato Relish

This sweet and hot pepper tomato relish is similar to Turkish Red-Hot Smoked Tomato Relish (page 223) and probably a derivative of it, since so many foods of North Africa have been influenced by the eastern Mediterranean. I like to keep a bowl of this in my refrigerator and use it as a condiment with grilled fish, chicken, lamb, and beef.

3 ripe medium tomatoes, peeled, seeded, and chopped (page 278)
3 large red peppers, roasted (page 278)
2 garlic cloves, minced
1 teaspoon cumin
¼ teaspoon *harissa* (page 241) or cayenne
1 tablespoon olive oil
2 tablespoons lemon juice
¼ cup chopped fresh parsley
Salt and freshly ground pepper
½ baguette, cut into ½-inch slices on the diagonal

1 Place the tomatoes in a skillet and sauté on high heat until they thicken, 6 to 8 minutes. Remove from the pan and place in a bowl.

2 Mince the roasted peppers and add to the tomatoes. Add the garlic, cumin, *harissa*, olive oil, lemon juice, and parsley. Mix well. Season with salt and pepper and place on a serving dish.

3 Serve with baguette slices.

Serves 6

NOTE: This can be made 1 day in advance. However, do not add the garlic until ready to use.

Baked Phyllo Triangles with Lamb and Moroccan Spices

My favorite Moroccan kitchen has to be the one at the palatial Mamounia Hotel in Marrakesh, where I learned to make warka, *the pastry used to make* briouats *and* bisteeya. *The dedicated and generous women chefs at the Mamounia made certain that I didn't leave the kitchen until I learned to make it perfectly. We rolled this* kefta *mixture of lamb, onions, and a pinch of just about every spice in the larder into the* warka *to make these fantastic* briouats *but I suggest that the reader who hasn't been tutored in* warka-making *substitute store-bought phyllo dough.*

¾ pound lean ground lamb

¼ cup minced onion

2 garlic cloves, minced

4 teaspoons cumin

1 teaspoon ginger

1 teaspoon paprika

¾ teaspoon cinnamon

Large pinch of cayenne

Large pinch of saffron threads, revived (page 279)

2 tablespoons chopped fresh parsley

2 tablespoons chopped fresh cilantro or coriander leaves

Salt and freshly ground pepper

1 egg, lightly beaten

½ pound phyllo dough

½ cup butter, melted

1 Combine the lamb, onion, garlic, cumin, ginger, paprika, cinnamon, cayenne, saffron, parsley, cilantro, salt, and pepper in a skillet and cook over medium heat, uncovered, stirring occasionally, until the lamb is cooked and the moisture has completely evaporated, 6 minutes. Drain off and discard the fat. Add the egg and continue to stir until it is cooked, 1 minute.

2 Preheat the oven to 375°F.

3 Cut 3-inch-wide strips of phyllo. Brush 1 strip with melted butter and place another one on top. Brush with butter. Place a heaping teaspoon of filling at one end. Fold the corner in to make a triangle. Fold along the line as you would in folding a flag. Repeat with the remaining phyllo and filling. Place on a greased baking sheet and bake until golden, 15 minutes.

4 Serve immediately, warm or at room temperature.

Makes 30 pastries to serve 6

NOTE: These can also be made into rolls. Cut 3-inch-wide strips of phyllo. Brush 1 strip lightly with butter and place another one on top. Brush lightly with butter. Place a heaping teaspoon of filling along the short end. Fold ½ inch of the long sides in and roll, forming a cigar shape. Brush lightly with butter and proceed as above to bake.

Tunisian Potato, Scallion, and Fried Egg Turnovers

The first time my Tunisian friend Abou made brik *for me I didn't understand. No one told me it was properly cooked when the egg yolk was still runny and dripped down my chin. Once this was established, I loved the challenge and the flavors of these peculiar turnovers. Try them yourself. They are simple to make and can be filled with all kinds of fillings. Use your imagination.*

¾ pound potatoes, peeled and stored in
    water
Salt and freshly ground pepper
6 scallions, white and green, finely chopped
2 tablespoons chopped fresh parsley
½ preserved lemon, cut in fine dice (page
    249) (optional, see Note)
7 tablespoons butter
6 sheets phyllo dough
6 small eggs
1 egg white, lightly beaten
Olive oil
Lemon wedges

1 Bring a saucepan of water to a boil. Add the potatoes and salt and simmer, uncovered, until soft, 20 minutes. Drain the potatoes and mash. Add the scallions, parsley, preserved lemon, 1 tablespoon butter, salt, and pepper. Mix well.

2 Melt the remaining 6 tablespoons butter. Place 1 sheet of phyllo on a work surface and brush the sheet lightly with butter. Fold the sheet in quarters to make an 8 × 6-inch rectangle. Brush lightly with butter and fold the short side in 2 inches to make a perfect square. Brush the folded 2-inch part lightly with butter. Divide the potato mixture into 6 equal parts and place one part on half of the square. Make a small indentation in the center of the potato and break an egg into it. Brush the edges of the pastry with egg white. Fold the square in half, making a triangle. Seal the edges by pressing firmly. Repeat with the remaining phyllo and filling.

3 Heat ¼ inch olive oil in a large skillet until it is hot. Immediately fry the turnovers until golden, 2 to 3 minutes per side. Remove with a slotted spoon and drain on paper towels. Serve immediately, garnished with lemon wedges.

Makes 6 turnovers to serve 6

NOTE: If preserved lemons are unavailable, substitute 1 teaspoon lemon juice and ½ teaspoon grated lemon zest.

Flaky Moroccan Chicken Pie

The crowning jewel of the Moroccan table is the bisteeya, *a glorious pie made with pigeon, lemon-flavored eggs, chopped almonds, and sugar. A very substantial first course,* bisteeya *is the most sophisticated and elaborate Moroccan dish. This recipe is lengthy but it is worth the effort.*

14 tablespoons butter

1 3- to 3½-pound chicken, cut into 4 pieces, skin removed

1 large onion, minced

Salt and freshly ground pepper

3¾ teaspoons cinnamon

1½ teaspoons ginger

1¼ teaspoons cumin

¼ teaspoon cayenne

½ teaspoon saffron threads

½ teaspoon turmeric

¼ cup chicken stock (page 272)

4 eggs, lightly beaten

¼ cup chopped fresh cilantro or coriander leaves

¼ cup chopped fresh parsley

1 cup whole almonds, blanched

4 tablespoons powdered sugar

¾ pound phyllo dough

1 In a large skillet, put 2 tablespoons butter, the chicken pieces, the onions, 1 teaspoon salt, 1 teaspoon pepper, 2 teaspoons cinnamon, the ginger, cumin, cayenne, saffron, turmeric, and chicken stock. Simmer gently, covered, until the chicken is cooked, 45 minutes. Remove the chicken from the sauce and let it cool. Remove all the bones and tear the chicken into 1-inch pieces. Bring the liquid to a simmer, add the eggs, and stir gently until the eggs are cooked and most of the liquid evaporates, 4 to 5 minutes. Add the chicken, cilantro, parsley, salt, and pepper and mix well.

2 Preheat the oven to 375°F.

3 Toast the almonds in the oven until very lightly golden and hot to the touch, 5 to 7 minutes. Coarsley chop them in a blender or food processor and mix with 3 tablespoons sugar and ¾ teaspoon cinnamon. Set aside. Reserve the remaining sugar and cinnamon for a garnish.

4 Melt the remaining 12 tablespoons butter. Brush a 12-inch pizza pan or pie plate lightly with butter. Place 1 sheet of phyllo on the bottom of the pie plate so that it completely covers the bottom of the plate and extends over one side by several inches. Brush the whole sheet lightly with butter. Continue with 7 more sheets, moving the sheets in a pinwheel effect, brushing butter on each sheet. Spread the chicken and egg mixture on the phyllo. Sprinkle with the almond mixture.

5 Fold the overhanging phyllo up over the chicken and almonds and brush with butter. Place 1 sheet of phyllo on the top of the pie plate so that it completely covers the top of the pie and extends over one side by several inches. Brush the whole sheet lightly with butter. Continue with 7 more sheets, layering them in a pinwheel effect, brushing butter on each sheet. Tuck the overhanging edges under the pie.

The pie can be prepared several hours in advance to this point.

6 Preheat the oven to 350°F.

7 Bake the pie 18 to 20 minutes, until golden brown. Remove from the oven. Pour off any excess butter. Place a larger plate on top and turn the pie over. Slide it back into the pie plate and continue to bake 18 to 20 minutes more, until golden brown. Remove from the oven and turn over onto a serving plate. Let cool 15 minutes before serving.

8 To serve, combine the remaining 1 teaspoon cinnamon and 1 tablespoon sugar and dust the top of the pie. Cut into wedges and serve.

Serves 6 to 8

NOTE: This can also be made on a baking sheet, maintaining a free form 12-inch circle in the end.

HAMED M'RAKAD

Preserved Lemons

Mounds of preserved or confit lemons are sold in the markets of Morocco. These lemons are indispensable in the Moroccan kitchen and offer a uniquely floral and fragrant aroma and taste. The lemons are pickled in salt and lemon juice, transforming the peel into an edible and essential ingredient in many dishes. They are used for tagines, *or stews, with olives as a condiment, and in vegetable salads. The pulp, used not nearly so frequently as the peel, provides an unusual flavor in vinaigrettes.*

8 Meyer lemons (see Note), washed
½ cup kosher salt
2 cinnamon sticks
4 bay leaves
Freshly squeezed lemon juice, if needed

1 Cut each lemon into quarters from the top to within ½ inch of the bottom, taking care to leave the 4 pieces joined at the stalk end. Sprinkle the insides of the lemon liberally with salt.

2 Place 1 tablespoon salt on the bottom of a canning jar and pack in the lemons, pushing them down and adding more salt as you go. Add the cinnamon sticks and bay leaves between the lemons. If the juice from the lemons isn't sufficient, add extra freshly squeezed juice almost to the top of the jar. Leave some airspace before closing the jar.

3 Let the lemons sit in a warm place for 3 weeks, turning the jar upside down periodically to distribute the salt and juices.

4 To use the lemons, remove from the brine and discard the pulp. Wash the peel and use. Some white crystals will form on the top of the lemons in the jar, which is normal, so do not discard the lemons. They do not need to be refrigerated. They will keep for 1 year.

Makes 1 quart

NOTE: Meyer lemons are used in Morocco but I have successfully substituted the commonly available Eureka and Lisbon lemons .

Moroccan Pizza Bread with Herb Salad

Salads are a way of life in the Maghreb because vegetables and fruits are so luscious and inexpensive. In this recipe, I have taken a traditional Moroccan herb salad called bekkoula and paired it with Moroccan bread called khobz for a non-traditional combination of great flavors.

Bread

1½ teaspoons active dry yeast

½ teaspoon sugar

1 cup warm water 115°F.

2 cups all-purpose flour

½ cup whole wheat flour

¼ cup cornmeal

1 teaspoon salt

1 teaspoon sesame seeds

¾ teaspoon aniseed, ground to a powder in a mortar and pestle or spice grinder

Salad

1¼ cups fresh arugula, stems removed, washed

¾ cup fresh Italian parsley leaves

¾ cup fresh cilantro or coriander leaves

Salt and freshly ground pepper

8 tablespoons extra virgin olive oil

4 tablespoons lemon juice

½ preserved lemon, cut in fine dice (page 249) (optional)

2 garlic cloves, minced

2 teaspoons paprika

Large pinch of cayenne

Rising and baking

2 tablespoons olive oil

2 tablespoons all-purpose flour

1 By hand, combine the yeast, sugar, water, and 1 cup all-purpose flour in a large bowl. Let proof for 1 hour.

2 Add the remaining all-purpose flour, whole wheat flour, cornmeal, salt, sesame seeds, and aniseed powder and mix well with a wooden spoon. Turn out onto a work surface and knead 7 to 10 minutes until smooth and elastic.

(Alternatively, this can be made in an electric mixer: In the mixer bowl, combine the yeast, sugar, water, and 1 cup all-purpose flour. Let proof 1 hour. Add the remaining all-purpose flour, whole wheat flour, cornmeal, salt, sesame seeds, and aniseed powder and on low speed, using a dough hook, mix for 5 to 7 minutes, until smooth and elastic.)

3 Place the dough in an oiled bowl and turn over to coat the top with oil. Cover with plastic wrap and let rise in a warm place (75°F.) for 1 to 1 ½ hours, until doubled in volume.

4 Preheat the oven to 375°F.

5 In the meantime, wash and spin dry the arugula, parsley, and cilantro. Chop the greens very coarsely and combine. Season with salt and pepper. In a small bowl, whisk together the olive oil, lemon juice, preserved lemon, garlic, paprika, cayenne, salt, and pepper.

6 Punch the bread down and form into a smooth ball. Place on an oiled sheet pan and flatten slightly. Let rest 10 minutes. Pat the dough into a 9-inch circle. Prick the loaf in 4 places with the tines of a fork. Bake until

golden, 20 to 25 minutes. Remove from the oven and place on a serving plate or board.

7 Toss the greens with the vinaigrette and place on top of the bread. Serve immediately, cut into wedges.

Makes one 9-inch round bread to serve 6

Ras El Hanout

*T*he familiar evocative musical sound of the Maghrebi kitchen comes from the brass mortar and pestle where the cook grinds *ras el hanout, a distinctive North African spice combination. Ras el hanout means "top of the shop" and constitutes as few as 8, or as many as 100, spices. Every cook has his own version of this highly aromatic mix, generally a combination of finely ground berries, roots, pods, seeds, and grains. Ras el hanout is used as a marinade or flavor enhancer, and some even boast of its aphrodisiacal qualities.*

5 bay leaves
1 tablespoon dried thyme
1 tablespoon black peppercorns
1 tablespoon nutmeg
1 tablespoon whole cloves (or ground cloves)
1 tablespoon ground cinnamon
1 teaspoon coriander seeds (or ground coriander)

½ teaspoon mace
½ teaspoon cardamom pods (or ground cardamom)
½ teaspoon ginger
½ teaspoon cumin seed (or ground cumin)
½ teaspoon allspice berries (or ground allspice)
½ teaspoon turmeric
¼ teaspoon aniseed
¼ teaspoon cayenne

Grind all of the ingredients with a mortar and pestle or spice mill for 1 minute. Store in a tightly closed jar.

Makes ¹/₂ cup

Couscous with Chick-peas and Caramelized Onions

In writing this book, I was fortunate enough to have an exceptional recipe tester, Anita Anderson. Anita, a quiet and fairly stoic woman, tested one recipe after another and we always tasted and talked about each dish. When we tasted this one, a smile broke across her face. All she could say was, "Wow!" Later that day, she admitted that of all the dishes she had worked on, this was her favorite. My thanks go to Paula Wolfert for her inspiration.

1 cup chick-peas

2 cups couscous

1 teaspoon *Ras el hanout* (page 251)

1 cinnamon stick

3 cups water

3 cups chicken stock (optional, water can be substituted)

Salt and freshly ground pepper

4 large onions, sliced

½ teaspoon cinnamon

¼ teaspoon allspice

2 tablespoons butter

⅓ cup honey

1 tablespoon sugar

¼ cup sultana or golden raisins

¼ cup dried apricots, cut in half

Harissa Sauce (recipe follows)

1 Pick over the chick-peas and discard any stones. Cover with water and soak overnight.

2 The next day, wash the couscous in cold water and drain immediately. Lift and rake the grains with your fingertips to separate them. Let rest at least 10 minutes.

3 Place the chick-peas in a soup pot that will also accommodate a steamer. Add the *ras el hanout,* cinnamon stick, and 6 cups water or water and chicken stock. Simmer, uncovered, until the skins begin to crack, 1 hour.

4 While the chick-peas are simmering, line a steamer with 3 layers of cheesecloth to cover the interior of the steamer and go up over the top. Make certain that the steamer fits snugly into the soup pot and that the bottom of the steamer won't touch the top of the chick-pea stew. When the chick-peas have cooked for about 40 minutes, add the couscous to the steamer and steam for 20 minutes, uncovered, fluffing the grains halfway through the cooking.

5 Remove the couscous from the steamer and dump it into a baking pan. Combine ⅔ cup cold water and ½ teaspoon salt. Sprinkle the couscous with the salt water. Lift and rake the grains with your fingertips to separate them. Let rest at least 10 minutes.

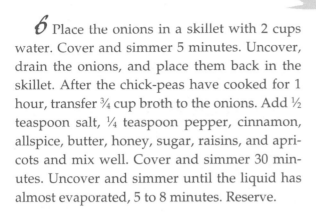

6 Place the onions in a skillet with 2 cups water. Cover and simmer 5 minutes. Uncover, drain the onions, and place them back in the skillet. After the chick-peas have cooked for 1 hour, transfer ¾ cup broth to the onions. Add ½ teaspoon salt, ¼ teaspoon pepper, cinnamon, allspice, butter, honey, sugar, raisins, and apricots and mix well. Cover and simmer 30 minutes. Uncover and simmer until the liquid has almost evaporated, 5 to 8 minutes. Reserve.

The recipe can be prepared to this point several hours ahead of time.

7 Twenty minutes before serving, place the steamer back on top of the soup pot and place the couscous in the cheesecloth-lined steamer. Simmer the chick-pea stew slowly, 15 minutes, until the couscous is hot. Remove the steamer and the couscous.

8 To serve, reheat the onions. Pour the couscous onto a serving platter and make a well in the center. With a slotted spoon, place the chick-peas in the well and cover with the onions. Season the remaining chick-pea broth. Moisten the couscous with a few spoonfuls of broth and serve at once with a bowl of Harissa Sauce and a bowl of chick-pea broth.

S e r v e s   6

Harissa Sauce

*A*lthough *this recipe for* harissa *sauce uses just a teaspoon of* harissa, *it is still very, very hot. It goes well with couscous, especially one with sweeter flavors like Couscous with Chick-peas and Caramelized Onions (page 252).*

1 cup chick-pea broth or chicken stock
(page 272)
2 to 3 teaspoons lemon juice
1 tablespoon olive oil
⅛ teaspoon cumin
1 tablespoon chopped fresh cilantro or
coriander leaves
1 teaspoon *harissa* (page 241)

Combine all the ingredients and bring to a boil in a small saucepan. Serve immediately with couscous.

M a k e s   a b o u t   1   c u p

AJJA

Tunisian Omelette with Hot Sausage, Peppers, and Eggplant

The French have left their mark in Tunisia with the introduction of the omelette and a ratatouillelike stew. When cooked together, the combination is hot and delicious.

1 small (½ pound) eggplant
Salt and freshly ground pepper
4 tablespoons olive oil
½ small onion, cut in ½-inch dice
1 green pepper, cored, and cut in ½-inch
  dice
½ pound spicy hot sausage (North African
  merguez—recipe follows—chorizo, or hot
  Italian), removed from casings and
  crumbled
2 garlic cloves, minced
¼ teaspoon *harissa* (page 241)
2 tomatoes, peeled, seeded, and chopped
  (page 278), or 1 cup canned Italian plum
  tomatoes, drained and chopped
8 eggs
1 tablespoon water

1 Preheat the oven to 375°F.

2 Peel the eggplant and cut into ½-inch cubes. Salt liberally, place in a colander, and let drain 30 minutes. Wash well and pat dry with paper towels. Toss with 2 tablespoons olive oil and place on an oiled baking sheet. Bake the eggplant until golden and cooked through, turning occasionally, 15 to 20 minutes.

3 Heat 1 tablespoon olive oil in a skillet. Add the onions, peppers, and sausage and sauté, uncovered, until the vegetables are almost soft, 10 minutes. Add the garlic and continue to sauté 1 minute. Add the eggplant, *harissa*, and tomatoes and simmer on high heat until most of the liquid in the pan has evaporated, 3 to 5 minutes. Season with salt and pepper.

4 Whisk the eggs with salt, pepper, and water until foamy. Heat the remaining 1 tablespoon oil in a large omelette pan until very hot and the oil is rippling, 1 minute. Add the egg mixture and let it cook 5 seconds. As the eggs begin to set, with a fork, lift up the outer edges of the omelette and let the liquid run underneath. Continue until it is almost set but still slightly soft inside, a total of 30 seconds. Quickly spread the eggs with the sausage and vegetable stew.

5 To serve, fold the omelette onto a serving plate to form a slight roll. Serve immediately.

*Makes 2 small omelettes
or 1 large omelette
to serve 6*

Maghreb Lamb Sausage

Merguez *sausage originated in Tunisia but to-day it is made in Algeria and Morocco as well. In Tunisia, they like very hot and spicy food and their* merguez *is murderous. It is tasty on its own grilled on a charcoal fire or stewed with sweet peppers and fresh summer tomatoes.*

1 pound lamb, cut into cubes (see Note)
¼ pound lamb or pork fat (available at a specialty butcher shop)
4 garlic cloves, minced
1 tablespoon paprika
1 teaspoon cumin
½ teaspoon *harissa* (page 241) or cayenne (or to taste)
½ teaspoon cloves
½ teaspoon cinnamon
¼ teaspoon nutmeg
Salt and freshly ground pepper
3 tablespoons chopped fresh cilantro or coriander leaves
1 tablespoon chopped fresh parsley
1 teaspoon chopped fresh thyme
¼ cup water
Sausage casings (optional, see Note)
2 tablespoons olive oil

1 Place the lamb, lamb fat, and garlic in a food processor and process until chopped well together. Add the paprika, cumin, *harissa*, cloves, cinnamon, nutmeg, 1½ teaspoons salt, and 1 teaspoon pepper. Process together until well mixed. Add the cilantro, parsley, thyme, and water and pulse several times.

2 Heat a small skillet. Make a small thin patty and sauté until cooked through, 1 to 2 minutes. Let cool. Taste and season the mixture with salt, pepper, and spices if needed.

3 If you have a sausage attachment on your electric mixer, stuff the sausages, twisting and tying at 3-inch intervals. Place on a sheet pan in the refrigerator for 24 hours. (Otherwise, see Note.)

4 Heat ¼ cup water in a skillet. Prick the sausages and simmer, uncovered, turning occasionally, until the water evaporates, the sausages render some fat, and they are cooked, 10 minutes. Alternatively, they can be brushed with oil and grilled on a charcoal grill, turning occasionally.

5 These can be served hot or at room temperature. Slice on the diagonal and serve. These sausages are a perfect combination with Tunisian Sweet and Hot Pepper Tomato Relish (page 223) or in the Tunisian Omelette with Hot Sausage, Peppers, and Eggplant (page 254).

Serves 6

NOTE: Beef and beef fat can be substituted.

The casings are optional. If they are not used, the sausage mixture can also be formed into long sausagelike shapes and threaded onto skewers. These can be brushed with oil and grilled on a charcoal grill or cooked under a hot broiler, turning occasionally.

Lamb Kefta Stewed with Hot Tomatoes

This dish is reminiscent of a tagine *I enjoyed at Palais Jamai in Fez, Morocco, made with lamb* kefta, *or spiced meatballs, tomatoes, and eggs. A* tagine *resembles a stew and in Morocco, Algeria, and Tunisia, there are a million different variations.* Tagines *are usually served as a main course but this recipe is witness to the fact that last night's leftovers are never discarded. Instead they are rewarmed and served on a smaller plate as today's first course.*

Kefta

1 pound ground lamb
½ cup coarsely grated onion
2 garlic cloves, minced
¼ cup chopped fresh parsley
5 tablespoons chopped fresh cilantro or
    coriander leaves
¾ teaspoon cumin
¾ teaspoon paprika
½ teaspoon ginger
¼ teaspoon cardamom
Salt and freshly ground pepper
¼ cup dry bread crumbs
3 tablespoons water

Tomato Sauce

1 28-ounce can Italian plum tomatoes,
    chopped
1 tablespoon tomato paste
½ cup chopped onion

1 garlic clove, minced
¼ teaspoon *harissa* (page 241)
4 tablespoons chopped fresh cilantro or
    coriander leaves
¼ teaspoon cumin
¼ teaspoon cinnamon
Pinch of saffron

1 In a bowl, mix the lamb, onions, garlic, parsley, cilantro, cumin, paprika, ginger, cardamom, ¾ teaspoon salt, 1 teaspoon pepper, bread crumbs, and water. Let stand 1 hour or overnight.

2 Place the tomatoes, tomato paste, onions, garlic, *harissa*, 3 tablespoons cilantro, cumin, cinnamon, saffron, salt, and pepper in a blender or food processor and puree until smooth. Pour the tomato sauce into a skillet and simmer 30 minutes. Season with salt and pepper if needed.

3 Preheat the oven to 450°F.

4 Form the lamb mixture into 1-inch oval-shaped balls. Place on a baking sheet and bake 10 minutes. Remove from the pan and place in the slowly simmering sauce. Simmer until done, 10 to 15 minutes.

5 Serve immediately, garnished with the remaining 1 tablespoon chopped cilantro.

Serves   6

Warm Spiced Lentils

In Morocco, I met dozens of Mohammeds—my guide, my butcher, my spice dealer, and my driver. Mohammed, my driver, was very quiet at the beginning, but after a week, he finally began to open up and a week after that, he invited me to his home on Friday for a traditional couscous lunch his wife had prepared. In the Moroccan home, there are a great many customs and I wanted to do everything right. When we walked into the room that doubled as a dining and living room, Mohammed removed his shoes, so I removed my shoes. When he ate these warm lentils with the first three fingers of his right hand, so did I. "Delicious!" I said. Mohammed smiled his usual shy way and handed me a piece of paper. His wife had already written out the recipe for me.

1½ cups lentils
4 cloves
1 medium onion, peeled
2 bay leaves
1 2-inch piece of lemon peel
¼ cup extra virgin olive oil
1 large red onion, minced
3 garlic cloves, minced
2 tomatoes, peeled, seeded, and chopped (page 278)
1 teaspoon cumin

1 teaspoon ginger
½ teaspoon turmeric
½ teaspoon paprika
¼ teaspoon cayenne
¼ cup chopped fresh parsley
¼ cup chopped fresh cilantro or coriander leaves
1 to 2 tablespoons lemon juice
Salt and freshly ground pepper
6 lemon wedges

1 Sort the lentils and discard any stones. Place the lentils in a large saucepan and cover with water by 2 inches. Stick the cloves in the onion and add to the lentils with the bay leaves and lemon peel. Bring to a boil, turn the heat down, and simmer until the lentils are just tender, 20 to 30 minutes. Remove and discard the onion, bay leaves, and lemon peel. Drain and discard the water.

2 Heat the olive oil in a large skillet and sauté the red onions until almost soft, 5 minutes. Add the garlic, tomatoes, cumin, ginger, turmeric, paprika, and cayenne and sauté 3 minutes. Add the parsley, cilantro, and lentils, stir together, and heat for 2 minutes. Season with the lemon juice, salt, and pepper. Garnish with the lemon wedges and serve immediately.

Serves 6 to 8

Fava Bean Puree

Bessara is certainly inspired by the Middle East, where they make hummus, *a puree of chick-peas, tahini, garlic, and lemon juice. This version is unique because spices are sprinkled on the bread, which is then dipped into the puree. Once you begin eating* bessara, *it is difficult to stop.*

1⅓ cups (½ pound) dried fava (see Note) or kidney beans
3 garlic cloves, minced
¼ cup extra virgin olive oil
1½ teaspoons cumin
1 teaspoon paprika
¼ teaspoon cayenne
1 tablespoon chopped fresh parsley
2 tablespoons chopped fresh cilantro or coriander leaves
3 to 4 tablespoons lemon juice
1 scallion, white and green, minced
Salt and freshly ground pepper

Garnish

1 tablespoon extra virgin olive oil
3 lemon wedges
2 tablespoons chopped scallions
1 tablespoon cumin
1 tablespoon paprika
1 small loaf rustic country-style bread

1 Pick over the fava or kidney beans and discard any stones. Cover with water and soak overnight. The next day, if you are using fava beans, remove the skins. Place the beans in a saucepan with enough water to cover by 2 inches. Simmer, uncovered, until the fava beans are tender, 1 to 1½ hours. If kidney beans are substituted, simmer 1 to ½ hours. Add additional water if necessary. Drain.

2 Place the beans, garlic, and olive oil in a food processor or blender and process until smooth. Remove and place in a bowl with the cumin, paprika, cayenne, parsley, cilantro, lemon juice, and scallions. Mix well and season with salt and pepper.

3 Place the puree on a serving platter and garnish with the olive oil, lemon wedges, and scallions. Serve the cumin and paprika in small bowls or on a separate plate.

4 To serve, sprinkle the bread liberally with cumin and paprika and then dip the bread into the bean puree or spread with a knife.

Serves 6

NOTE: Fava beans can be purchased in a food store that specializes in Italian ingredients.

Algerian Eggplant Jam

Eggplant jam is made all over the Maghreb but this version comes from Algeria. In this recipe, the eggplant slices are brushed with olive oil and baked in the oven, but very often in North Africa, the eggplant slices are fried in olive oil. I have changed the eggplant cooking method to reduce the amount of olive oil and create a lighter, more palatable dish, definitely one of my favorites.

3 medium eggplants (3 pounds total)
Salt and freshly ground pepper
7 tablespoons olive oil
3 garlic cloves, minced
2 teaspoons sweet paprika
1 ¼ teaspoons ground cumin
½ cup water
¼ teaspoon cayenne or ⅛ teaspoon *harissa*
  (page 241) (optional)
3 to 4 tablespoons lemon juice
1 tablespoon chopped fresh parsley
3 lemon slices or tomato wedges
Crusty country-style bread

1 Preheat the oven to 375°F.

2 Cut the stems off the eggplants. With a vegetable peeler or sharp knife, peel the skin in ½-inch-wide strips vertically so you get a striped eggplant. Discard the peel. Slice the eggplant horizontally into ½-inch slices. Place in a colander and salt each slice. Let stand 30 minutes. Rinse well and pat dry with paper towels.

3 Using 3 tablespoons olive oil, brush a baking sheet liberally. Brush the eggplant slices lightly with 2 tablespoons oil. Place the eggplant slices in a single layer on the baking sheet. Bake, turning occasionally, until they are a light golden brown on both sides, 20 to 30 minutes.

4 Place the eggplant slices in a bowl and with a fork or potato masher, mash the eggplant with the garlic, paprika, cumin, water, salt, and pepper. Heat the remaining 2 tablespoons olive oil in a large skillet. Fry the mashed eggplant very slowly, uncovered, turning the eggplant over occasionally until the moisture evaporates, 20 minutes. Stir the lemon juice into the eggplant jam and cook 1 minute longer. Season with salt and pepper.

5 Place warm or room temperature eggplant on a platter and garnish with the parsley and lemon slices or tomato wedges. Serve with warm bread.

S e r v e s   6

NOTE: This can be prepared 1 day in advance. Store in the refrigerator until ready to use. Bring to room temperature before serving.

Warm Olives
with Preserved Lemons

Dar Marjana is an enchanting restaurant tucked into the labyrinth of Marrakesh. Chouki, the hospitable proprietor, greeted us at the door as though it was his home. We were seated in the courtyard, already crowded with palm and olive trees. Music serenaded our ears with its rhythmic beat. Chouki brought a glass of light green fig liquor, a potent aperitif, and a small plate of these sumptuous olives. I looked up to a clear blue-black sky and a full moon.

¾ cup cracked green olives

¾ cup Kalamata or Niçoise olives

¼ cup extra virgin olive oil

2 garlic cloves, minced

½ teaspoon cumin

¼ teaspoon paprika

⅛ teaspoon *harissa* (page 241)

1 whole preserved lemon (page 249), diced

1 to 2 tablespoons lemon juice

1 tablespoon chopped fresh cilantro or
    coriander leaves

1 tablespoon chopped fresh parsley

1 Place the olives in a saucepan and cover with water. Bring to a boil and immediately drain. Repeat the process 1 more time.

2 Heat the olive oil in a small saucepan. Add the garlic, cumin, paprika, *harissa*, preserved lemons, and olives. Cook over medium heat uncovered, 1 minute. Remove from the heat, and place in a bowl. Add the lemon juice, cilantro, and parsley and toss together.

Makes 1½ cups to serve 6

NOTE: These can be made 3 to 4 days in advance and stored in the refrigerator. Add the fresh herbs at the last minute. Bring to room temperature or warm when ready to serve.

SHELADA BAIBA ALCHIN
WA'L GHARGHAA

Beet, Orange, and Walnut Salad

Salads are the catch-all in Morocco, Algeria, and Tunisia and consist of everything: fried lamb's brains; grilled liver, potatoes, scallions, and lemon; leftover lamb kefta *meatballs stewed with hot tomatoes; and this excellent and colorful combination of wedges of beets, oranges, toasted walnuts, and romaine lettuce.*

1 pound beets
3 tablespoons olive oil
3 oranges
½ cup walnut halves
2 tablespoons walnut oil (see Note)
Pinch of sugar
Salt and freshly ground pepper
1 medium head of romaine lettuce
1 ½ tablespoons red wine vinegar

1 Preheat the oven to 375°F.

2 Wash the beets and place in a baking dish. Drizzle with 1 tablespoon olive oil. Cover the dish with foil and bake 45 to 60 minutes, until a skewer can be inserted easily into the beets. Remove from the oven and cool. Slip off the beet skins and discard. Cut the beets into wedges.

3 With a knife, cut off the top and bottom of 2 oranges. Do not peel. Cut off the skin with a knife, leaving no white pith remaining. Cut the oranges into sections between the membrane, leaving the core and membrane intact. Juice the remaining orange and reserve separately.

4 Toss the walnuts in 1 tablespoon walnut oil, sugar, salt, and pepper. Place on a baking sheet and toast until they are very hot to the touch and smell nutty, 5 to 7 minutes. Chop very coarsely.

5 Wash the lettuce, discard the outer leaves, and cut in half crosswise.

6 Whisk together the orange juice, the remaining 2 tablespoons olive oil and 1 tablespoon walnut oil, red wine vinegar, salt, and pepper.

7 Toss the lettuce with three-quarters of the vinaigrette and place on a platter. Toss the beets with the remaining vinaigrette. Garnish the salad with the beets, orange sections, and walnuts. Serve immediately.

Serves 6

NOTE: Other nut oils can be substituted. Hazelnut, walnut, and almond oil are all available at specialty food stores.

Couscous Salad with Tomatoes and Hot Green Peppers

Couscous is the pillar of North African cookery. It is a staple of the table the same way that rice or bulgur is to the Middle East, pasta, polenta, and rice are to Italy, and rice is to Greece and Spain. Couscous is a fine pellet made from semolina flour, each golden grain a bit larger than the head of a pin. Some even call it "Moroccan pasta" because it is a starch and made with the same durum wheat grain that pasta is made from. Here, cooked couscous is combined with roasted green peppers, tomatoes, and cucumbers. The resulting salad is similar to Middle Eastern tabouleh *and perfect for a summer picnic.*

1½ cups couscous
6 cups water
Salt and freshly ground pepper
2 green peppers, roasted (page 278), and cut in ½-inch dice
2 large tomatoes, peeled, seeded (page 278), and cut in ½-inch dice
1 small cucumber, peeled, seeded, and cut in ½-inch dice
1 hot green or red chili pepper (jalapeño or serrano), minced
¼ cup chopped fresh parsley
¼ cup chopped fresh cilantro or coriander leaves
5 tablespoons extra virgin olive oil
2 to 4 tablespoons lemon juice

1 teaspoon cumin
¼ teaspoon paprika
3 garlic cloves, minced

1 Wash the couscous in cold water and drain immediately. Lift and rake the grains with your fingertips to separate them. Let rest 10 minutes.

2 Heat the water in the bottom of a soup pot fit with a steamer. Line the steamer with 3 layers of cheesecloth to cover the interior of the steamer and go up over the top. Make certain that the steamer fits snugly into the soup pot and that the bottom of the steamer doesn't touch the top of the water. Add the couscous to the steamer and steam for 20 minutes, uncovered, fluffing the grains halfway through the cooking.

3 Remove the couscous from the steamer and dump it into a baking pan. Combine ½ cup water and ½ teaspoon salt. Sprinkle the couscous with the salt water. Lift and rake the grains with your fingertips to separate them. Let rest 10 minutes.

4 Place the steamer back on top of the soup pot and place the couscous in the cheesecloth-lined steamer. Simmer slowly, 15 minutes. Remove the steamer and the couscous. Let the couscous cool completely.

The couscous can be prepared up to 2 days ahead of time to this point.

♪ Place the couscous in a bowl and add the peppers, tomatoes, cucumbers, chili pepper, parsley, and cilantro.

6 In a small bowl, combine the olive oil, lemon juice, cumin, paprika, and garlic. Season with salt and pepper. Toss with the couscous and vegetables. Taste and season with salt and pepper.

Serves 6

SHELADA BEL MATESHA, BASLLA W'L'HAMED M'RAKHED

Tomato, Onion, and Preserved Lemon Salad

The first time I had this first-course salad, I couldn't get enough. When the main course, mechoui, *arrived, the salad was left on the table and I was delighted. Mechoui is a whole roasted lamb served golden brown and crisp on the outside and tender and moist inside, sprinkled with cumin and coarse salt. To go back and forth from the cool refreshing tomato salad to the lamb was a revelation to me. I was witness to the simplicity and harmony of Moroccan cooking.*

10 ripe tomatoes, peeled, seeded (page 278), and cut in ½-inch dice
1 small red onion, cut in ¼-inch dice
1½ preserved lemons (page 249)
6 tablespoons olive oil
4 tablespoons lemon juice
2 large garlic cloves, minced

¼ cup chopped fresh parsley
¼ cup chopped fresh cilantro or coriander leaves
¾ teaspoon cumin
¼ teaspoon paprika
Salt and freshly ground pepper

1 Combine the tomatoes, onions, and preserved lemons in a bowl.

2 Whisk together the olive oil, 3 tablespoons lemon juice, garlic, parsley, cilantro, cumin, and paprika. Season with ¾ teaspoon salt, pepper, and additional lemon juice if needed. Toss the vinaigrette with the vegetables and marinate 30 minutes.

3 Serve at room temperature.

Serves 6

Fennel Salad with Preserved Lemons and Garlic

We had been driving for hours when we came to the beautiful white hilltop town of Moulay Idriss, which lies in the countryside between Fez and Rabat. We were famished. It was a beautiful day, sunny and very warm, so we decided to eat our lunch outside at one of the cafés in the town square. My first bite of this cool and refreshing salad revealed assertive flavors combined with such simplicity, the true qualities of the Moroccan kitchen and table.

2 to 3 large bulbs fennel, trimmed
¼ preserved lemon (page 249), diced
2 garlic cloves, minced
2 to 3 tablespoons lemon juice
3 tablespoons extra virgin olive oil
Salt and freshly ground pepper
¼ cup fresh cilantro or coriander leaves

1 Cut the fennel into paper-thin slices and toss with the preserved lemon.

The fennel can be sliced ahead of time. If so, toss with lemon juice to prevent discoloration.

2 In a small bowl, whisk together the garlic, lemon juice, olive oil, salt, and pepper. Add the vinaigrette to the fennel and toss well. Garnish with cilantro leaves.

Serves 6

Moroccan Carrot, Radish, and Orange Salad

When I was young, I used to steal the orange flower water from the kitchen cabinet and dab it behind my ears, making believe it was perfume. Orange flower water comes from the blossoms of the Bergamot orange tree. In Morocco, it is often mixed with warm water and splashed on the hands to perfume them after a meal. Orange flower water is also used in many North African recipes like this one, where it provides a lovely and unusual floral scent and taste.

2 oranges
2 carrots, peeled and cut into paper-thin rounds
12 red radishes, trimmed, and cut into paper-thin rounds
Juice of ½ orange
Juice of ½ lemon
2 tablespoons extra virgin olive oil
1 teaspoon orange flower water
¼ teaspoon cinnamon
Small pinch of cayenne
1 tablespoon powdered sugar
Salt and freshly ground pepper
2 tablespoons coarsely chopped fresh parsley

1 With a knife, cut the top and bottom off of the oranges. Do not peel. Cut off the skin with a knife, leaving no white pith remaining. Cut the oranges into ¼-inch slices. Place in a bowl with the carrots and radishes.

2 In a small bowl, whisk together the orange juice, lemon juice, olive oil, orange flower water, cinnamon, cayenne, sugar, salt, and pepper.

3 Add the vinaigrette to the oranges, carrots, and radishes and toss together. Place on a platter, garnish with parsley, and serve.

Serves 6

Orange, Black Olive, and Cilantro Salad

Orange and olive groves compete for space all along the Mediterranean coast. This symbiotic relationship produces wonderful first course salads like Corfu Salad of Orange Slices, Red Onions, and Kalamata Olives (page 180) and this salad of oranges, black olives, preserved lemons, and cilantro, so distinctive of North Africa.

6 oranges
¼ cup extra virgin olive oil
1 small garlic clove, minced
Pinch of cayenne
Salt and freshly ground pepper
½ cup Kalamata or Niçoise olives
½ small red onion, thinly sliced
½ preserved lemon (page 249), diced
    (optional)
6 tablespoons cilantro or coriander leaves

1 With a knife, cut the top and bottom off of 5 oranges. Do not peel. Cut off the skin with a knife, leaving no white pith remaining. Cut the oranges into ¼-inch slices.

2 Juice the remaining orange and add to the olive oil. Whisk together with the garlic, cayenne, salt, and pepper.

3 Place the orange slices on a platter. Garnish with the olives, onions, and diced preserved lemon. Drizzle with the vinaigrette and garnish with the cilantro leaves. Serve immediately.

Serves 6

Mussels Steamed with Cumin and Tomatoes

Mussels are more readily available than clams in the Maghreb. I love this dish just as it is, served with a loaf of crusty bread or as a sauce tossed together with pasta.

2 pounds mussels, washed, beards removed

3 tablespoons extra virgin olive oil

½ cup water or bottled clam juice

1 small onion, minced

2 garlic cloves, minced

2 tomatoes, peeled, seeded, and chopped (page 278), or 1 cup canned Italian plum tomatoes, drained and chopped

1 tablespoon tomato paste

2 tablespoons chopped fresh parsley

1 teaspoon cumin

1 teaspoon paprika

¼ teaspoon crushed red pepper

Salt and freshly ground pepper

¼ teaspoon grated lemon zest

2 to 3 teaspoons lemon juice

6 lemon wedges

1 Heat a large skillet over high heat. Add the mussels, olive oil, water or clam juice, onion, garlic, tomatoes, tomato paste, parsley, cumin, paprika, and crushed red pepper. Cover and simmer until the mussels open, 3 to 4 minutes. As the mussels open, remove them from the pan and place in a bowl. When all of the mussels have opened, uncover the pan, increase the heat to high, and reduce the tomato sauce by one-quarter, 3 to 5 minutes.

2 Add the salt, pepper, lemon zest, and lemon juice to taste. Add the mussels and toss well.

3 Serve immediately, warm or at room temperature, garnished with the lemon wedges.

Serves 6

Braised Clams with Preserved Lemons and Cilantro

Preserved lemons are a flavor enhancer that provides a bit of sweet, acid, and salt to an otherwise simply flavored dish. Here, preserved lemons pair well with clams, coriander, parsley, and garlic for this quick and easy dish.

3 tablespoons extra virgin olive oil
¾ cup water
¾ cup bottled clam juice
1 small red onion, minced
2 garlic cloves, minced
¼ cup chopped fresh parsley
½ preserved lemon (page 249), diced
3 pounds clams, scrubbed well
Salt and freshly ground pepper
¼ cup chopped fresh cilantro or coriander
  leaves
1 teaspoon lemon juice
6 lemon wedges

1 Heat a large skillet over high heat. Add the olive oil, water, clam juice, onion, garlic, and parsley. Simmer slowly, uncovered, 5 minutes. Add the preserved lemon and clams and simmer, covered, until the clams open, 3 to 5 minutes. As the clams open, remove them from the pan and place in a bowl. When all of the clams have opened, add the salt, pepper, cilantro, and lemon juice to taste. Add the clams and juice on the bottom of the bowl and toss well.

2 Serve immediately, warm or at room temperature, garnished with the lemon wedges.

Serves 6

Grilled Tuna Skewers with Moroccan Spices

Chermoula is a Moroccan marinade used to enhance the flavors of the food, not mask them. The recipe for chermoula varies from cook to cook, but usually it is made of parsley, cilantro, garlic, onions, saffron, sweet and hot pepper, cinnamon, and cumin. Chermoula is a natural with grilled tuna, but it also goes well with swordfish, cod, shellfish, and all kinds of poultry. Keep in mind, it is best to marinate the fish or poultry for at least 2 hours. This recipe is simple and just wonderful.

1¼ pounds fresh tuna
1 teaspoon cumin
1 teaspoon paprika
½ teaspoon turmeric
¼ teaspoon cayenne
2 garlic cloves, minced
¼ cup coarsely grated onion
1 teaspoon coarse salt
Freshly ground pepper
¼ cup chopped fresh cilantro or coriander
    leaves
¼ cup chopped fresh parsley
¼ cup lemon juice
3 tablespoons extra virgin olive oil
12 4- to 5-inch bamboo skewers
Lemon wedges

1 Cut the tuna into 1-inch cubes and reserve.

2 With a mortar and pestle, or in a blender or food processor, mix together the cumin, paprika, turmeric, cayenne, garlic, onion, salt, pepper, cilantro, parsley, lemon juice, olive oil, and 1 tablespoon water. Pour over the tuna and mix well. Let marinate 2 hours.

3 Start a charcoal grill (see Note).

4 Divide the tuna into 12 parts and thread the tuna onto the skewers. Set the brochettes on a platter until ready to grill. Reserve the marinade.

The recipe can be done 6 hours ahead to this point.

5 Grill the tuna brochettes over a medium-hot fire for 5 to 8 minutes, turning every few minutes and brushing occasionally with the marinade. Remove from the fire and place on a platter. Garnish with the lemon wedges and serve immediately.

Serves 6

NOTE: These brochettes can also be cooked under the broiler for 5 to 8 minutes. Turn every few minutes and brush occasionally with the marinade.

Mediterranean Basics

Beef, Veal, or Lamb Stock

Chicken Stock

Fish Stock

Mayonnaise

Provençal Garlic Mayonnaise

Spicy Hot Garlic Mayonnaise

Spanish Garlic Mayonnaise

Crème Fraîche

Mascarpone

Pizza Dough

Toasting Nuts

Toasting Pine Nuts

Smoked Eggplant

Peeling and Seeding Tomatoes

Cleaning Artichokes

Roasting Peppers

Pitting Olives

Sectioning Oranges

Reviving Saffron

Cleaning Squid

Beef, Veal, or Lamb Stock

5 pounds beef, veal, or lamb bones (see
Note)
10 to 12 cups water
1 large onion, unpeeled, quartered
1 large carrot, peeled and coarsely chopped
12 parsley stems
Pinch of dried thyme
1 bay leaf

1 Preheat the oven to 375°F.

2 Place the bones on a baking sheet, leaving space between each one so they can brown evenly. Bake 1½ to 2 hours, until russet on all sides. Remove from the oven. Transfer the bones from the baking sheet to a stockpot. Discard any accumulated fat. Pour 1 cup water onto the baking sheet and place on the burners of the stove. With a spatula, scrape any cooked bits that have accumulated on the baking sheet. When all of the bits have been loosened, pour everything into the stockpot. Add the onion, carrot, parsley, thyme, bay leaf, and enough water to cover the bones and vegetables by a good 2 inches. Bring to a boil. Skim the foam from the top and discard. Reduce the heat and simmer very slowly, uncovered, for 4 to 5 hours. As the liquid evaporates, replenish to the original level in the stockpot.

3 When the meat has fallen off the bone and the stock is a deep rich brown, strain the stock. Discard the bones. Place the stock in the refrigerator. The following day, skim the fat from the top and discard it.

4 The stock can be frozen for 1 to 2 months.

Makes 10 to 12 cups

NOTE: To make a beef stock, use knuckle, neck, shin and other marrow bones. For veal, use breast bones, which have been cut completely between each rib. For lamb, use shank, shoulder, knuckle, or shin bones.

If a lighter-flavored broth is desired, mix 1 part stock to one part water.

Chicken Stock

5 pounds chicken parts (backs, necks,
    wings), excess fat removed
10 to 12 cups water
1 large onion, peeled and quartered
1 carrot, peeled and coarsely chopped
12 parsley stems
Pinch of dried thyme
1 bay leaf

1 Place all of the ingredients in a stockpot.
Add enough water to cover the chicken and
vegetables by 2 inches.

2 Bring to a boil. Skim foam from the top
and discard. Reduce the heat and simmer very
slowly, uncovered, for 3 to 4 hours. As the liquid evaportes, replenish to the original level in
the stockpot.

3 When the meat has fallen off the bone
and the stock smells good and strong, strain the
stock. Discard the bones. Place the stock in the
refrigerator. The following day, skim the fat
from the top and discard it.

4 The stock can be frozen for 1 to 2
months.

Makes 10 to 12 cups

NOTE: If a lighter-flavored broth is desired, mix
1 part stock to 1 part water.

Fish Stock

2 to 2½ pounds fish bones, such as snapper,
    grouper, cod, perch, sole, trout, pike, or
    salmon
1 cup dry white wine
1 small onion, coarsely chopped
1 small carrot, coarsely chopped
12 parsley stems
Pinch of fresh or dried thyme
1 bay leaf

1 Remove the flippers, liver, gills, fat, skin,
tail, and any traces of blood. Wash the bones
and put in a stockpot. Fill the pot with water to
the level of the bones. Add white wine to cover by
1 inch. Add the remaining ingredients.

2 Bring to a boil. Skim the foam from the
top and discard. Turn the heat down and simmer, uncovered, 40 minutes. During cooking,
crush the bones with a wooden spoon occasionally. Strain immediately through a fine-mesh
strainer. Remove the fat from the surface by
running a spoon over the surface or place a paper towel over the top and lift to remove the fat.

Makes 5 cups

Mayonnaise

Mayonnaise is the basis for many sauces around the Mediterranean: aioli and rouille from France and allioli negat from Spain. The process is very simple as long as a few guidelines are followed: All ingredients must be at room temperature. An emulsion must be formed with the egg yolk, mustard, and 1 tablespoon oil at the start of making the mayonnaise. Then add the oil slowly, a few drops at a time, whisking constantly to maintain an emulsion. Do not add the oil too quickly or it will flood the emulsion and the mayonnaise will "break," resembling egg yolks floating in oil. If you do "break" the emulsion, do not discard the mixture. Place another egg yolk in a clean bowl and whisk in the broken emulsion a few drops at a time, whisking constantly. One egg yolk will hold 1 cup of oil. For flavor, I usually make mayonnaise with half olive oil and half lighter-flavored oil like corn, peanut, safflower, or vegetable. And of course, once you have mastered the technique of making mayonnaise by hand, you can make mayonnaise in a food processor or blender.

1 egg yolk
2 teaspoons Dijon mustard
½ cup olive oil
½ cup peanut oil
Salt and freshly ground pepper
Juice of ½ lemon

In a bowl, whisk the egg yolk, mustard, and 1 tablespoon olive oil together until an emulsion is formed. Combine the remaining olive oil and the peanut oil. Drop by drop, add the oil to the emulsion, whisking constantly. Continue to do this, drop by drop, in a steady stream, whisking, until all of the oil has been added. Season with salt, pepper, and lemon juice.

Makes 1¼ cups

AIOLI
Provençal Garlic Mayonnaise

1 recipe Mayonnaise (recipe above)
3 to 4 garlic cloves, mashed with a mortar and pestle

Once you have made the mayonnaise, add the garlic and whisk together well.

Makes 1¼ cups

Spicy Hot Garlic Mayonnaise

Rouille means "rusty" and is used to describe the color of this spicy garlic mayonnaise, colored by roasted red pepper puree and often seen as a garnish to bouillabaisse and seafood soup. If this pungent sauce doesn't provide a jolt of flavor, it may need to be spiked with more mashed garlic and hot pepper.

1 red bell pepper, roasted (page 278)

1 slice coarse white bread, crusts removed

2 tablespoons bottled clam juice

Large pinch of saffron threads

Large pinch of cayenne or to taste

3 garlic cloves, mashed in a mortar and pestle

1 tablespoon Dijon mustard

2 egg yolks

¾ cup olive oil

¾ cup peanut oil

Juice of 1 lemon

Salt and freshly ground pepper

¼ cup chopped fresh parsley

1 tablespoon tomato paste

1 Puree the pepper until it is a fine paste. Reserve.

2 Drizzle the slice of bread with the clam juice. Sprinkle with the saffron and cayenne. Add the mashed garlic to the bread and mash with a fork to make a paste.

3 Combine the mustard, egg yolks, and 1 tablespoon olive oil in a bowl. Mix very well until an emulsion is formed. Combine the remaining olive oil and the peanut oil. Drop by drop, add the oil to the emulsion, whisking constantly. Do not add the oil too quickly, and be sure that the emulsion is homogeneous before adding more oil. Season with the lemon juice, salt, pepper, parsley, tomato paste, red pepper puree, mashed bread and garlic, and more cayenne, if desired.

Makes 2 cups

Spanish Garlic Mayonnaise

1 egg yolk, at room temperature
1 cup olive oil
5 garlic cloves
Salt and freshly ground pepper
2 to 3 teaspoons white wine vinegar

Place the egg yolk in a bowl and mix well with 1 tablespoon oil. Drop by drop, add the remaining oil to the egg yolk, whisking constantly until all the oil has been added before making another addition. Mash the garlic and a pinch of salt in a mortar and pestle and add to the mayonnaise. Season with salt, pepper, and vinegar.

Makes 1¼ cups

NOTE: This garlic mayonnaise can be made up to 6 hours ahead of time.

Crème Fraîche

1 cup heavy cream
2 tablespoons buttermilk

1 Warm the cream in a saucepan to 95° F. Stir in the buttermilk. Pour into a glass jar and cover loosely. Let sit in a warm place (75° F.), until the cream has thickened slightly, 12 to 14 hours. Cover and store in the refrigerator. It will keep for 10 days in the refrigerator.

2 If you've got some *crème fraîche* and you want to make more, follow the directions above but substitute 2 tablespoons of the *crème fraîche* for the buttermilk.

Makes 1 cup

Mascarpone

Mascarpone can be purchased at specialty Italian or cheese stores or made at home. Note that it takes 2 to 3 days to prepare.

2 cups heavy cream
⅛ teaspoon tartaric acid (see Note)

1 Place the cream in the top of a double boiler and heat it to 180° F. Remove the double boiler from the heat. Stir in the tartaric acid and stir continuously for 30 seconds. Remove the top of the double boiler and continue to stir for 3 minutes.

2 Place a kitchen towel–lined strainer over a deep bowl. Slowly pour the mascarpone into the strainer. It should not seep through the cloth but instead stay in the strainer. Place the bowl and strainer in the refrigerator and let cool undisturbed for 12 hours. Cover with plastic wrap and let the mascarpone sit in the refrigerator for 1 to 2 days before using.

Makes 2 cups

NOTE: Tartaric acid is available at pharmacies.

Pizza Dough

1½ teaspoons active dry yeast
Pinch of sugar
¼ cup lukewarm water (110° F.)
2 cups all-purpose flour
¾ teaspoon salt
3 tablespoons olive oil
½ cup water

1 By hand, combine the yeast, sugar, ¼ cup lukewarm water, and ¼ cup flour in a large bowl. Let proof for 10 minutes.

2 Add the remaining 1¾ cups flour, salt, olive oil, and water and mix well with a wooden spoon. Turn out onto a work surface and knead 7 to 10 minutes, until smooth and elastic. The dough should feel moist to the touch.

(Alternatively, this dough can be made in a food processor or electric mixer. If you're using a mixer, mix the dough for 5 to 7 minutes. In the food processor, process the dough for one minute.)

3 Place the dough in an oiled bowl and turn over to coat the top with oil. Cover with plastic wrap and let rise in a warm place (75° F.), for 1 to 1 ½ hours until doubled in volume. It is now ready to use.

Makes two 9-inch pizzas or 1 large rectangular pizza

Toasting Nuts

1 cup nuts: pecans, walnuts, or almonds
1 tablespoon vegetable, nut, or olive oil
Salt and freshly ground pepper

1 Preheat the oven to 350° F.

2 Toss the nuts with the oil, salt, and pepper. Place on a baking sheet and bake until they smell nutty, 5 to 7 minutes.

Makes 1 cup

Toasting Pine Nuts

Do not toast pine nuts in the oven because they brown too quickly. Always toast them in a skillet on top of the stove.

1 teaspoon vegetable or olive oil
1 cup pine nuts

Heat the oil in a skillet and add the pine nuts. Stir constantly until golden, 2 to 3 minutes.

Makes 1 cup

Smoked Eggplant

Pierce the eggplant several times with a fork. If you have a gas stove, you can rest the eggplant directly over the gas jets or skewer the eggplant with a large fork and turn it over the gas flame. Alternatively, you can place the eggplant on a charcoal-fired grill, turning occasionally, until the outside skin is completely black and blistered all over. Using any one of these methods, it will take 20 to 25 minutes to achieve a very smoky flavor, 15 minutes for a medium smoky flavor, and 5 minutes for a lightly smoky flavor. If neither a gas stove nor a charcoal-fired grill is available, the eggplant can be broiled, turning periodically, until the skin is black and blistered, 10 to 15 minutes. However, the result will not taste as smoky.

Peeling and Seeding Tomatoes

Bring a large pot of water to a boil. Place the tomatoes in the water for 30 seconds. Remove with a slotted spoon. With a knife, core the tomatoes from the stem end, then peel off the skin (the skin will come off easily). With the stem end up, cut the tomatoes in half horizontally. Cupping each half in the palm of your hand, squeeze out the seeds. Discard the seeds, skin, and core. Use accordingly.

Cleaning Artichokes

With a serrated knife, cut through the leaves of the artichoke crosswise (perpendicular to the stem), removing about half of the body just above the choke. Discard the top half of the artichoke. Tear off the outer dark green leaves all around the base of the artichoke until you get to the light green leaves. Discard the dark green torn leaves. With a paring knife, trim the torn edges of the base of the artichoke. Scoop and scrape out the hairy choke. Discard the parings and the hairy choke. Set the artichoke hears in a bowl of water with the juice of 1 lemon added to prevent discoloration.

Roasting Peppers

1 Preheat the broiler.

2 Cut the peppers in half and place them, cut side down, on a baking pan. Broil the peppers until they are completely black, 6 to 10 minutes. Alternatively, the peppers can be pierced with a large fork and held directly over the gas jets of a gas stove, turning occasionally, until the skin on all sides is completely black, 5 to 6 minutes. Place the charred peppers in a plastic bag, close the bag, and steam them for 10 minutes. When the peppers are soft, remove them from the plastic bag and with a knife, scrape off and discard the black skin. (I prefer not to wash them under running water as some of the flavor is lost.) If you haven't already done so, cut the peppers in half and remove and discard the membrane and seeds.

Pitting Olives

Place the olive on a work surface and with your thumb, press the olive until you feel the pit. This loosens the pit and makes it much easier to remove with your fingers, feel the pit and remove. Discard pits. (Alternatively, larger olives like Greek Kalamata olives can be pitted with a cherry pitter.)

Sectioning Oranges

With a knife, cut the top and bottom off the orange. Place one of the cut sides down on a work surface. Starting at the top and following the contour of the orange down, cut off the skin, leaving no white pith remaining. Cut the peeled orange into sections between the remaining membranes.

Reviving Saffron

I recommend buying saffron threads as opposed to saffron powder. The best method for bringing out the flavor is to crush the threads with a mortar and pestle and then soak them in a small amount of warm water. Use both the water and the ground saffron threads.

Cleaning Squid

Wash the squid. Separate the body from the head by tugging gently. (If the ink is needed for the recipe, reserve the black ink sacs intact and place in a cheesecloth-lined strainer. With the back of a spoon, press to extract the ink into a bowl.) With your fingers, pull any remaining insides and the transparent quill bone from the body and discard. Remove the tentacles by cutting just below the eyes of the head. Remove the beak by turning the head inside out and pressing the center. This small round beak can be discarded. Remove the skin from the body by scraping with a knife.

List of Restaurants

While writing this book I traveled to the Mediterranean several times. I include here a list of restaurants whose chefs and owners not only got excited about my book project but also gave me their time, cooked some excellent special dishes, and provided me with the recipes. Without them, this book would not be.

SPAIN

La Truchas, Madrid
Egipte, Barcelona
Los Caracoles, Barcelona
Es Pla, Barcelona
El 7 Portes, Barcelona
Mare Nostrum, Sitges
Cal Pinxo, Sitges
L'Avi Pau, Cunit
L'Ampurdan, Figueras
Ca La Maria, Mollet de
    Paralada
Rincon de Pepe, Murcia
Bar Las Mulas, Murcia
Los Lebrillas, Murcia
Venezuela, Mar Menor
Las Tinajas, Granada
El Convento, Arcos de la
    Frontera
Altamirano, Seville
La Albariza, Seville

FRANCE

Auberge d'Aillane, Aix-en-
    Provence
Heily, Avignon
Liautaud, Cassis
Maurice Brun, Marseilles
Le Beaugravière, Mondragon

Le Bistrot du Paradou,
    Le Paradou
Feurie, Lourmarin
La Mère Besson, Cannes
Auberge de Port, Bandol
L'Ane Rouge, Nice
La Barale, Nice
La Merenda, Nice
Chez Josie, Porto Vecchio,
    Corsica
Chez Bliancine, Sartene,
    Corsica

ITALY

Otello alla Concordia, Rome
Relais de Picine Alsrovandi,
    Rome
Piperno, Rome
Ciro a Margellina, Naples
L'Antica Trattoria, Sorrento
Primi Piatti, Cocumella,
    Sorrento
Da Antonietta, Martina Franca
Dei Trulli, Alberobello
Luna Rossa, Terranova di
    Pollino
La Posada, Taormina, Sicily
Ristorante Majore,
    Chiaramonte Gulfi, Sicily
Pescomare, Siracusa, Sicily
Arlecchino, Siracusa, Sicily
Trattoria del Porto, Trapani,
    Sicily
Cortile di Venere, Erice, Sicily
Trattoria Mamma Carmela,
    Palermo, Sicily
Antica Focacceria San Fran-
    cesco, Palermo, Sicily
Trattoria Stella, Palermo, Sicily
Shanghai, Palermo, Sicily

GREECE

Apagio, Athens
Renatis Ftelias, Athens
Kefeneion, Athens
Bukios, Zakynthos
Oyzepi o Tzimhe, Agria
Fotis Papadis Ouzeri, Volos
Bacchus, Katerini
Makethonikon, Thessaloniki
Aplototeaous, Thessaloniki
Veneto, Iraklion, Crete

TURKEY

Kiyi, Tarabya
Pandeli, Istanbul
Sarnic, Istanbul
Konyali, Istanbul
Siribom, Istanbul
Ilyada, Kalkan
Kalkan Han, Kalkan
Ahtapot, Antalya
Aphrodit, Side
Sifa, Konya
Dalma, Konya
Han Ciragan, Urgup
Mahmet Pasa, Goreme
Merek Pension, Goreme

MOROCCO

Le Restaurant Morocain du
    Mamounia, Marrakesh
Dar Marjana, Marrakesh
Stylia, Marrakesh
Al Fassia, Fez
Restaurant al Andalous, Fez
Kanoun Grill, Rabat
Dar Rbatia, Rabat
La Mer, Casablanca

Bibliography

Algar, Ayla. *Classic Turkish Cooking* (New York: HarperCollins, 1991).

Andrews, Colman. *Catalan Cuisine* (New York: Atheneum, 1988).

Apicius. *Cooking and Dining in Imperial Rome*, translation by Joseph D. Vehling (New York: Dover, 1977).

Armush, Anne Marie Weiss. *Arabian Cuisine* (Beirut: Dar An-Nafaes, 1984).

Barron, Rosemary. *Flavors of Greece* (New York: Morrow, 1991).

Beck, Simone. *Simca's Cuisine* (New York: Knopf, 1972).

Bennani-Smires, Latifa. *Moroccan Cooking* (Casablanca: Al Madariss, 1984).

Bertolli, Paul, with Alice Waters: *Chez Panisse Cooking* (New York: Random House, 1988).

Bettoja, Jo. *Southern Italian Cooking* (New York: Bantam, 1991).

Boni, Ada. *Italian Regional Cooking* (New York: Bonanza, 1969).

Boulestin, X.M. *Having Crossed the Channel . . .* (Great Britain: Windmill Press, 1934).

Bugialli, Giuliano. *Bugialli on Pasta* (New York: Simon & Schuster, 1988).

Calera, Ana Maria. *Cocina Andaluza* (Madrid: Everest, 1990).

———. *Cocina Catalana* (Madrid: Everest, 1988).

Carrier, Robert. *A Taste of Morocco* (New York: Clarkson N. Potter, 1987).

Carter, Elizabeth. *Majorcan Food* (London: Prospect, 1989).

Casas, Penelope. *The Foods and Wines of Spain* (New York: Knopf, 1979).

———. *Tapas* (New York: Knopf, 1985).

Chamberlain, Samuel. *Bouquet de France* (New York: Rand McNally, 1952).

Chatto, James, and W. L. Martin. *A Kitchen in Corfu* (London: Weidenfeld & Nicolson, 1987).

Corey, Helen. *Syrian Cookery* (New York: Doubleday, 1962).

David, Elizabeth. *French Provincial Cooking* (New York: Harper and Row, 1960).

———. *Italian Food* (London: MacDonald, 1954).

———. *Mediterranean Food, French Country Cooking, and Summer Cooking* (New York: Knopf, 1980).

Davidson, Alan. *Mediterranean Seafood* (London: Penguin, 1981).

Day, Irene. *Kitchen in the Kasbah* (London: Andre Deutsch, 1976).

Deschamps, Marion. *Travels in Provence* (London: Merehurst Press, 1988).

Escudier, Jean-Noel, and Peta J. Fuller. *The Wonderful Food of Provence* (New York, Harper and Row, 1968).

Field, Carol. *Celebrating Italy* (New York: Morrow, 1990).

Fisher, M. F. K. *Two Towns in Provence* (New York: Vintage, 1964).

Ford, Ford Madox. *Provence* (New York: Ecco Press, 1935).

Gray, Patience. *Honey from a Weed* (San Francisco: North Point Press, 1990).

Gumus, Dogan. *The Art of Turkish Cookery* (translation) (Istanbul: Do-Gu Yayinlari, 1988).

Gunur, M. Isin. *Turkish Cookery* (translation) (Istanbul: Net Turistik Yayinlar, 1990).

Haroutunian, Arto der. *The Turkish Cookbook* (London: Ebury Press, 1987).

Hazan, Marcella. *Marcella's Italian Kitchen* (New York: Knopf, 1987).

International Olive Oil Council. *The Tree The Oil The Olive* (Madrid: International Olive Council).

Kamman, Madeleine. *When French Women Cook* (New York: Atheneum, 1976).

Khayat, Marie Karam. *Food from the Arab World* (Beirut: Khayats, 1959).

Kochilas, Diane. *The Food and Wine of Greece* (New York: St. Martin's Press, 1990).

Lomonte, Mimmetta. *Classic Sicilian Cooking* (New York: Simon & Schuster, 1990).

Man, Rosamond. *The Complete Meze Table* (London: Ebury Press, 1986).

Manjon, Maite, with Jan Read and Hugh Johnson. *The Wine and Food of Spain* (Boston: Little, Brown, 1987).

Maurois, Andre. *La Belle France* (New York: Golden Press, 1964).

McConnell, Carol, and Malcolm McConnell. *The Mediterranean Diet* (New York: Norton, 1987).

Middle Eastern Cooking (New York: Time-Life Books, 1969).

Morse, Kitty. *Come with Me to the Kasbah* (Casablanca: Serar, 1989).

Moryoussef, Viviane, and Nina Moryoussef. *Moroccan Jewish Cookery* (Casablanca: Sochepress, 1983).

Mourdjis, Marios. *The Cypriots at Table* (Athens: C.A.L. Graphics).

Olney, Richard. *Simple French Food* (New York: Atheneum, 1983).

———. *The French Menu Cookbook* (Boston: David R. Godine, 1985).

Orga, Irfan. *Turkish Cooking* (London: Andre Deutsch, 1958).

Paradissis, Chrissa. *Greek Cookery* (Athens: Efstathiadis, 1976).

Perl, Lila. *Rice, Spice and Bitter Oranges* (Cleveland: The World Publishing Company, 1967).

A Quintet of Cuisines (New York: Time-Life Books, 1970).

Ramazanoglu, Gulseren. *Turkish Cooking* (Istanbul: Ramazanoglu, 1990).

Roden, Claudia. *Mediterranean Cookery* (New York: Knopf, 1987).

———. *The Book of Middle Eastern Food* (New York: Knopf, 1974).

———. *The Good Food of Italy* (New York: Knopf, 1991).

———. *The Food of Italy* (New York: Vintage, 1971).

———. *The Food of France* (New York: Knopf, 1958).

Semeti, Mary Taylor. *Pomp and Sustenance* (New York: Knopf, 1989).

Seranne, A. *Near Eastern Cookery* (New York: Doubleday, 1964).

Skoura, Sophia. *The Greek Cookbook* (New York: Crown, 1967).

Smouha, P. *Middle Eastern Cooking* (London: Andre Deutsch, 1955).

Stavroulakis, Nicholas. *Cookbook of the Jews of Greece* (Athens: Lycabettus, 1990).

Times *World History* (Maplewood, N.J.: Hammond, 1989).

Torres, Marimar. *The Catalan Country Kitchen* (New York: Aris, 1992).

———. *The Spanish Table* (New York: Doubleday, 1986).

Wolfert, Paula. *Couscous and Other Good Food from Morocco* (New York: Harper and Row, 1973).

———. *The Cooking of the Southwest of France* (New York: Dial Press/ Doubleday, 1983).

———. *Mediterranean Cooking* (New York: Ecco Press, 1977).

———. *World of Food* (New York: Harper and Row, 1988).

Yacoubi, Ahmed. *Alchemist's Cookbook* (Tucson, Ariz.: Omen, 1972).

Index

CONVERSION CHART
Equivalent Imperial and Metric Measurements

American cooks use standard containers, the 8-ounce cup and a tablespoon that takes exactly 16 level fillings to fill that cup level. Measuring by cup makes it very difficult to give weight equivalents, as a cup of densely packed butter will weigh considerably more than a cup of flour. The easiest way therefore to deal with cup measurements in recipes is to take the amount by volume rather than by weight. Thus the equation reads:

1 cup = 240 ml = 8 fl. oz.   ½ cup = 120 ml = 4 fl. oz.

It is possible to buy a set of American cup measures in major stores around the world.

In the States, butter is often measured in sticks. One stick is the equivalent of 8 tablespoons. One tablespoon of butter is therefore the equivalent to ½ ounce / 15 grams.

Liquid Measures

Fluid ounces	U.S.	Imperial	Milliliters
	1 teaspoon	1 teaspoon	5
¼	2 teaspoon	1 dessert spoon	7
½	1 tablespoon	1 tablespoon	15
1	2 tablespoon	2 tablespoon	28
2	¼ cup	4 tablespoon	56
4	½ cup or ¼ pint		110
5		¼ pint or 1 gill	140
6	¾ cup		170
8	1 cup or ½ pint		225
9			250, ¼ liter
10	1¼ cups	½ pint	280
12	1½ cups	¾ pint	340
15	¾ pint		420
16	2 cups or 1 pint		450
18	2¼ cups		500, ½ liter
20	2½ cups	1 pint	560
24	3 cups or 1½ pints		675
25		1¼ pints	700
27	3½ cups		750
30	3¾ cups	1½ pints	840
32	4 cups or 2 pints or 1 quart	900	
35		1¾ pints	980
36	4 ½ cups		1000, 1 liter
40	5 cups or 2½ pints	2 pints or 1 quart	1120
48	6 cups or 3 pints		1350
50		2½ pints	1400
60	7½ cups	3 pints	1680
64	8 cups or 4 pints or 2 quarts		1800
72	9 cups		2000, 2 liters

Solid Measures

U.S. and Imperial Measures		Metric Measures	
OUNCES	POUNDS	GRAMS	KILOS
1		28	
2		56	
3	½	100	
4	¼	112	
5		140	
6		168	
8	½	225	
9		250	¼
12	¾	340	
16	1	450	
18		500	½
20	1¼	560	
24	1½	675	
27		750	¾
28	1¾	780	
32	2	900	
36	2¼	1000	1
40	2½	1100	
48	3	1350	
54		1500	1½
64	4	1800	
72	4½	2000	2
80	5	2250	2¼
90		2500	2½
100	6	2800	2¾

Oven Temperature Equivalents

Fahrenheit	Celsius	Gas Mark	Description
225	110	¼	Cool
250	130	½	
275	140	1	Very Slow
300	150	2	
325	170	3	Slow
350	180	4	Moderate
375	190	5	
400	200	6	Moderately Hot
425	220	7	Fairly Hot
450	230	8	Hot
475	240	9	Very Hot
500	250	10	Extremely Hot

Linear and Area Measures

1 inch	2.54 centimeters
1 foot	0.3048 meters
1 square inch	6.4516 square centimeters
1 square foot	929.03 square centimeters

Equivalents for Ingredients

all-purpose flour—plain flour
arugula—rocket
confectioner's sugar—icing sugar
cornstarch—cornflour
eggplant—aubergine
granulated sugar—caster sugar

lima beans—broad beans
scallion—spring onion
squash—courgettes or marrow
unbleached flour—strong, white flour
zest—rind

zucchini—courgettes
light cream—single cream
heavy cream—double cream
half and half—12% fat milk
buttermilk—ordinary milk